Radical Technologies

Radical Technologies

The Design of Everyday Life

Adam Greenfield

VERSO

London • New York

First published by Verso 2017
© Adam Greenfield 2017

1 3 5 7 9 10 8 6 4 2

Verso
UK: 6 Meard Street, London W1F 0EG
US: 20 Jay Street, Suite 1010, Brooklyn, NY 11201

versobooks.com

Verso is the imprint of New Left Books

ISBN-13: 978-1-78478-043-2
ISBN-13: 978-1-78663-449-8 (EXPORT)
ISBN-13: 978-1-78478- 047-0 (US EBK)
ISBN-13: 978-1-78478- 046-3 (UK EBK)

British Library Cataloguing in Publication Data
A catalogue record for this book is available from the British Library

Library of Congress Cataloging-in-Publication Data

Names: Greenfield, Adam, author.
Title: Radical technologies : the design of everyday
life / Adam Greenfield.
Description: Brooklyn, NY : Verso, 2017. | Includes
bibliographical
   references and index.
Identifiers: LCCN 2017011127| ISBN 9781784780432
(hardback) | ISBN
   9781786634498 (export) | ISBN 9781784780470
(US ebk) | ISBN 9781784780463
   (Uk ebk)
Subjects: LCSH: Ubiquitous computing. | Electronic
data processing—Social
   aspects. | Technological innovations—Social
aspects. | Telematics. | Work
   design.
Classification: LCC QA76.5915 .G745 2017 | DDC
004—dc23
LC record available at
https://lccn.loc.gov/2017011127

Typeset in Sabon by MJ&N Gavan, Truro, Cornwall
Printed in the UK by CPI Mackays, UK

For N., the light on your door to show that you're home.

One has to become a cybernetician to remain a humanist.

Peter Sloterdijk

Contents

Introduction

Paris year zero

It's a few moments before six in Paris, on a damp evening in early spring. From Montreuil in the east to Neuilly-sur-Seine in the west, streetlights wink on in a slow wave as their sensors register the falling dusk. There's a rush-hour backup approaching the Porte d'Orléans exit on the Périphérique; in front of a BNP Paribas ATM in the Rue de Sèvres, a brief scuffle breaks out between supporters of the Paris Saint-Germain and Olympique de Marseille football clubs. Two friends from Sciences-Po laugh abashedly, as they recognize one another before one of the few tatty multiplexes remaining on the Champs-Élysées—they're in line to pick up tickets for the 6:15 showing of an American blockbuster. Not far away, in the Avenue Carnot, a *flic* pins a suspected purse-snatcher to the wall; affecting nonchalance as he waits for a van to come pick them up, he leans into the man's back, putting all his weight behind the point of his elbow.

A municipal street-cleaner churns slowly through the streets of the Marais, hosing the day's grit and dust from the asphalt. Across town, on the Boulevard Ney in the 18th Arrondissement, a bored Ghanaian streetwalker seeks shelter from a brief downpour beneath the awning of a pharmacy, her emerald-daubed nails clacking on the screen of her phone as she checks her messages. In the Rue Saint-Honoré, a fashion executive urges her two matched Standard Poodles from the back of the black Mercedes that has just deposited her in front of her office. An American backpacker on a post-collegiate month abroad strides forth from the marble gate of Père Lachaise with a shoplifted Gide wedged in the cargo pocket of his fatigue pants. And way out in Torcy, RER cars are being switched from a siding to the main rail line, bound for Les Halles and the other stations of the center.

In this city, everyone with a mobile phone reveals their location—whether or not the phone is equipped with explicitly locative technology, whether or not the phone is even turned on. Every transaction in the bistros and shops and cafés generates a trail, just as every bus and car and Vélib bicycle throws its own data shadow. Even the joggers in the Bois du Boulogne cast a constant, incrementing tally of miles logged and calories burned.

This is Paris: all of it, all at once. In any previous epoch, all of these events might have transpired unobserved and unmarked. Even the most sensitive observer could never hope to witness or impress upon their recollection more than the tiniest fraction of them, however long they watched the city go by. And any information or potential insight bound up in the flow of events fell to the ground like a silent, diffuse drizzle, forever lost to introspection, analysis, and memory.

But now these flows can be traced, at least in principle, and plotted in space and time. Latent patterns and unexpected correlations can be identified, in turn suggesting points of effective intervention to those with a mind to exert control. All of the living city's rhythms make themselves plain, more rhythms than anyone would have dared to dream of: anticipations, reversals, slight returns. Stutters, stops, and lags; doublings and crashes. And all of this is possible because of the vast array of data-collecting devices that have been seeded throughout the quotidian environment, the barely visible network that binds them, and the interface devices just about everyone moving through the city carries on their person.

Which rhythms, precisely? Traffic cameras and roadway sensors log the slowdown on the Périphérique; it shows up as a thick red line splashed across a hundred thousand electronic road signs, dashboard navigation units and smartphone screens, and as a new weighting in the routing algorithms that guide whatever trips are planned at that hour. Here are the rhythms of daily mobility and, by extension, the broader economy.

The ATM's security camera captures the precise details of who did what to whom in the scuffle, and when; the identities of the participants can be reconstructed later on, if need be, by a state-sanctioned trawl of the transaction records. Those identity files will almost certainly note an individual's allegiance to a particular football club, that they've been photographed at a Nuit Debout assembly, or have social or familial links to suspected jihadists. As with the traffic, here too we can begin to make correlations, mapping outbreaks of aggression against other observed phenomena—the league schedule, perhaps, or the phase of the moon, or the unemployment index. Or even something comparatively unexpected, like the price of discount-airline tickets. Here are the rhythms of collective mood.

The friends who were so embarrassed to run into one another at a superhero movie? They reserved their tickets online using their phones, and in so doing broadcast their choice for all to see, at least in aggregate; they might be surprised to learn that those who purchase tickets in this way in the streets around their campus appear to have a marked fondness for Hollywood action flicks. Here are correlated geographical patterns of socialization and economic activity, and the rhythms of media consumption.

The Avenue Carnot is nowhere to be found in any official record of the bag-snatching incident. In all the relevant entries, the offense is associated with the location where it was reported, a few blocks away in the rue de Tilsitt, and so that is how it shows up in both the city's official statistics and a citizen-generated online map of risk in Paris; in fact, this kind of slippage between an event that happens in the world and the event's representation in the networked record is routine. But the arrogant insouciance of the arresting flic's posture bothers a *lycée* student passing by, who snaps a picture with her phone and submits it, time- and location-stamped, to the Commission Citoyens Justice Police, a civilian review board. In this constellation of facts, we can see something about the frequency with which particular kinds of crimes are committed in a given location, the type and density of policing resources deployed to address them, and the frictions between the police and the communities in which they operate. Here, then, are the contrapuntal rhythms of crime, its control and the response to that control.

The nature of the streetwalker's trade could perhaps be inferred from the multiple daily orbits her cellphone describes between her regular patch on the sidewalk and a cheap rented room nearby. If not this, then her frequent purchases of condoms would certainly help to flesh out the picture—even though she pays cash, the pharmacy where she buys them retains a service that uses each phone's unique IMEI number to track customers' trajectories through the store, and this service maps her path to the Durex display with unerring precision. Here in these ghostly trails are the rhythms of the informal economy, surfacing through seemingly innocuous patterns of fact.

The streetcleaner, of course, has a GPS transponder; its moment-to-moment route through the city is mapped by the Mairie, and provided to citizens in real time as part of a transparency initiative designed to demonstrate the diligence and integrity of civil servants (and very much resented by the DPE workers' union). Unless they are disrupted by some external force—should sanitation workers, for example, happen to go on strike, or a particularly rowdy *manif* break out—here are the metronomic rhythms of the municipal.

The fashion executive had her assistant book an Uber for her; while there's certainly something to be inferred from the fact that she splurged on the Mercedes as usual instead of economizing with a cheaper booking, there's still some question as to whether this signifies her own impression of her status, or the assistant's. Even if the car hadn't been booked on the corporate account, it is also equipped with GPS, and that unit's accuracy buffer has been set such that it correctly identifies the location at the moment it pulls up to the curb, and tags the booking with the name of the house the executive works for. Here can be gleaned solid, actionable business intelligence: both the cycling of particular enterprises and sectors of the economy, and by extension possibly even some insight into the rhythms of something as inchoate and hard to grasp as taste.

What might we learn from the American backpacker? The pedometer app on his phone is sophisticated enough to understand his pause of eleven minutes in a location in the Rue de Rivoli as a visit to the WHSmith bookstore, but other facets of his activity through the day slip through holes in the mesh. That boosted volume of Gide, notably, will remain an unexplained lacuna on the bookstore's inventory-tracking software. And, bizarrely, his few hours contemplating greatness and mortality in Père Lachaise, which resolve against a flaky location database as having been passed instead in the aisles of a Franprix market a few blocks to the east. (Indeed, so often does this same error happen that after a few months, the Franprix starts getting recommended to other tourists as a destination frequently visited by people like them, and enjoys a slight but detectable bump in revenues as a result. The manager is pleased, but mystified.)

As for the commuters passing through the turnstiles of the RER at day's end, each of them increments a register in the capacity-management systems of the RATP, and in doing so helps to clarify the contours of one final picture. The city's population at 4 AM may be half what it is at 4 PM, revealing the true Paris as something that has only a casual relationship with its administrative boundaries. Here is the rhythm of the city itself.

Where previously everything that transpired in the fold of the great city evaporated in the moment it happened, all of these rhythms and processes are captured by the network, and retained for inspection at leisure. Basins of attraction or repulsion can readily be visualized, shedding light on the relationships between one kind of flow and another, and this gives the optimists among us reason to hope that administrators might learn to shape the evolution of such flows with a lighter hand. By the same token, though, that which had once been liminal becomes clear; what was invisible is made self-evident, even painfully obvious; the circumstances we generally prefer to ignore or dissemble stand forth, plain as day. The embarrassing, the informal, the nominally private and the illegal become subject to new and perhaps unbearable kinds of scrutiny. The gaze of the state intensifies—but the state may find, to its surprise, that its subjects command many of the same capabilities, and are gazing right back upon it.

On this evening in the City of Light, a hundred million connected devices sing through the wires and the aether. Of the waves that ripple through the urban fabric, at whatever scale, very few escape being captured by them, and represented in bursts of binary data. Enciphered within are billions of discrete choices, millions of lives in motion, the cycling of the entire economy, and, at the very edge of perception, the signs and traces of empire's slow unwinding.

This city may seem strange. It's yours, the one you live in—described from a series of unusual perspectives and vantage points, perhaps, but still recognizably your own, whether you should happen to live in Paris, Seoul or Santiago.

And this way of seeing a city is so startling, so new to us and so beguiling that we risk reading it the wrong way, and learning the wrong lessons. Yes, we can now perceive the rhythms of the city through the use of our technology. But more pertinently, *networked digital information technology has become the dominant mode through which we experience the everyday.* In some important sense this class of technology now mediates just about everything we do. It is simultaneously the conduit through which our choices are delivered to us, the mirror by which we see ourselves reflected, and the lens that lets others see us on a level previously unimagined.

A series of complex technological systems shapes our experience of everyday life, in a way that simply wasn't true in any previous era, and we barely understand anything about them: neither how they work, nor where they come from, nor why they take the forms they do. Insight into their functioning is distributed unequally across society, as is the power to intervene meaningfully in their design. And this is a set of circumstances we choose to hold at arm's length in our definitions of the situation before us, both in private or in public.

And this is troublesome, because none of the processes set loose in our world are static, none of them will fail to evolve. And so before long the fashion executive's car service has been automated, and its drivers let go. Its cars prowl the boulevards in patterns unintelligible to anyone with the ordinary complement of human senses, orbiting, waiting for a call; as more and more of the vehicles on the road likewise surrender to algorithmic control, traffic evaporates. The fashion house goes away— pointless in a time when design is generated by algorithmic engines, and clothing fabricated on the desktop—and with it the great contribution of couture to the French economy. The ATM in the Rue de Sèvres goes away, like all of the others strewn around the city, as money comes to reside in the direct transit of encrypted digits from one device to another. The streetwalker goes away; she stops patrolling the Boulevard Ney the moment that virtual erotics are perfected, and the bottom drops out of the market for physical intimacy. The union goes away—hard to organize for solidarity, or press claims on power, when fewer than two out of every ten people retain anything we'd recognize as a job. The Mairie goes away, supplanted by an autonomous entity that lives entirely in code, and yet makes plans, issues contracts and hires workers just like any other municipal government. Increasingly the landscape itself is tuned, simplified, shaped for the needs of its posthuman inhabitants. Here we can see one final rhythm propagating through the space of the city—a long wave that carries away all the timeless verities of metropolitan life, before setting us back down on a far shore whose details remain hard to discern.

What will it mean for us to live in that place and time? How will we understand the bargains it offers us, as individuals or societies? If we've barely begun to reckon with the construction of the ordinary in our own moment, how will we ever make sense of it in the city to come? Let's be clear: none of our instincts will guide us in our approach to the next normal. If we want to understand the radical technologies all around us, and see just how they interact to produce the condition we recognize as everyday life, we'll need a manual.

That is the project of this book. In the pages to come, we will explore a wide band of the technologies that are already implicated in our everyday lives, and will be to a still greater extent in the years just ahead: the smartphone and the internet of things; augmented and virtual reality; 3D printing and other technologies of digital fabrication; cryptocurrency and the blockchain; and the dense complex of ideas surrounding algorithms, machine learning, automation and artificial intelligence.

We'll see what commitments were made in the design of these systems. We'll try to puncture the hype that surrounds them, and evaluate the claims made about their function and effect more closely than is generally the case. And we'll pay particular attention to the ways in which these allegedly disruptive technologies leave existing modes of domination mostly intact, asking if they can ever truly be turned to liberatory ends.

Networked digital information technology looms ever larger in all of our lives. It shapes our perceptions, conditions the choices available to us, and remakes our experience of space and time. It requires us to master arcane bodies of knowledge, forcing us into a constant cycle of obsolescence and upgrade that, with startling rapidity, makes nonsense of our most diligent attempts to reckon with it. It even inhibits our ability to think meaningfully about the future, tending to reframe any conversation about the reality we want to live in as a choice between varying shades of technical development. The extent to which it organizes the everyday is one of the defining characteristics of our era, and for all the apparent power it offers us, our attempts to master it observably leave most of us feeling overwhelmed and exhausted. If we are to have any hope of retaining our agency and exerting some measure of control over the circumstances of our being in the years to come, we will need to know a lot more about where these radical technologies came from, how they accomplish their work in the world, and why they appear to us in the way that they do. What follows is an attempt to shed light on all of these questions.

1

Smartphone

The networking of the self

The smartphone is the signature artifact of our age. Less than a decade old, this protean object has become the universal, all-but-indispensable mediator of everyday life. Very few manufactured objects have ever been as ubiquitous as these glowing slabs of polycarbonate.[1]

For many of us, they are the last thing we look at before sleep each night, and the first thing we reach for upon waking. We use them to meet people, to communicate, to entertain ourselves, and to find our way around. We buy and sell things with them. We rely on them to document the places we go, the things we do and the company we keep; we count on them to fill the dead spaces, the still moments and silences that used to occupy so much of our lives.

They have altered the texture of everyday life just about everywhere, digesting many longstanding spaces and rituals in their entirety, and transforming others beyond recognition. At this juncture in history, it simply isn't possible to understand the ways in which we know and use the world around us without having some sense for the way the smartphone works, and the various infrastructures it depends on.

For all its ubiquity, though, the smartphone is not a simple thing. We use it so often that we don't see it clearly; it appeared in our lives so suddenly and totally that the scale and force of the changes it has occasioned have largely receded from conscious awareness. In order to truly take the measure of these changes, we need to take a step or two back, to the very last historical moment in which we negotiated the world without smartphone in hand.

There are few better guides to the pre-smartphone everyday than a well-documented body of ethnographic research carried out circa 2005, by researchers working for Keio University and Intel Corporation's People and Practices group.[2] Undertaken in London, Tokyo and Los Angeles, the study aimed to identify broad patterns in the things people carried in their wallets, pockets and purses on a daily basis. It found a striking degree of consistency in what Londoners, Angelenos and Tokyoites thought of as being necessary to the successful negotiation of the day's challenges:

Pictures, firstly, and similar mementoes of family, friends and loved ones. Icons, charms and other totems of religious or spiritual significance. Snacks. Personal hygiene items, breath mints, chewing gum—things, in other words, that we might use to manage the bodily dimensions of the presentation of self. Things we used to gain access of one sort or another: keys, identity cards, farecards and transit passes. Generally, a mobile phone, which at the time the research was conducted was just that, something used for voice communication and perhaps text messaging. And invariably, money in one or more of its various forms.

If the Intel/Keio study found in the stuff of wallets and handbags nothing less than circa-2005 in microcosm, its detailed accounting provides us with a useful and even a poignant way of assessing just how much has changed in the intervening years. We find that a great many of the things city dwellers once relied upon to manage everyday life as recently as ten years ago have by now been subsumed by a single object, the mobile phone. This single platform swallowed most all the other things people once had floating around in their pockets and purses, and in so doing it became something else entirely.

Once each of the unremarkable acts we undertake in the

course of the day—opening the front door, buying the groceries, hopping onto the bus—has been reconceived as a digital transaction, it tends to *dematerialize*. The separate, dedicated chunks of matter we needed to use in order to accomplish these ends, the house keys and banknotes and bus tokens, are replaced by an invisible modulation of radio waves. And as the infrastructure that receives those waves and translates them into action is built into the ordinary objects and surfaces all around us, the entire interaction tends to disappear from sight, and consequently from thought.

Intangible though this infrastructure may be, we still need some way of communicating with it. The 2005-era mobile phone was perfect in this role: a powered platform the right shape and size to accommodate the various antennae necessary to wireless communication, it was quite literally ready-to-hand, and best of all, by this time most people living in the major cities of the world already happened to be carrying one. And so this one device began to stand in for a very large number of the material objects we previously used to mediate everyday urban life.

Most obviously, the smartphone replaced conventional telephones, leading to the widespread disappearance from streetscapes everywhere of that icon of midcentury urbanity, the telephone booth, and all the etiquettes of negotiated waiting and deconfliction that attended it. Where phone booths remain, they now act mostly as a platform for other kinds of services—WiFi connectivity, or ads for sex workers.

In short order, the smartphone supplanted the boombox, the Walkman and the transistor radio: all the portable means we used to access news and entertainment, and maybe claim a little bubble of space for ourselves in doing so. Except as ornamentation and status display, the conventional watch, too, is well on its way to extinction, as are clocks, calendars and datebooks. Tickets, farecards, boarding passes, and all the other tokens of access are similarly on the way out, as are the keys, badges and other physical means we use to gain entry to restricted spaces.

The things we used to fix cherished memory—the dogeared, well-worried-over Kodachromes of lovers, children, schoolmates

and pets that once populated the world's plastic wallet inserts—
were for the most part digitized at some point along the way,
and long ago migrated to the lockscreens of our phones.

Most of the artifacts we once used to convey identity are
not long for this world, including among other things name
cards, calling cards and business cards. Though more formal
identity-authentication documents, notably driver's licenses and
passports, are among the few personal effects to have successfully resisted assimilation to the smartphone, it remains to be
seen how much longer this is the case.

What else disappears from the world? Address books,
Rolodexes and "little black books." The directories, maps and
guidebooks of all sorts that we used to navigate the city. Loyalty
and other stored-value cards. And finally money, and everything
it affords its bearer in freedom of behavior and of movement.
All of these have already been transfigured into a dance of ones
and zeroes, or are well on their way to such a fate. Of all the discrete artifacts identified by the Intel/Keio studies, after a single
decade little more remains in our pockets and purses than the
snacks, the breath mints and the lip-balm.

Time flows through the world at different rates, of course,
and there are many places where the old ways yet reign. We
ourselves are no different: some of us prefer the certainty of
transacting with the world via discrete, dedicated objects, just
as some still prefer to deal with a human teller at the bank. But
as the smartphone has come to stand between us and an ever-
greater swath of the things we do in everyday life, the global
trend toward dematerialization is unmistakable. As a result, it's
already difficult to contemplate objects like a phone booth, a
Filofax or a Palm Pilot without experiencing a shock of either
reminiscence or perplexity, depending on the degree of our past
acquaintance with them.

However clumsy they may seem to us now, what's important about such mediating artifacts is that each one implied an
entire way of life—a densely interconnected ecosystem of commerce, practice and experience. And as we've overwritten those

ecosystems with new and far less tangible webs of connection based on the smartphone, the texture of daily experience has been transformed. The absorption of so many of the technics of everyday life into this single device deprives us of a wide variety of recognizably, even distinctively urban sites, gestures and practices. Stepping into the street to raise a hand for a cab, or gathering in front of an appliance-shop window to watch election results or a championship game tumble across the clustered screens. Stopping at a newsstand for the afternoon edition, or ducking into a florist shop or a police booth to ask directions. Meeting people at the clock at Grand Central, or the Ginza branch of the Wako department store, or in the lobby of the St. Francis Hotel. What need is there for any of these metropolitan rituals now?

It isn't particularly helpful to ask whether this new everyday life is "better" or "worse"; I very much doubt we'd have permitted the smartphone to supplant so many other objects and rituals in our lives if we didn't, on balance, perceive some concrete advantage in doing so. But there are a few circumstances that arise as a result of this choice that we might want to take careful note of.

Firstly, the most basic tasks we undertake in life now involve the participation of a fundamentally different set of actors than they did even ten years ago. Beyond the gargantuan enterprises that manufacture our devices, and the startups that develop most of the apps we use, we've invited technical standards bodies, national- and supranational-level regulators, and shadowy hackers into the innermost precincts of our lives. As a result, our ability to perform the everyday competently is now contingent on the widest range of obscure factors—things we'd simply never needed to worry about before, from the properties of the electromagnetic spectrum and our moment-to-moment ability to connect to the network to the stability of the software we're using and the current state of corporate alignments.

Secondly, all of the conventions and arrangements that constitute our sense of the everyday now no longer evolve at any speed we'd generally associate with social mores, but at the far faster rate of digital innovation. We're forced to accommodate some degree of change in the way we do things every time the newest version of a device, operating system or application is released.

And thirdly, and perhaps most curiously of all, when pursuits as varied as taking a photograph, listening to music and seeking a romantic partner all start with launching an app on the same device, and all of them draw on the same, relatively limited repertoire of habits and mindsets, a certain similarity inevitably comes to color each of them. We twitch through the available options, never fully settling on or for any one of them.

This is our life now: strongly shaped by the detailed design of the smartphone handset; by its precise manifest of sensors, actuators, processors and antennae; by the protocols that govern its connection to the various networks around us; by the user interface conventions that guide our interaction with its applications and services; and by the strategies and business models adopted by the enterprises that produce them.

These decisions can never determine our actions outright, of course, but they do significantly condition our approach to the world, in all sorts of subtle but pervasive ways. (Try to imagine modern dating without the swipe left, or the presentation of self without the selfie.) Fleshing out our understanding of the contemporary human condition therefore requires that we undertake a forensic analysis of the smartphone and its origins, and a detailed consideration of its parts.

Though its precise dimensions may vary with fashion, a smartphone is fundamentally a sandwich of aluminosilicate glass, polycarbonate and aluminum sized to sit comfortably in the adult hand, and to be operated, if need be, with the thumb only. This requirement constrains the device to a fairly narrow range of shapes and sizes; almost every smartphone on the market at present is a blunt slab, a chamfered or rounded rectangle between eleven and fourteen centimeters tall, and some six to seven wide. These compact dimensions permit the device to live comfortably on or close to the body, which means it will only rarely be misplaced or forgotten, and this in turn is key to its ability to function as a proxy for personal identity, presence and location.

The contemporary smartphone bears very few, if any, dedicated ("hard") controls: generally a power button, controls for audio volume, perhaps a switch with which to silence the device entirely, and a "home" button that closes running applications and returns the user to the top level of the navigational hierarchy. On many models, a fingerprint sensor integrated into the home button secures the device against unauthorized access.

Almost all other interaction is accomplished via the device's defining and most prominent feature: a shatter-resistant glass touchscreen of increasingly high resolution, covering the near entirety of its surface. It is this screen, more than any other component, that is responsible for the smartphone's universal appeal. Using a contemporary touchscreen device is almost absurdly easy. All it asks of us is that we learn and perform a few basic gestures: the familiar tap, swipe, drag, pinch and spread[3]. This interaction vocabulary requires so little effort to master that despite some tweaks, refinements and manufacturer-specific quirks, virtually every element of the contemporary smartphone interface paradigm derives from the first model that featured it, the original Apple iPhone of summer 2007.

Beneath the screen, nestled within a snug enclosure, are the components that permit the smartphone to receive, transmit, process and store information. Chief among these are a multi-core central processing unit; a few gigabits of nonvolatile storage (and how soon that "giga-" will sound quaint); and one or more ancillary chips dedicated to specialized functions. Among the latter are the baseband processor, which manages communication via the phone's multiple antennae; light and proximity sensors; perhaps a graphics processing unit; and, of increasing importance, a dedicated machine-learning coprocessor, to aid in tasks like speech recognition. The choice of a given chipset will determine what operating system the handset can run; how fast it can process input and render output; how many pictures, songs and videos it can store on board; and, in proportion to these capabilities, how much it will cost at retail.

Thanks to its Assisted GPS chip—and, of course, the quarter-trillion-dollar constellation of GPS satellites in their orbits twenty million meters above the Earth—the smartphone knows where it is at all times. This machinic sense of place is further refined by the operation of a magnetometer and a three-axis microelectromechanical accelerometer: a compass and gyroscope that together allow the device to register the bearer's location, orientation and inclination to a very high degree of precision. These sensors register whether the phone is being held vertically or oriented along some other plane, and almost incidentally allow it to accept more coarsely grained gestural input than that mediated by the touchscreen, i.e. gestures made with the whole device, such as turning it upside down to silence it, or shaking it to close applications and return the user to the home screen.

A microphone affords voice communication, audio recording and the ability to receive spoken commands, while one or more speakers furnish audible output. A small motor allows the phone to produce vibrating alerts when set in silent mode; it may, as well, be able to provide so-called "haptics," or brief and delicately calibrated buzzes that simulate the sensation of pressing a physical button.

Even cheap phones now come with both front and rear cameras. The one facing outward is equipped with an LED flash, and is generally capable of capturing both still and full-motion imagery in high resolution; though the size of the aperture limits the optical resolution achievable, current-generation cameras can nonetheless produce images more than sufficient for any purpose short of fine art, scientific inquiry or rigorous archival practice. The user-facing camera generally isn't as capable, but it's good enough for video calls, and above all selfies.

Wound around these modules, or molded into the chassis itself, are the radio antennae critical to the smartphone's basic functionality: separate ones for transmission and reception via cellular and WiFi networks, an additional Bluetooth antenna to accommodate short-range communication and coupling to accessories, and perhaps a near-field communication (NFC) antenna for payments and other ultra-short-range interactions. This last item is what accounts for the smartphone's increasing ability to mediate everyday urban interactions; it's what lets you tap your way onto a bus or use the phone to pay for a cup of coffee.

Finally, all of these components are arrayed on a high-density interconnect circuit board, and powered by a rechargeable lithium-ion or lithium-polymer battery capable of sustaining roughly 1,500 charging cycles. This will yield just about four years of use, given the need to charge the phone daily, though experience suggests that few of us will retain a given handset that long.

There is one final quality of the smartphone that is highly significant to its ability to mediate everyday experience: it is incomplete at time of purchase. For all its technical capability, the smartphone as we currently conceive of it remains useless unless activated by a commercial service provider. In the business of mobile telephony, the process by which this otherwise-inactive slab of polycarbonate and circuitry is endowed with functionality is called "provisioning." A user account is established, generally with some means of payment authenticated, and only once this credential has been accepted do you find that the object in your hands has come alive and is able to transact with the things around it.

Even once provisioned, the smartphone is not particularly useful. It can be used to make voice calls, certainly; it generally comes loaded with a clock, a calendar, weather and map applications, a web browser, and—rather tellingly—a stock ticker. But the overwhelming balance of its functionality must be downloaded from the network in the form of "apps," designed and developed by third parties with wildly differing levels of craft, coding ability and aesthetic sensibility.

This immediately confronts the would-be user with a choice to make about which corporate ecosystem they wish to participate in. The overwhelming majority of smartphones in the world run either on Apple's iOS or on some flavor of the open-source Android operating system, and these are incompatible with one another. Apps designed to work on one kind of device and operating system must be acquired from the corresponding marketplace—Apple's App Store, Google Play—and cannot be used with any other. In this light, we can see the handset for what it truly is: an aperture onto the interlocking mesh of technical, financial, legal and operational arrangements that constitutes a contemporary device and service ecosystem.

The smartphone as we know it is a complicated tangle of negotiations, compromises, hacks and forced fits, swaddled in a sleekly minimal envelope a few millimeters thick. It is, by any reckoning, a tremendously impressive technical accomplishment. Given everything it does, and all of the objects it replaces or renders unnecessary, it has to be regarded as a rather astonishing bargain. And given that it is, in principle, able to connect billions of human beings with one another and the species' entire stock of collective knowledge, it is in some sense even a utopian one.

But behind every handset is another story: that of the labor arrangements, supply chains and flows of capital that we implicate ourselves in from the moment we purchase one, even before switching it on for the first time.

Whether it was designed in studios in Cupertino, Seoul or somewhere else, it is highly probable that the smartphone in your hand was assembled and prepared for shipment and sale at facilities within a few dozen kilometers of Shenzhen City, in the gritty conurbation that has sprawled across the Pearl River Delta since the Chinese government opened the Shenzhen Special Economic Zone for business in August 1980.[4] These factories operate under circumstances that are troubling at best. Hours are long; the work is numbingly repetitive, produces injuries at surreal rates,[5] and often involves exposure to toxic chemicals.[6] Wages are low and suicide rates among the workforce are distressingly high.[7] The low cost of Chinese labor, coupled to workers' relative lack of ability to contest these conditions, is critical to the industry's ability to assemble the components called for in each model's bill of materials, apply a healthy markup[8] and still bring it to market at an acceptable price point. Should Chinese wages begin to approximate Western norms,[9] or local labor win for itself anything in the way of real collective bargaining power, we may be certain that manufacturers will find other, more congenial places to assemble their devices. But for now Shenzhen remains far and away the preeminent global site of smartphone manufacture.

Take a step or two further back in the production process, and the picture gets bleaker still. To function at all, the smartphone—like all electronic devices—requires raw materials that have been wrested from the Earth by ruthlessly extractive industries. The cobalt in its lithium-ion batteries was mined by hand in the Congo, often by children; the tin in the soldered seams that bind it together most likely comes from the Indonesian island of Bangka, where the water table is irreparably fouled, 70 percent of the coral reefs have been destroyed by mine runoff, and on average one miner a week is killed on the job.[10] The damage caused by the processes of extraction fans out across most of a hemisphere, mutilating lives, human communities and natural ecosystems beyond ready numbering. And so the polluted streams, stillborn children and diagnoses of cancer, too, become part of the way in which the smartphone has transformed everyday life, at least for some of us.

Though these facts might give us pause in just about any other context, we don't appear to be too troubled by them when it comes to the smartphone. The smartphone *isn't* like any other product, and in fact ranks among the most rapidly adopted technologies in human history.[11] And so we suppress whatever qualms we may have about the conditions in the mines and factories, the environmental footprint, the energetic cost of the extended supply chain, or the authoritarian governments we ultimately support through our act of purchase. To the degree that we're even aware of it, we leave this deniable prehistory behind the moment we plunk down our cash and take home our new phone.

And for whatever it may be worth, our desire for the smartphone has yet to reach its saturation point. As prices fall, an ever-higher proportion of the planetary population acquires some sort of device with this basic feature set. It is always dangerous to imagine futures that are anything like linear extrapolations from the present, but if the augurs can be relied upon, we balance on the cusp of an era in which every near- or fully adult person on Earth is instrumented and connected to the global network at all times.[12] Though we've barely begun to reckon with what this implies for our psyches, our societies, or our ways of organizing the world, it is no exaggeration to say that this capability—and all the assumptions, habits, relations of power and blindspots bound up in it—is already foundational to the practice of the everyday.

Part of the difficulty in approaching the smartphone analytically is that there is so very much to say about it. Entire books could be written, for example, about how the constant stream of notifications it serves up slices time into jittery, schizoid intervals, and may well be eroding our ability to focus our attention in the time between them.[13] Or how its camera has turned us all into citizen photojournalists, and in so doing significantly altered the social dynamics surrounding police violence. We might find some purchase, though, by considering a single one of its functions: the ability it grants us to locate ourselves.

Consider that for the entire history of cartography, using a map effectively meant decoding a set of abstract symbols that had been inscribed on a flat surface, and then associating those symbols with the various three-dimensional features of the local environment. The ability to do so, and therefore to successfully determine one's position, was by no means universally distributed across the population, and this scarcity of knowledge was only compounded by the fact that until relatively recently, maps themselves were rare (and occasionally militarily sensitive) artifacts.

But the maps we see on the screen of a phone cut across all this. Everyone with a smartphone has, by definition, a free, continuously zoomable, self-updating, high-resolution map of every part of the populated surface of the Earth that goes with them wherever they go, and this is in itself an epochal development. These maps include equally high-resolution aerial imagery that can be toggled at will, making them just that much easier for the average user to comprehend and use. Most profoundly of all—and it's worth pausing to savor this—they are the first maps in human history that follow our movements and tell us where we are on them in real time.

It's dizzying to contemplate everything involved in that achievement. It fuses globally dispersed infrastructures of vertiginous scale and expense—the original constellation of American NAVSTAR Global Positioning System satellites, and its Russian, European and Chinese equivalents; fleets of camera- and Lidar-equipped cars, sent to chart every navigable path on the planet; map servers racked in their thousands, in data centers on three continents; and the wired and wireless network that yokes them all together—to a scatter of minuscule sensors on the handset itself, and all of this is mobilized every time the familiar blue dot appears on the screen. By underwriting maps of the world that for the first time include our real-time position, center on us, and move as we do, two dollars' worth of GPS circuitry utterly transforms our relationship to place and possibility. Thanks to a magnetometer that costs another dollar or so, they automatically orient themselves to the direction we're looking in and pivot as we turn, helping us perform the necessary cognitive leap between the abstraction on screen and the real world we see around us. And in a neatly Borgesian maneuver, the touch-screen controller and the onboard RAM let us fold a map that would otherwise span some 30 miles from side to side, if the entire world were rendered at the highest level of detail, into an envelope small and light enough to be gripped in a single hand and carried everywhere.

The maps we see on the screen of a smartphone help us rebalance the terms of our engagement with complex, potentially confounding spatial networks, allowing newcomers and tourists alike to negotiate the megacity with all the canniness and aplomb of a lifelong resident. By furnishing us with imagery of places we've never yet been, they can help to banish the fear that prevents so many of us from exploring unfamiliar paths or districts. They are the most generous sort of gift to the professional lover of cities, and still more so to everyone whose livelihood and wellbeing depends on their ability to master the urban terrain. But they also furnish us with a great deal of insight into the networked condition.

Most obviously, in using them to navigate, *we become reliant on access to the network to accomplish ordinary goals.* In giving ourselves over to a way of knowing the world that relies completely on real-time access, we find ourselves at the mercy of something more contingent, more fallible and far more complicated than any paper map. Consider what happens when someone in motion loses their connection to the network, even briefly: lose connectivity even for the time it takes to move a few meters, and they may well find that they have been reduced to a blue dot traversing a featureless field of grey. At such moments we come face to face with a fact we generally overlook, and may even prefer to ignore: the performance of everyday life as mediated by the smartphone depends on a vast and elaborate infrastructure that is ordinarily invisible to us.

Beyond the satellites, camera cars and servers we've already identified, the moment-to-moment flow of our experience rests vitally on the smooth interfunctioning of all the many parts of this infrastructure—an extraordinarily heterogeneous and unstable meshwork, in which cellular base stations, undersea cables, and microwave relays are all invoked in what seems like the simplest and most straightforward tasks we perform with the device. The very first lesson of mapping on the smartphone, then, is that the handset is primarily a tangible way of engaging something much subtler and harder to discern, on which we have suddenly become reliant and over which we have virtually no meaningful control.

We ordinarily don't experience that absence of control as a loss. Simultaneously intangible and too vast to really wrap our heads around, the infrastructure on which both device and navigation depend remains safely on the other side of the emotional horizon. But the same cannot be said for what it feels like to use the map, where our inability to make sense of what's beneath our fingertips all too frequently registers as frustration, even humiliation. Here we're forced to reckon with the fact that *the conventions of interaction with the device are obscure or even inexplicable to many.* Spend even a few minutes trying to explain basic use of the device to someone picking it up for the first time, and you'll realize with a start that what manufacturers are generally pleased to describe as "intuitive" is in fact anything but. When we do fail in our attempts to master the device, we are more likely to blame ourselves than the parties who are actually responsible. And while there will no doubt come a point at which everyone alive will have been intimately acquainted with such artifacts and their interface conventions since earliest childhood, that point remains many years in the future. Until that time, many users will continue to experience the technics of everyday life as bewildering, overwhelming, even hostile.

If we are occasionally brought up short by the complexities of interacting with digital maps, though, we can also be badly misled by the very opposite tendency, the smoothness and naturalness with which they present information to us. We tend to assume that our maps are objective accounts of the environment, diagrams that simply describe what is there to be found. In truth, they're nothing of the sort; *our sense of the world is subtly conditioned by information that is presented to us for interested reasons, and yet does not disclose that interest.*

Even at its highest level of detail, for example, it's generally not feasible to label each and every retail store or other public accommodation that may appear on the map. Decisions have to be made about which features to identify by name, and increasingly, those decisions are driven by algorithms that leverage our previous behavior: where we've been in the past, the websites we've visited, what we've searched for, the specific apps we have installed, even who we've spoken with. As a result, it may never be entirely clear to us why a particular business has been highlighted on the map we're being offered. It would be a mistake to think of this algorithmic surfacing as somehow incidental, or lacking in economic consequence: according to Google, four out of every five consumers use the map application to make local searches, half of those who do so wind up visiting a store within twenty-four hours, and one out of every five of these searches results in a "conversion," or sale.[14]

There are two aspects of this to take note of: the seamless, all-but-unremarked-upon splicing of revenue-generating processes into ordinary behavior, which is a pattern that will crop up time and again in the pages to come, and the fact that by tailoring its depiction of the environment to their behavior, the smartphone presents each individual user with a different map. Both of these qualities are insidious in their own way, but it is the latter that subtly erodes an experience of the world in common. We can no longer even pretend that what we see on the screen is a shared, consistent representation of the same, relatively stable underlying reality. A map that interpellates us in this way ensures, in a strikingly literal sense, that we can only ever occupy and move through our own separate lifeworlds.

This is not the only way in which the smartphone sunders us from one another even as it connects. For in the world as we've made it, *those who enjoy access to networked services are more capable than those without.* Someone who is able to navigate the city in the way the smartphone allows them to will, by and large, enjoy more opportunities of every sort, an easier time availing themselves of the opportunities they are presented with, and more power to determine the terms of their engagement with everything around them than someone not so equipped—and not by a little way, but by a great deal.

This will be felt particularly acutely wherever the situations we confront are predicated on the assumption of universal access. If the designers (or funders) of shared space become convinced that "everyone" has a phone to guide them, we may find that other aids to wayfinding—public maps, directional signage, cues in the arrangement of the physical environment—begin to disappear from the world. Under such circumstances, the personal device is no longer an augmentation but a necessity; under such circumstances, design that prevents people from understanding and making full use of their devices is no longer simply a question of shoddy practice, but of justice.

There's something of an ethical bind here, because if the smartphone is becoming a *de facto* necessity, it is at the same time *impossible to use the device as intended without, in turn, surrendering data to it* and the network beyond. In part, this is simply a function of the way mobile telephony works. Most of us know by now that our phones are constantly tracking our location, and in fact have to do so in order to function on the network at all: the same transaction with a cellular base station or WiFi router that establishes connectivity suffices to generate at least a low-resolution map of our whereabouts. But it is also a function of business model. Your location can be used to refine real-time traffic reports, tailor targeted advertising, or otherwise bolster the map vendor's commercial imperatives, and this means that high-resolution tracking will invariably be enabled by default.

Unless you explicitly go into your device's settings menu and disable such tracking, and possibly several other application-specific functions as well, it's continuously shedding traces of your movement through the world—and the terms and conditions you assented to when you set your phone up for the first time permit those traces to be passed on to third parties. (Here, again, the interface's inherent opacity crops up as an issue: many people don't know how to find the controls for these functions, or even that they can be switched off in the first place.) On top of the map you yourself see, then, superimpose another: the map of your peregrinations that is at least in principle available to the manufacturers of your phone, its operating system and mapping application, and any third-party customers they may have for that data.

That map can be combined with other information to build up detailed pictures of your behavior. Algorithms applied to the rate at which you move are used to derive whether you're on foot or in a vehicle, even what kind of vehicle you're in, and of course such findings have socioeconomic relevance. More point-edly still, when latitude and longitude are collapsed against a database of "venues," you're no longer understood to be occu-pying an abstract numeric position on the surface of the Earth, but rather Père Lachaise cemetery, or Ridley Road Market, or 30th Street Station. And just like our choice of transportation mode, a list of the venues we frequent is not in any way a neutral set of facts. There are any number of places—an Alcoholics Anonymous meeting, a fetish club, a betting shop or a psycho-therapist's practice—that may give rise to inferences about our behavior that we wouldn't necessarily want shared across the network. And yet this is precisely what leaches off the phone and into the aether, every time you use the map.

Whenever we locate ourselves in this way, whether we're quite aware of it or not, *we are straightforwardly trading our privacy for convenience.* For most of us, most of the time, the func-tionality on offer is so useful that this is a bargain we're more than happy to strike, yet it remains distressing that its terms are rarely made explicit.

And however much one may believe that it's an ethical imper-ative to ensure that people are aware of what their smartphone is doing, this is by no means a straightforward proposition. It is complicated by the fact that *a single point of data can be mobilized by the device in multiple ways.* For example, the map is not the smartphone's only way of representing its user's loca-tion. The suite of sensors required to produce the map—the GPS, the accelerometer, the magnetometer and barometer—can also pass data to other applications and services on the device via a structured conduit called an API, or application programming interface. Through the API, the same data that results in the familiar blue dot being rendered on the map lets us geotag photos and videos, "check in" to venues on social media, and receive weather forecasts or search results tailored for the particular place in which we happen to be standing. Depending on the applications we have running, and the degree of access to location data we've granted them, place-specific information can be served to us the moment we traverse a "geofence," the digitally defined boundaries demarcating some region of the Earth's surface, and this might mean anything from vital safety alerts to discount coupons to new powers in a game.

When we move through the world with a smartphone in hand, then, we generate an enormous amount of data in the course of our ordinary activities, and we do so without noticing or thinking much about it. In turn, that data will be captured and leveraged by any number of parties, including handset and operating system vendors, app developers, cellular service providers, and still others; those parties will be acting in their interests, which may only occasionally intersect our own; and it will be very, very difficult for us to exert any control over any of this.

What is true of the map is true of the device it resides on, as it is of the broader category of networked technologies to which both belong: whatever the terms of the bargain we entered into when we embraced it, this bargain now sets the conditions of the normal, the ordinary and the expected. Both we ourselves and the cultures we live in will be coming to terms with what this means for decades to come.

The familiar glowing rectangles of our smartphone screens are by now unavoidable, pretty much everywhere on Earth. They increasingly dominate social space wherever we gather, not even so much an extension of our bodies as a prosthesis grafted directly onto them, a kind of network organ. Wherever you see one, there too is the vast ramified array of the planetary network, siphoning up data, transmuting it into a different form, returning it to be absorbed, acted upon, ignored entirely. Equipped with these devices, we're both here and somewhere else at the same time, joined to everything at once yet never fully anywhere at all.

The individual networked in this way is no longer the autonomous subject enshrined in liberal theory, not precisely. Our very selfhood is smeared out across a global mesh of nodes and links; all the aspects of our personality we think of as constituting who we are—our tastes, preferences, capabilities, desires—we owe to the fact of our connection with that mesh, and the selves and distant resources to which it binds us.

How could this do anything but engender a new kind of subjectivity? Winston Churchill, in arguing toward the end of the Second World War that the House of Commons ought to be rebuilt in its original form, famously remarked that "we shape our buildings, and afterwards our buildings shape us."[15] Now we make networks, and they shape us every bit as much as any building ever did, or could.

It's easy, too easy, to depict the networked subject as being isolated, in contact with others only at the membrane that divides them. But if anything, the overriding quality of our era is *porosity*. Far from affording any kind of psychic sanctuary, the walls we mortar around ourselves turn out to be as penetrable a barrier as any other. Work invades our personal time, private leaks into public, the intimate is trivially shared, and the concerns of the wider world seep into what ought to be a space for recuperation and recovery. Above all, horror finds us wherever we are.

This is one of the costs of having a network organ, and the full-spectrum awareness it underwrites: a low-grade, persistent sense of the world and its suffering that we carry around at all times, that reaches us via texts and emails and Safety Check notices. The only way to hide from that knowledge is to decouple ourselves from the fabric of connections that gives us everything else we are. And that is something we clearly find hard to do, for practical reasons as much as psychic ones: network connectivity now underwrites the achievement of virtually every other need on the Maslovian pyramid, to the extent that refugees recently arriving from warzones have been known to ask for a smartphone before anything else, food and shelter not excluded.[16]

We need to understand ourselves as nervous systems that are virtually continuous with the world beyond the walls, fused to it through the juncture of our smartphones. And what keeps us twitching at our screens, more even than the satisfaction of any practical need, is the continuously renewed opportunity to bathe in the primal rush of communion.

Whether consciously or otherwise, interaction designers have learned to stimulate and leverage this desire: they know full well that every time someone texts you, "likes" your photo or answers your email, it changes you materially, rewiring neurotransmitter pathways, lighting up the reward circuits of your brain, and enhancing the odds that you'll trigger the whole cycle over again when the dopamine surge subsides in a few seconds. This clever hack exploits our most primal needs for affirmation, generally from the most venal of motivations. But it can also sensitize us to the truth of our own radical incompleteness, if we let it, teaching us that we are only ever ourselves in connection with others. And as we have never been anything but open and multiple and woven of alterity—from the DNA in our cells, to the microbes in our guts, to the self-replicating modules of language and learned ideology that constitute our very selves—in the end maybe the network we've wrought is only a clunky way of literalizing the connections that were always already there and waiting to be discovered.

It remains to be seen what kind of institutions and power relations we will devise as selves fully conscious of our interconnection with one another, though the horizontal turn in recent politics might furnish us with a clue. Whatever form they take, those institutions and relations will bear little resemblance to the ones that now undergird everyday experience, even those that have remained relatively stable for generations. The arrangements through which we allocate resources, transact value, seek to exert form on the material world, share our stories with one another, and organize ourselves into communities and polities will from now on draw upon a fundamentally new set of concepts and practices, and this is a horizon of possibilities that first opened up to us in equipping ourselves with the smartphone.

2

The internet of things

A planetary mesh of perception and response

In Copenhagen, a bus running two minutes behind schedule transmits its location and passenger count to the municipal traffic signal network, which extends the green light at each of the next three intersections long enough for its driver to make up some time. In Davao City in the Philippines, an unsecured webcam overlooks the storeroom of a fast-food stand, allowing anyone equipped with its address to peer in at will on all its comings and goings. In San Francisco, a young engineer hopes to "optimize" his life through sensors that track his heart rate, respiration and sleep cycle.

What links these wildly different circumstances is a vision of connected devices now being sold to us as the "internet of things," in which a weave of networked perception wraps every space, every place, every thing and every body on Earth. The technologist Mike Kuniavsky, a pioneer and early proponent of this vision, characterizes it as a state of being in which "computation and data communication [are] embedded in, and distributed through, our entire environment."[1] I prefer to see it for what it is: the colonization of everyday life by information processing.

Like the smartphone, the internet of things isn't a single technology, but an unruly assemblage of protocols, sensing regimes, capabilities and desires, all swept under a single rubric for the sake of disciplinary convenience. Just about all that connects the various devices, services, vendors and efforts involved is the ambition to raise awareness of some everyday circumstance to the network for analysis and response.

Though it can often feel as if this colonization proceeds of its own momentum, without any obvious driver or particularly pressing justification beyond the fact that it is something our technology now makes possible, it always pays to remember that distinct ambitions are being served wherever and however the internet of things appears, whether as rhetoric or reality. Some of these ambitions speak to the needs of commercial differentiation, and the desire to instill the qualities of surprise and delight into otherwise banal products. Others are founded in a much more concrete and pragmatic set of concerns, having to do with the regulation of energy consumption or the management of municipal infrastructure. Inevitably, some of these ambitions involve surveillance, security and control. But whatever the context in which these connected devices appear, what unites them is the inchoate terror that a single event anywhere might be allowed to transpire unobserved, uncaptured and unleveraged.

This, then, is the internet of things. If the endeavor retains a certain sprawling and formless quality, we can get a far more concrete sense of what it involves, what it invokes and what it requires by looking at each of the primary scales at which it appears to us: that of the body, that of the room, and that of public space in general. Though they all partake of the same general repertoire of techniques, each of these domains of activity has a specific, distinguishing label associated with it. The quest to instrument the body, monitor its behavior and derive actionable insight from these soundings is known as the "quantified self"; the drive to render interior, domestic spaces visible to the network "the smart home"; and when this effort is extended to municipal scale, it is known as "the smart city." Each of these scales of activity illuminates a different aspect of the challenge presented to us by the internet of things, and each of them has something distinct to teach us.

At the most intimate scale, the internet of things manifests in the form of wearable biometric sensors: devices that collect the various traces of our being in the world, and submit them to the network for inspection and analysis. The simplest of these are little more than networked digital pedometers. Using the same kind of microelectromechanical accelerometer found in our smartphones, these count steps, measure overall distance traversed, and furnish an estimate of the calories burned in the course of this activity. More elaborate models measure heart rate, breathing, skin temperature and even perspiration— biological primitives from which higher-order, harder-to-define psychoemotional states like stress, boredom or arousal can be inferred.

We can understand these devices as hinges between the body and the network: ways of raising the body's own processes directly to the network, where they can be stored or mined for insight like any other data set. These latent indicators of biological performance, otherwise so hard to discern, are made legible in order that they may be rendered subject to the exercise of will, and brought under at least some semblance of control.

While the various models of Fitbit are probably the most widely used wearable biometric monitors, the Apple Watch is currently the most polished example of the category—indeed, lower-than-anticipated sales when initially marketed as a fashion accessory have spurred Apple to reposition its offering as a high-performance fitness device. With its obsessively detailed design, precision machining and luxury-grade materials, the Watch looks and feels a good deal less "technical" than its competitors. But it is every bit as capable of harvesting biometric data across multiple regimes, if not more so, and its colorful visualizations, trend lines and insistent reminders incorporate the latest findings of motivational psychology. It may be the long-awaited breakthrough in wearables: both the enabler and the visible symbol of a lifestyle in which performance is continuously monitored and plumbed for its insights into further improvements.

Nobody has embraced this conception of instrumented living more fervently than a loose global network of enthusiasts called the Quantified Self, whose slogan is "self-knowledge through numbers."[2] Founded by *Wired* editor Gary Wolf and *Whole Earth Review* veteran Kevin Kelly in 2007, the Quantified Self currently boasts a hundred or so local chapters, and an online forum where members discuss and rate the devices mobilized in their self-measurement efforts. (It can be difficult to disentangle this broader movement from a California company of the same name also founded by Wolf and Kelly, which mounts conferences dedicated to proselytizing for the practice of self-measurement.)

In their meetups and on their forum, the stalwarts of the Quantified Self discuss the theory and practice of the measured life, mulling everything from the devices most effective at capturing REM sleep to the legalities involved in sharing data. One forum thread goes quite a bit further; entitled "Can You Quantify Inner Peace?," it discusses metrics that the instrumented aspirant might use to measure their progress toward heights of consciousness previously understood as the preserve of Zen meditators and yogic adepts.

As an individual lifestyle choice, none of this is properly anyone else's to question, and there's no doubt that the effort can occasionally yield up some provocative insights. Consider the young cognitive neuroscientist who cross-referenced her online purchases, entertainment choices and dating decisions against her menstrual cycle,[3] and found among other things that she only ever purchased red clothing when she was at her most fertile.

What almost never seems to be addressed in these forums and meetups, though, are questions about what this self-knowledge is being mobilized for, and just where the criteria against which adherents feel they need to optimize their performance come from in the first place. While there are some fascinating questions being explored in the Quantified Self community, a brutal regime of efficiency operates in the background. Against the backdrop of late capitalism, the rise of wearable biometric monitoring can only be understood as a disciplinary power traversing the body itself and all its flows. This is a power that Frederick Taylor never dreamed of, and Foucault would have been laughed out of town for daring to propose.

It's clear that the appeal of this is overwhelmingly to young workers in the technology industry itself, the control they harvest from the act of quantification intended to render them psychophysically suitable for performance in a work environment characterized by implacable release schedules and a high operational tempo. (Not for nothing is there a very significant degree of overlap between the Quantified Self and the "lifehacking" subculture—the same people who brought you Soylent[4], the flavorless nutrient slurry that is engineered to be a time-and-effort-efficient alternative to actual meals.) And of course what is most shocking about all of this is that it is undertaken voluntarily. Here, a not-insignificant percentage of the population has so decisively internalized the values of the market for their labor that the act of resculpting themselves to better meet its needs feels like authentic self-expression. They are willing to do whatever it takes to reengineer the body so it gets more done in less time, is easier and more pleasant to work with—to render themselves, as the old Radiohead lyrics put it, "calm, fitter, healthier and more productive," and in so doing transform themselves into all-but-fungible production units, valued only in terms of what they offer the economy.

What may be unproblematic as the niche interest of a technical subculture becomes considerably more worrisome when its tenets are normalized as a way of life appropriate for the rest of us. But it is of yet greater concern when it becomes mandated by actors that operate at societal scale, and have the leverage to impose these choices upon us.

For now, this takes the form of a carrot: health insurance companies, including Aetna in the United States and Vitality in the United Kingdom,[5] have already extended their customers steep discounts on the Apple Watch, and offer reduced premiums for those whose Watches continue to report a high and regular level of exercise. But it isn't hard to see how this way of eliciting compliance could easily be transformed into a stick, with punitively higher rates—or even the refusal of coverage altogether—for those customers unwilling to share these most intimate facts of the body over the global network.

If these practices of the Quantified Self ever do spur any one individual to genuine introspection, impelling them to reckon with the true nature of their self as it manifests in this body and this life, then so much the better. But the Delphic injunction to "know thyself" hardly seems honored in the decision to strap on a Fitbit. And whatever gains may accrue to the occasional individual, they pale in comparison with everything that is sure to be lost when the posture of the body and all the details of its situation in space and time are used collectively, to construct models of nominal behavior we're all thereafter forced to comply with.

If wearable biometric devices are aimed, however imperfectly, at rigorous self-mastery, the colonization of the domestic environment by similarly networked products and services is intended to deliver a very different experience: convenience. The clear aim of such "smart home" efforts is to as nearly as possible short-circuit the process of reflection that stands between one's recognition of a desire and its fulfillment via the market.

The apotheosis of this tendency is a device currently being sold by Amazon, the Dash Button. Many internet-of-things propositions are little more than some more or less conventional object with networked connectivity tacked on, and their designers have clearly struggled to imagine what that connectivity could possibly be used for. The Dash Button is the precise opposite, a thing in the world that could not possibly have existed without the internet—and not merely some abstract network of networks, but the actual internet we have, populated by the precise mix of devices and services the more privileged among us habitually call upon in the course of their lives. I cannot possibly improve on Amazon's own description of this curious object and how it works, so I'll repeat it in full here:

> Amazon Dash Button is a Wi-Fi connected device that reorders your favorite item with the press of a button. To use Dash Button, simply download the Amazon App from the Apple App Store or Google Play Store. Then, sign into your Amazon Prime account, connect Dash Button to Wi-Fi, and select the product you want to reorder. Once connected, a single press on Dash Button automatically places your order. Amazon will send an order confirmation to your phone, so it's easy to cancel if you change your mind. Also, the Dash Button Order Protection doesn't allow a new order to be placed until the prior order ships, unless you allow multiple orders.[6]

So: a branded, single-purpose electronic device, and quite an elaborate one at that, whose entire value proposition is that you press it when you're running out of detergent, or toilet paper, or coffee beans, and it automatically composes an order request to Amazon. I don't for a second want to downplay the value of a product like this for people who have parents to look after, or kids to drop off at daycare, or who live amid social and spatial conditions where simply getting in the car to go pick up some laundry detergent may take an hour or more out of their day. But the benefit is sharply differential. You get your detergent on time, yes, but Amazon gets so much more. They get data on the time and place of your need, as well as its frequency and intensity, and that data has value. It is, explicitly, an asset, and you can be sure they will exploit that asset in every way their terms and conditions permit them to—including by using it to develop behavioral models that map the terrain of our desires, so as to exploit them with even greater efficiency in the future.

Again, the aim of devices like the Dash Button is to permit the user to accomplish commercial transactions as nearly as possible without the intercession of conscious thought, even the few moments of thought involved in tapping out commands on the touchscreen of a phone or tablet. The data on what the industry calls "conversion" is as clear as it is unremitting: for every box to tick, form to fill or question that needs to be answered, the percentage of remaining users that makes it all the way to checkout tumbles.

For the backers of commercial internet-of-things ventures, this falloff is the stuff of sleepless nights and sour stomachs. And yet manufacturers, enticed by the revenue potential inherent in a successful conquest of the domestic environment, keep trying, in the hope that sooner or later one of the connected products and services on offer will be embraced as something as essential to everyday life as the smartphone. We can understand the recent industry push toward the "smart home" as simply the latest version of this: a conscious, coherent effort to enlist our intimate spaces as a site of continuous technological upgrade, subscription-based services and the perpetual resupply of consumables. Perhaps the promise of effortless convenience can succeed in convincing consumers to sign on, where the sheer novelty of being connected did not.

For the moment, this strategy has come to center on so-called smart speakers, a first generation of which have now reached the market—products like the Amazon Echo and Google Home, each of which is supposed to function as a digital hub for the home. As we might by now expect of networked things, nothing about the physical form of these objects goes any way at all toward conveying their purpose or intended mode of function: Amazon's Echo is a simple cylinder, and its Echo Dot that same cylinder hacked down to a puck, while the Google Home presents as a beveled ovoid. The material form of such speakers is all but irrelevant, though, as their primary job is to function as the physical presence of and portal onto a service—specifically, a branded "virtual assistant."

Google, Microsoft, Amazon and Apple each offer their own such assistant, based on natural-language speech recognition; no doubt further competitors and market entrants will have appeared by the time this book sees print. Almost without exception, these assistants are given female names, voices and personalities, presumably based on research conducted in North America indicating that users of all genders prefer to interact with women.[7] Apple's is called Siri, Amazon's Alexa; Microsoft, in dubbing their agent Cortana, has curiously chosen to invoke a character from their *Halo* series of games, polluting that universe without seeming to garner much in return. For now, at least, Google has taken a different tack, refreshingly choosing not to give their assistant offering any token of gendered personal identity, even in the rudimentary form of a name.[8] One simply addresses it as "Google."

Gendered or otherwise, these assistants live in a smart speaker the way a genie might in its bottle, from where they are supposed to serve as the command hub of a connected home. The assistant furnishes an accessible, easy-to-use front end on what might otherwise be an overwhelming number of controls scattered in different places throughout the home, subsuming those for lighting and entertainment, security functions, and heating, cooling and ventilation systems; through a selection of APIs, it also reaches out to engage third-party commercial services. Whether or not this scenario appeals to a significant audience, or corresponds to the way in which anyone actually lives, it is of powerful interest to the manufacturers, who in this way establish a beachhead in the home for the brand—a point of presence, and a means of considerable leverage.

At first blush, devices like these seem harmless enough. They sit patiently in the periphery of attention, never pressing any kind of overt claim on their users, and are addressed in the most natural way imaginable: conversationally. But the details of implementation shed some light on just what this is all for. This is how Google's assistant works: you mention to it that you're in the mood for Italian, and it "will then respond with some suggestions for tables to reserve at Italian restaurants using, for example, the OpenTable app."[9] This scenario was most likely offered off the top of the head of the journalist who wrote it. But it's instructive, a note-perfect illustration of the principle that though the choices these assistants offer us are presented as neutral, they invariably arrive prefiltered through existing assumptions about what is normal, what is valuable, and what is appropriate. Their ability to channel a nascent, barely articulated desire into certain highly predictable kinds of outcomes bears some scrutiny.

Ask restaurateurs and front-of-house workers what they think of OpenTable, for example, and you'll swiftly learn that one person's convenience is another's accelerated work tempo, or worse. You'll learn that restaurants offering reservations via the service are "required to use the company's proprietary floor management system, which means leasing hardware and using OpenTable-specific software," and that OpenTable retains ownership of all the data generated in this way.[10] You'll also learn that OpenTable takes a cut on reservations made of one dollar per seated diner, which obviously adds up to a very significant amount on a busy night. Conscientious diners (particularly those with some experience working in the industry) have therefore been known to bypass the ostensible convenience of OpenTable, and make whatever reservations they have to by phone. By contrast, Google Home's all but frictionless default to making reservations via OpenTable normalizes that option, the same way the appearance of Uber as a default option in the Google Maps interface sanctifies the choice to use that service.

This is hardly accidental. It reflects the largely preconscious valuations, priorities and internalized beliefs of the people who devised Home—at Google, as throughout the industry, a remarkably homogeneous cohort of young designers and engineers, still more similar to one another psychographically and in terms of their political commitments than they are demographically alike.[11] But as with those who have embraced the practices of the Quantified Self, what is more important than the degree of similarity they bear to one another is how different they are from everyone else.

I don't think it's unfair to say that at this moment in history, internet-of-things propositions are generally imagined, designed and architected by a group of people who have completely assimilated services like Uber, Airbnb and Venmo into their daily lives, at a time when Pew Research Center figures suggest that a very significant percentage of the population has never used (or even heard of) them.[12] And all of their valuations get folded into the things they design. These propositions are normal to them, and so become normalized for everyone else as well.

There are other challenges presented by this way of interacting with networked information. It's difficult, for example, for a user to determine whether the options they're being offered by a virtual assistant result from what the industry calls an "organic" return—something that legitimately came up in the result of a search process—or from paid placement. But the main problem with the virtual assistant is that it fosters an approach to the world that is literally thoughtless, leaving users disinclined to sit out any particularly prolonged frustration of desire, and ever less critical about the processes that result in the satisfaction of their needs and wants.

Whatever artifact they happen to be embedded in at any given moment, virtual assistants are literally listening to us at all times, and to everything that is said in their presence. But then, of course they are: as voice-activated interfaces, they must by definition be constantly attentive in this way, in order to detect when the "wake word" rousing them to action is spoken. That they are in this way enabled to harvest data that might be used to refine targeted advertising, or for other commercial purposes, is something that is only disclosed deep in the terms and conditions that govern their use.[13] The logic operating here is that of preemptive capture: the notion that as a service provider you might as well trawl up everything you can, because you never know what value might be derived from it in the future.

This leads to situations that might be comical, were they not so very on-the-nose in what they imply about the networking of our domestic environments. These stories circulate in the internet of things community as cautionary tales; one of the best-known concerns the time the National Public Radio network aired a story about the Echo, and various cues spoken aloud on the broadcast were interpreted as commands by Echos belonging to members of the audience. (One listener reported that just such a command had caused his Echo to reset the thermostat it was connected with to a balmy, and expensive, 70 degrees.)[14]

Here we see something that was intended as a strategy for the reduction of cognitive overload threatening to become one of its main drivers. What the designers of these experiences failed to imagine was that while an calming experience of use might have been narrowly achievable in a research lab, where total control might be imposed on every artifact and service operating in the local environment, it is virtually impossible to realize in a home where the things at play come from any number of vendors, with each interactive object in the space most likely designed from the tacit assumption that it would be the only one with a claim on anyone's attention.

Put to the side for one moment the question of disproportionate benefit—the idea that you as the user derive a little convenience from your embrace of a virtual assistant, while its provider gets *everything*, all the data and all the value latent in it. Let's simply consider what gets effaced in the ideology of ease[15] that underlies this conception of the internet of things, this insistence that all tasks be made as simple as possible, at all times. Are the constraints presented to us by life in the non-connected world *really* so onerous? Is it really so difficult to wait until you get home to pre-heat the oven? And is it worth trading away so much, just to be able to do so remotely?

Like the Dash Button, connected products that are intended for consumers generally make great emphasis on their "plug-and-play" quality: a simplicity in use so refined that one might bring a product home, turn it on for the first time and step back as it autoconfigures itself. In emphasizing the appeal of this, manufacturers have correctly intuited that most people have neither the time, the knowledge nor the inclination to manage the details of a device's connection with the internet. But the push toward ease often effaces something critical, and one of the things that all too frequently gets elided in the logic of plug-and-play is any consideration for network security.

This is especially the case where networked cameras are concerned. A cheap plug-and-play webcam, the kind of marginally adequate Shenzhen product you can currently pick up for around $10, broadcasts to the internet in just the same way that an industrial-grade model costing ten or fifteen times as much would. But unlike that more considered product, it will lack even the most rudimentary means of controlling access to its feed. And this in turn means that when you use a specialized internet of things search engine like Shodan to seek out devices that are broadcasting unsecured, you turn up hundreds of thousands of them, located all over the planet.

Such feeds can be discovered by anyone with a mind to, and they open onto scenes you'd imagine people would treat with far greater discretion: illegal marijuana grow ops, secure areas of bank branches, military base housing, and column after column of babies lying in their cribs, asleep or otherwise.[16] The sense of boundary transgression is intense. As I write these words, I have a tab open with a view onto what looks like the stock room of a Jollibee fast-food restaurant in Davao City in the Philippines; I wonder how the two young women on camera would react if they realized that their movements and actions were fully visible, albeit in low resolution, to a writer watching them from 7,300 miles away. Even cameras that do technically offer more elaborate security provisions are often left vulnerable as a consequence of that most human and persistent of blunders, the failure to change the default password that a device ships with. A search site based in Russia compiles links to some 73,000 cameras mounted in locations around the world, both outdoor and indoor, that are left unsecured in just this way.[17]

This tendency toward laziness is near-universal throughout the internet of things world, and beyond cameras it afflicts just about any class of objects that can be connected to the network. A security researcher named Matthew Garrett described his March 2016 stay in a London hotel,[18] for example, where the guest-room light switches had been replaced with touchscreen Android tablets, presumably in the misguided pursuit of contemporary cool. With a few minutes' work, Garrett was able to determine not only that the heating, cooling, lighting and entertainment controls for his room faced the global network unsecured, but that the last four digits of the IP address for every room in the hotel transparently mapped onto floor and room number. A digital intruder could take control of any room they desired to, at will—whether from the room next door, or from halfway around the world—simply by substituting the relevant digits in the IP address.

Every networked device that goes unprotected in this way isn't simply exposing its own controls. It can be suborned as a point of access to the entire local network and every other device connected to it,[19] offering intruders an aperture through which they might install backdoors, intercept traffic passing across the network, or launch denial-of-service attacks.[20]

My concern here isn't so much to point out that the internet of things is a security nightmare, although it certainly is. What I want to emphasize is that, in very large part, this is a direct consequence of commercial decisions, and a problem of business model. It's not all that expensive to furnish networked devices with security elaborate enough to defeat the more obvious exploits—but at the low end of the market, where profit margins are reed-thin, any additional increment of cost is intolerable. Similarly, the hotel with the Android-tablet light switches wanted bragging rights to an cutting-edge guest experience, but evidently wasn't prepared to invest in an effective security plan, or an addressing scheme that might prevent the controls in each room from being trivially guessed.

This is the open secret of the internet of things—each instance of which is, by definition, coupled to the same internet that carries by far the greater share of our civilization's communications, news, entertainment, and financial traffic. The price of connection is vulnerability, always and in every context, and it is no different here: every single device that is connected to the network offers an aperture, a way in, what the security community calls an "attack vector." Taken together, these trillion unpatched vulnerabilities raise the specter of swarms of zombie machines directed to spam the internet infrastructure, and overwhelm it with spurious traffic to the point that no legitimate message can get through. This is known as a "distributed denial of service" attack, or DDoS, and while it's by no means sophisticated, it can be devastatingly effective.

If ever there were a situation in which a little bit of paranoia might be advisable, it's this one. Understand, too, that the overwhelming majority of such vulnerabilities will never be patched. As internet security legend Bruce Schneier argues, the parties that understand the vulnerabilities—device manufacturers—aren't incentivized to fix them, while the end user doesn't have the expertise to do so.[21]

The reigning internet security paradigm was developed in an age where almost all networked devices were operated by institutions with full-fledged IT departments. The security conventions we rely on are predicated on the assumption that knowledgeable staff would always be available to patch vulnerabilities and ensure that firmware remained current. By contrast, the internet of things business model consists precisely in selling devices too cheap to have functional security provisions, to people who don't know what firmware is or why it might present a vulnerability.

Every time someone buys a low-end device of this type off a pallet at Costco or PCWorld, takes it home and plugs it in, they expand the property of their local network that security professionals call its "attack surface," or the total scope of exposure it presents to the world. And until someone manages to develop a security paradigm appropriate to these circumstances, this vulnerability will afflict every class and category of networked object. The lesson here is that the security crisis of the internet of things was effectively inevitable, implicit in the ideology of ease and the fundamental proposition of billions of cheap devices installed and managed by ordinary people.

If we are to make our way in a world populated with them, we need to learn how to see these connected things as sites of interest—and particularly as places where our own interests come into contention with those of multiple other parties, the moment we connect an object with the network that animates it and gives it force.

Consider that staple of the smart home, the networked camera or webcam, whose capacity for remote oversight is generally invoked to secure the people, places or things within its field of vision. This was clearly the intention of the camera installed in the Davao City stockroom, for example, whose operator presumably wished to monitor worker behavior, prevent inventory shrinkage, gather evidence in the event of a theft, and perhaps remind employees that they were visible at all times. Taken together, these aims constitute the interest of the person who installed the camera. Its manufacturer, however, had an interest in keeping its price low, and that meant that the camera shipped without effective provisions for controlling access to it. This in turn served yet another party's interest: that of an intruder, who could probe the local network through this unsecured point of access, and see if there might not be something connected to it worth corrupting, or mobilizing as part of a botnet. These interests all contend in the camera from the first moment it's plugged in, just as your interests and OpenTable's and Google's and a restaurateur's all contend in the Home interface.

What is being gathered together in a Tide-branded Amazon Dash Button? Crack open the case,[22] and you'll find a WiFi module and a microcontroller, a microphone, a memory chip and an LED, along with some other harder-to-identify components, all sandwiched on a printed circuit board. The cost of this bill of materials is such that Amazon almost certainly loses a little money with each unit sold—and that's even before considering that they chose to subsidize its purchase in full with a $5 rebate on the first order made with it.[23] So the first thing that's folded up in the Dash Button is a business model: Amazon wouldn't sell it at all if they didn't know perfectly well they'll be making a healthy profit on everything you buy, on each of the thousand or so occasions you'll be able to press the button before its welded-in battery succumbs.

But what you will also find coiled up in the Dash Button, if you look carefully enough, is a set of standards and protocols that enfold the agreements of obscure industry working groups on how wireless networking ought to work, incorporating all the tacit assumptions they've made about what a home looks like, what other networked objects you might have at hand, and how bandwidth might be apportioned between them. In fact everything in this proposition seems contingent on something else, everything cascades and invokes some set of settled conventions still further down the line: at minimum the Dash Button assumes that you have a wireless base station at home, and a phone that can run the Amazon app, and most obviously that you have an Amazon account and a line of credit to feed it.

Other facts about the world unavoidably get wound in, too. The temperature in Amazon's fulfillment center, passing-out hot in the summer months because leaving the doors open to let in a breeze would also admit some possibility of theft. The prevalence of miscarriages and cancers among workers in the plant where the gallium arsenide in the LED was made. The composition of leachate in springs fed by runoff from the landfill where the Dash Button will inevitably come to rest in just a few years' time. Your relationship with and feelings about brands—the degree to which you've let the thought "Tide" supplant that of "detergent" in your ordinary awareness, as well as the degree to which you're willing to give that brand real estate in your house. And all of this invoked every time you press the button, just to ensure you never run out of laundry detergent.

There is one more thing that is hidden in the gathering of forces and potentials represented by this little button, more than simply shabby labor relations and some measure of degradation inflicted on the land. It is something that would likely bother a great many of Amazon's customers more than any such nebulous concerns, if they were ever made fully aware of it: that the products sold in this way are subject to Amazon's dynamic pricing algorithm, and therefore that their prices may fluctuate by as much as 25 percent in either direction, anywhere up to several times each day. Strictly speaking, this means that the Dash Button does something a little different every time it is pushed. Anyone wanting to ascertain precisely what it is that they are paying for their Tide Smart Pouch Original Scent HE Turbo Clean Liquid Laundry Detergent, Pack of Two 48 oz. Pouches will have to seek out that information on the website proper, and this is of course precisely the interaction the Dash Button is designed to forestall and prevent.

The philosopher Graham Harman reminds us that "we live in a world in which things withdraw from awareness, silently enabling our more explicit deeds."[24] But what he doesn't mention is that very often some party is counting on that withdrawal because it serves their interests. It is not merely for reasons of philosophical curiosity that it is worth our while to haul these reticent things back into the light of day, and open them up for a more considered inspection.

If this imperative holds at the scale of domestic objects and the smart home, it becomes more urgent still when the same set of techniques and practices is applied to the management of urban experience. At this largest scale, the internet of things appears to us as a body of rhetoric around the performance and behavior of the so-called "smart city." This is a place where the instrumentation of the urban fabric, and of all the people moving through the city, is driven by the desire to achieve a more efficient use of space, energy and other resources. If the ambition beneath the instrumentation of the body is a nominal self-mastery, and that of the home convenience, the ambition at the heart of the smart city is nothing other than control.

Most of us are by now at least distantly aware that our phones, smart or otherwise, are constantly harvesting information about our whereabouts and activities. But we tend to be relatively ignorant of the degree to which the contemporary streetscape itself has also been enabled to collect information. Just as our bodies and homes have become comprehensively instrumented, so too has the terrain through which we move.

The broadest range of networked information-gathering devices are already deployed in public space, including cameras; load cells and other devices for sensing the presence of pedestrians and vehicles; automated gunshot-detection microphones and other audio-spectrum surveillance grids; advertisements and vending machines equipped with biometric sensors; and the indoor micropositioning systems known as "beacons," which transact directly with smartphones.

Perhaps mercifully, the average pedestrian is at best only liminally aware of the presence or operation of these sensors. From the sidewalk, they appear as a retrofitted profusion of little-noticed and more or less inexplicable pods on façades and lampposts, a fractal encrustation built up from devices of wildly varying age, type and provenance. With the exception of CCTV cameras—most of which are very much meant to be seen[25]— these devices are not of any particularly obvious telltale shape. Some are literally embedded in the walls; others are sealed away beneath the street surface, with nothing more than the occasional shiny seam in the paving or the Day-Glo annotations of utility personnel to betray their presence. Very often, they're quite literally black boxes, mute little oblongs of polycarbonate lampreyed to a building-front, easy to overlook in the rush of daily life. However opaque they may be, though, and whatever the original inspiration underlying their placement, all of these things are ultimately there for a single purpose: to gather facts about some condition or activity transpiring in the public way, and raise them to the network.

Given the enduring, if not increasing, significance of weather in our lives, it should surprise nobody that many urban sensors are intended to gather meteorological information. These measure ambient temperature, precipitation levels and barometric pressure; wind velocity and direction; and multiple indices of air quality, including ozone level and pollen and particulate count. Increasingly often, such meteorological stations are equipped with sniffers designed to scan for the molecular traces of nuclear, chemical, biological, radiological or high-explosive weapons of mass destruction.

Inevitably, a great deal of such sensor deployments have to do with the daily exigencies of municipal administration, whether these be the detectors that measure the average speed of traffic and the velocity of individual vehicles; the soil moisture and pH monitors that give maintenance crews insight into the health of street trees and plantings; or the automated gunshot-detection systems that recognize the distinctive acoustic signature of a firearms discharge, and (at least in principle) dispatch public-safety resources to investigate.

Many systems in this category are intended to regulate or manage the behavior of another infrastructure. Water-distribution and sewerage networks are increasingly provisioned with their own dedicated grid of sensing devices, in the hope that emergent anomalies in their behavior or performance can be detected early, and dealt with while they're still of manageable scale. The same can be said for the infrastructural networks we more ordinarily encounter directly: the networked bollards and gates that block the flow of traffic into arterials generally rely on some kind of inductive sensor grid, buried beneath the pavement, to register the presence of vehicles. Similarly, the sensors for detecting that a parking space is available, a shared bicycle has been returned to its rack, or a recycling bin is full and needs to be emptied.

Other systems are emplaced in the street because they help administrators regulate behavior more indirectly. This is the intention behind most of the CCTV systems we encounter in public space, whether municipal or private in ownership; over time, these will be tend to be provisioned with advanced capabilities like face-detection and -recognition and gaze tracking.[26] Similar things can be said for the automated license-plate readers many police departments now equip their fleets with, surprising nobody with the revelation that they are disproportionately likely to be deployed in poor neighborhoods.[27] We can think of these as devices that embody, articulate and concretize the gaze of the state, and of other interested parties, as it is brought to bear on people moving through the public way.

Newer systems aim to discover patterns of fact pertinent to commercialization of the sidewalk frontage, detecting how many people are present at each given hour of the day; what they are paying attention to; and, if possible, what demographic or psychographic categories they belong to. Typical of these is Placemeter, an "open urban intelligence platform" which promises its users the ability to "see how busy places are in real time."

An increasing number of sensors find their way to the street thanks to the prerogatives of citizen science, and the desire to gather data that supplements (or for that matter, corrects) the official government line on air quality, decibel levels, or radiation. The best-known example of this is the rooftop air-quality station maintained by the US Embassy in Beijing, whose readings are broadcast worldwide over Twitter, making it one of the few sources of information about pollution available to Chinese citizens beyond reach of interference from their government. This is entirely laudable, as are the sensors that underwrite assistive technologies—for example, the beacons deployed in the hope that they might enable visually impaired people to make their way through the city independently.

Sometimes it's not quite clear why a sensor is there at all. This may be because some party has arrived at a reasoned judgment that the cost of deployment is likely to be outweighed by the potential future value of the data collected, even if it's not yet clear what that value is. It may be because the sensor is little more than a gesture in the direction of contemporaneity and hipness. Or it may well be that the instrumentation is all but pointless, betraying a profound misunderstanding of what networked data is or how it might be used.

Often, a party pursuing some higher-order ambition fuses sensors of multiple types into a single functional ensemble. New York City's Midtown traffic management system,[28] for example, integrates data from lamppost-mounted cameras[29] and microwave traffic-detection arrays, taxicab GPS units, inductive loops in the roadway, and the EZPass electronic toll collection system.[30] This is the case in Copenhagen as well, where the adaptive traffic signals integrate data garnered from sources as varied as mobile phones, bicycle sensors in the roadway, and hardware installed in the light standards themselves.

And finally, not everything drawing data off activity on the street is a sensor *per se*. An example, and an important exception to the general rule of imperceptibility, is that class of systems designed to be overt precisely because they function primarily as interfaces with a networked service of some sort. The classic example would be an ATM, but we can include parking meters, transit-fare kiosks and even vending machines in this category. The data produced by such devices tends to be incidental to their primary purpose, but it is produced and uploaded to the network nonetheless: who was in this place to use this device, at what time, to achieve what end?

The picture we are left with is that of an urban fabric furiously siphoning up information, every square meter of seemingly banal sidewalk yielding so much data about its uses and its users that nobody quite yet knows what to do with it all. And it is at this scale of activity that the guiding ideology of the whole internet of things enterprise comes into clearest focus.

We see the strongest and most explicit articulation of this ideology in the definition of a smart city offered by the multinational technology vendor Siemens[31]: "Several decades from now cities will have countless autonomous, intelligently functioning IT systems that will have perfect knowledge of users' habits and energy consumption, and provide optimum service ... The goal of such a city is to optimally regulate and control resources by means of autonomous IT systems."[32]

There is an implicit theory, a clear philosophical position, even a worldview, behind all of this effort. We might think of it as an unreconstructed logical positivism, which among other things holds that the world is in principle perfectly knowable, its contents enumerable and their relations capable of being meaningfully encoded in the state of a technical system, without bias or distortion. As applied to the affairs of cities, this is effectively an argument that there is one and only one universal and transcendently correct solution to each identified individual or collective human need; that this solution can be arrived at algorithmically, via the operations of a technical system furnished with the proper inputs; and that this solution is something which can be encoded in public policy, again without distortion. (Left unstated, but strongly implicit, is the presumption that whatever policies are arrived at in this way will be applied transparently, dispassionately and in a manner free from politics.)

Every single aspect of this argument is problematic.

Perhaps most obviously, the claim that anything at all is perfectly knowable is perverse. When Siemens talks about a city's autonomous systems acting on "perfect knowledge" of residents' habits and behaviors, what they are suggesting is that everything those residents ever do—whether in public, or in spaces and settings formerly thought of as private—can be sensed accurately, raised to the network without loss, and submitted to the consideration of some system capable of interpreting it appropriately. And furthermore, that all of these efforts can somehow, by means unspecified, avoid being skewed by the entropy, error and contingency that mark everything else that transpires inside history. The greatest degree of skepticism is advisable here. It's hard to see how Siemens, or anybody else, might avoid the slippage that's bound to occur at every step of this process, even under the most favorable circumstances imaginable.

However thoroughly sensors might be deployed in a city, they'll only ever capture the qualities about the world that are amenable to capture. As the architect and critical-data scholar Laura Kurgan has argued, "we measure the things that are easy to measure ... the things that are cheap to measure,"[33] and this suggests that sensors, however widely deployed, will only ever yield a partial picture of the world. So what if information crucial to the formulation of sound civic policy is somehow absent from their soundings, resides in the space between them, or is derived from the interaction between whatever quality of the world we set out to measure and our corporeal experience of it?

Other distortions may creep into the quantification of urban processes. Actors whose performance is subject to measurement may consciously adapt their behavior to produce metrics favorable to them in one way or another. For example, a police officer under pressure to "make quota" may issue citations for infractions she would ordinarily overlook,[34] while conversely, her precinct commander, squeezed by City Hall to present the city as an ever-safer haven for investment, may downwardly classify a felony assault as a simple misdemeanor. This is the phenomenon known to viewers of *The Wire* as "juking the stats," and it's particularly likely to occur when financial or other incentives are contingent on achieving some nominal performance threshold.[35] Nor is this manipulation the only factor likely to skew the act of data collection; long, sad experience suggests that the usual array of all-too-human pressures will continue to condition any such effort—consider the recent case in which Seoul Metro operators were charged with using CCTV cameras to surreptitiously ogle women passengers, rather than scan platforms and cars for criminal activity as intended.[36]

What about those human behaviors, and they are many, that we may for whatever reason wish to hide, dissemble, disguise or otherwise prevent being disclosed to the surveillant systems all around us? "Perfect knowledge," by definition, implies either that no such attempts at obfuscation will be made, or that any and all such attempts will remain fruitless. Neither one of these circumstances sounds very much like any city I'm familiar with.

And what about the question of interpretation? The Siemens scenario amounts to a bizarre compound assertion that each of our acts has a single salient meaning, which is always and invariably straightforwardly self-evident—in fact, so much so that this meaning can be recognized, made sense of and acted upon remotely by a machinic system, without any possibility of mistaken appraisal. The most prominent advocates of this approach appear to believe that the contingency of data capture is not an issue, nor is any particular act of interpretation involved in making use of whatever data is retrieved from the world in this way.

When discussing their own smart-city venture, senior IBM executives argue,[37] in so many words, that "the data is the data": transcendent, limpid and uncompromised by human frailty. This mystification of "the data" goes unremarked upon and unchallenged in the overwhelming majority of discussions of the smart city. But surely these intelligent and experienced professionals know better. Different values for air pollution in a given location can be produced by varying the height at which a sensor is mounted by a few meters. Perceptions of risk in a neighborhood can be transformed by slightly altering the taxonomy used to classify reported crimes.[38] And anyone who's ever worked in opinion polling knows how sensitive the results are to the precise wording of a survey. The fact is that the data is never "just" the data, and to assert otherwise is to lend inherently political and interested decisions regarding the act of data collection an unwonted gloss of neutrality and dispassionate scientific objectivity.

The bold claim of perfect knowledge appears incompatible with the messy reality of all known information-processing systems, the human individuals and institutions that make use of them and, more broadly, with the world as we experience it. In fact, it's astonishing that any experienced engineer would ever be so unwary as to claim "perfection" on behalf of any computational system, no matter how powerful.

The notion that there is *one and only one solution* to urban problems is also deeply puzzling. With their inherent diversity and complexity, we can usefully think of cities as *tragic*. As individuals and communities, the people who live in them hold to multiple competing and equally valid conceptions of the good, and it's impossible to fully satisfy all of them at the same time. A wavefront of gentrification can open up exciting new opportunities for young homesteaders, small retailers and craft producers, in other words, but tends to displace the very people who'd given a neighborhood its desirable character and identity in the first place. An increased police presence on the streets of a district reassures some residents, but makes others uneasy, and puts yet others at definable risk. Even something as seemingly straightforward and honorable as an anticorruption initiative can undo a fabric of relations that offered the otherwise voiceless at least some access to local power. We should know by now that there are and can be no Pareto-optimal solutions for any system as complex as a city.[39]

That such a solution, if it even existed, could be *arrived at algorithmically* is also subject to the starkest doubt. Assume, for the sake of argument, that there did exist a master formula capable of resolving all resource allocation conflicts and balancing the needs of all of a city's competing constituencies. It certainly would be convenient if this golden mean could be determined automatically and consistently, via the application of a set procedure—in a word, algorithmically.

In urban planning, the idea that certain kinds of challenges are susceptible to algorithmic resolution has a long pedigree. It's present in the Corbusian doctrine that the ideal and correct ratio of spatial provisioning in a city can be calculated from nothing more than an enumeration of the population, it underpins the complex composite indices Jay Forrester devised in his groundbreaking 1969 *Urban Dynamics*, and it lay at the heart of the RAND Corporation's (eventually disastrous) intervention in the management of 1970s New York City.[40] No doubt part of the idea's appeal to smart-city advocates, too, is the familial resemblance such an algorithm would bear to the formulae by which commercial real-estate developers calculate air rights, the land area that must be reserved for parking in a community of a given size, and so on.

These are tools developers already know how to use, and in the right context and at the appropriate scale, they are surely helpful. But the wholesale surrender of municipal management to an algorithmic toolset seems to repose an undue amount of trust in the party responsible for authoring the algorithm. At least, if the formulae at the heart of the Siemens scenario turn out to be anything at all like the ones used in the current generation of computational models, critical, life-altering decisions will hinge on the interaction of poorly defined and surprisingly subjective values: a "quality of life" metric, a vague category of "supercreative" occupations, or other idiosyncrasies along these lines.[41] The output generated by such a procedure may turn on half-clever abstractions, in which a complex circumstance resistant to direct measurement is represented by the manipulation of some more easily determined proxy value: average walking speed stands in for the more inchoate "pace" of urban life, while the number of patent applications constitutes an index of "innovation."

Quite simply, we need to understand that the authorship of an algorithm intended to guide the distribution of civic resources is itself an inherently political act. And at least as things stand today, nowhere in the extant smart-city literature is there any suggestion that either algorithms or their designers would be subject to the ordinary processes of democratic accountability.

And finally, it's supremely difficult to believe that any such findings would ever be encoded in public policy, and applied transparently, dispassionately and in a manner free from politics. Even the most cursory review of the relevant history suggests that policy recommendations derived from computational models are only rarely applied to questions as politically sensitive as resource allocation without some intermediate tuning taking place. Inconvenient results may be suppressed, arbitrarily overridden by more heavily weighted decision factors, or simply ignored.

The best-documented example of this tendency remains the work of the New York City-RAND Institute, explicitly chartered to implant in the governance of New York City "the kind of streamlined, modern management that Robert McNamara applied in the Pentagon with such success" during his tenure as secretary of defense (1961–68).[42] The statistics-driven approach that McNamara's Whiz Kids had so famously brought to the prosecution of the war in Vietnam, variously thought of as "systems analysis" or "operations research," was first applied to New York in a series of studies conducted between 1973 and 1975, in which RAND used FDNY incident response-time data to determine the optimal distribution of fire stations.

Methodological flaws undermined the effort from the outset. RAND, for simplicity's sake, chose to use the time a company arrived at the scene of a fire as the basis of their model, rather than the time at which that company actually began fighting the fire. (Somewhat unbelievably, for anyone with the slightest familiarity with New York City, RAND's analysts then compounded their error by refusing to acknowledge traffic as a factor in response time.)[43]

Again, we see some easily measured value used as a proxy for a reality that is harder to quantify, and again we see the distortion of ostensibly neutral results by the choices made by an algorithm's designers. But the more enduring lesson for proponents of data-driven policy has to do with how the study's results were applied. Despite the mantle of coolly "objective" scientism that systems analysis preferred to wrap itself in, RAND's final recommendations bowed to factionalism within the Fire Department, as well as the departmental leadership's need to placate critical external constituencies; the exercise, in other words, turned out to be nothing if not political.

The consequences of RAND's intervention were catastrophic. Following their recommendations, fire battalions in some of the sections of the city most vulnerable to fire were decommissioned, while the department opened other stations in low-density, low-threat neighborhoods—neighborhoods, we may note, which just happened to be disproportionately wealthy and white. The resulting spatial distribution of fire-fighting assets actually prevented resources from being applied where they were most critically needed. Great swaths of the city's poorest neighborhoods burned to the ground as a direct consequence: most memorably the South Bronx, but immense tracts of Manhattan and Brooklyn as well. Hundreds of thousands of residents were displaced, many permanently, and the unforgettable images that emerged fueled perceptions of the city's nigh-apocalyptic unmanageability that impeded its prospects well into the 1980s. Might a less-biased model, or an application of the extant findings that was less skewed by the needs of political expediency, have produced a more favorable outcome? Like all counterfactual exercises, the answers to such questions are unknowable, forever beyond reach. But the human and economic calamity that actually did transpire is a matter of public record.

Examples like this counsel us to be wary of claims that any

autonomous system will ever be entrusted with the regulation and control of civic resources—just as we ought to be wary of claims that the application of some single master algorithm could result in an Pareto-efficient distribution of resources, or that the complex urban ecology might be sufficiently characterized in data to permit the effective operation of such an algorithm in the first place. As matters now stand, the claim of perfect competence that is implicit in most smart-city rhetoric is incommensurate with everything we know about the way technical systems work.

But it also flies in the face of everything we know about how *cities* work. The architects of the smart city have utterly failed to reckon with the reality of power, and the perennial ability of various elites to suppress policy directions they find uncongenial to—that word again—their interests. At best, the technocratic notion that the analysis of sensor-derived data would ever be permitted to drive resource-allocation decisions and other acts of municipal policy is naive. At its worst, though, it is culpably negligent of the lessons of history.

That the available evidence strongly suggests that most such data is never leveraged in this way—that, in fact, the formation of municipal policy is guided by just about any concern other than what the data determines—is immaterial. There will always be an enterprise willing to make these arguments, and in this historical period, anyway, there will always be municipal administrations desperate enough for some insight that they're willing to sign on the dotted line. There seems to be little that any of us can do to prevent this. But the rest of us are best advised to approach all claims about the smart city and its ostensible benefits with the greatest caution.

At present, the internet of things is the most tangible material manifestation of a desire to measure and control the world around us. But as an apparatus of capture, it is merely means to an end. The end remains the quantification of the processes of life at every scale; their transformation into digital data; and the use of that data for analysis, the development of projective simulation and the training of machine-learning algorithms. It behooves us to spend some time thinking about what comes along for the ride, every time we invoke this complex of ideas, to consider where it might have come from and what kind of world it is suggesting we live in.

For me, many years of thinking and working in this domain have left behind a clear and vivid picture of that world. It seems strange to assert that anything as broad as a class of technologies might have a dominant emotional tenor, but the internet of things does. That tenor is *sadness*. When we pause to listen for it, the overriding emotion of the internet of things is a melancholy that rolls off of it in waves and sheets. The entire pretext on which it depends is a milieu of continuously shattered attention, of overloaded awareness, and of gaps between people just barely annealed with sensors, APIs and scripts.

Implicit in its propositions is a vision of inner states and home lives alike savaged by bullshit jobs, overcranked schedules and long commutes, of intimacy stifled by exhaustion and the incapacity or unwillingness to be emotionally present. The internet of things in all of its manifestations so often seems like an attempt to paper over the voids between us, or slap a quick technical patch on all the places where capital has left us unable to care for one another.

But for all the reservations we may have along these lines, however sincerely held, they still don't speak to the most sobering circumstance we are confronted with by this class of technologies. This concerns who it is that winds up in possession of the data we shed onto the internet of things, and what they choose to do with it.

Here, heartbreakingly, history furnishes us with a directly relevant case study. In 1936, it became mandatory for each Dutch municipality to maintain a demographic record of its inhabitants; by 1939, each citizen had to carry a *persoonskaart*, or personal identity card. Both included a field for "heritage," or ethnic origin, and this finding was entered alongside all the other facts by which the state Bureau of Statistics characterized its population. This registry was maintained on punched Hollerith cards, the most advanced data-storage and -processing system available at the time.[44]

We may believe that the collection of such facts is fundamentally innocuous, if not an essential aspect of modern statecraft. We may further repose a significant degree of trust in the institutions responsible, and rest easy in the thought that they have our best interests in mind. Perhaps you feel sufficiently assured of the good intentions of our own duly-elected democratic government, and of the checks on its exercise of power imposed by the rule of law, that the mere existence of tools infinitely more powerful than a Hollerith card reader does not trouble you.

But history is replete with reasons for doubt on all of these counts. Regimes, after all, do change, and closely held state secrets are spilled into the open air. Businesses fail, or are acquired, and whatever property belonged to them passes from their control. "Eternal vigilance" sounds stirring enough, but turns out to be rather hard to maintain over time. So what happens when datasets harvested by institutions we trust pass into other, less benevolent hands—as history suggests they demonstrably and reliably do, whether through systems intrusion, corporate acquisition, or simple human clumsiness?

The Dutch experience is instructive. Both the Hollerith cards on which the civil registry of 1936 was tabulated, and the machines necessary to sort and read them, immediately fell under German control after the invasion of 1940. The same data that was innocuous when provided to the Bureau of Statistics turned out to be lethal in the hands of the Gestapo.

Information that under a liberal administration would have been perfectly harmless was literally weaponized by the Germans and their Dutch collaborators, permitting comprehensive roundups and targeted, efficient door-to-door searches for named individuals. In June 1942, mass deportations began. Approximately 107,000 Dutch Jews were sent to the Mauthausen and Bergen-Belsen concentration camps and the death camps of Sobibor and Auschwitz beyond, the latter places where organized murder took place at industrial scale.[45] Fewer than five percent of the deportees survived to the end of the Second World War.

What this precedent reminds us is that data can be acted upon to shape the world, leveraged to produce such an outcome. But also: that in some way *this outcome was always already nestled within the data*, from the moment of its collection. This is the grim reality underneath the pat Foucauldian formulation "power/knowledge," and it stands in sharp rebuke to an age in which we not merely submit to the continuous siphoning of information from our cities, spaces and bodies, but do so willingly and even enthusiastically. As for the commonplace assertion that those who have nothing to hide have nothing to fear, consider the sentiment often attributed to Richelieu, and salient whatever its actual provenance: "If you give me six lines written by the hand of the most honest of men, I will find something in them with which to hang him." This has never been truer than it is in our age of metadata, when analysis of large bodies of data may turn up correlations we weren't ourselves aware of, when drone strikes and acts of extraordinary rendition have been authorized for the most glancing and seemingly coincidental constellations of fact.

So, yes: the internet of things is a sprawling and complex domain of possibility, and it would be foolish to avoid investigating it energetically and in good faith. But we would be wise to approach that investigation with an unusually strong leavening of skepticism, and in particular to resist its attempts to gather data regarding ourselves, our whereabouts, our activities and our affiliations, whatever the blandishments of ease, convenience or self-mastery on offer. The Serbian human rights activist Jasmina Tešanović recently described the internet of things as the "project of a technical elite that aspires to universality,"[46] and in truth that description could apply with as much justice to every technology discussed in this book. Wherever a project has such overtly imperial designs on the everyday as this one, though, it's imperative for us to ask just what vision of universality is being evoked in it—what vision, and whose.

3

Augmented reality

An interactive overlay on the world

Early on the morning of July 8, 2016, a young woman named Shayla Wiggins slipped on a pair of sandals, left her mother's home in the B&K Trailer Park in Riverton, Wyoming, and walked a block or so south, toward the place where State Highway 789 crosses the Wind River.[1] She came to a chainlink fence, climbed over it, and made her way down to the riverbank on the east side of the highway bridge. There she noticed something bobbing in the water, no more than ten feet from shore. What she saw turned out to be the body of a man, later identified by the Fremont County Sheriff's Office as Jeffrey Day, 28, of nearby Arapahoe. This is how Shayla Wiggins became the first person in human history known to have discovered a body while present in two places at once.

What dragged her out of her home that Friday morning was Pokémon Go, an augmented reality (AR) game that had launched just two days before, and immediately became an unprecedented success. Like all AR applications, Pokémon Go furnishes its users with some order of information about the world and the objects in it, superimposing it on the visual field in the form of a location-specific graphic overlay. But where other applications mostly use this overlay to provide pragmatic information—directions from one place to another, historical facts about a given locale, and so on—Pokémon Go presents players with an alternative reality in which monsters of various types inhabit the Earth. You advance in the game by capturing them, and to capture them you must be physically occupying the place where the in-game map says they are.

Shayla Wiggins may have been standing with her sandaled feet planted on the gravelly bank of the Wind River, but in a very real sense she was also present somewhere else: in that dimension only visible to her through the screen of her iPhone 6, where the riverbank south of the trailer park was a perfectly reasonable place to go looking for the Water-element monster she needed to collect.

The conceptual shear between the physical world and the realm overlaid onto it led to more than stumbling onto corpses, of course. The game's enormous popularity pulled people out into the streets en masse, in a startling disruption of all the usual urban patterns—a Situationist fantasy of boundary transgression made completely and wonderfully real. Within hours of the game's release in any given market, you could find knots of players ranging the city in search of virtual monsters, bumping into other clusters of people doing the very same thing, and their mutual delight was palpable. Palpable, as well, was the total mystification of passersby, unable to imagine why so many people should suddenly be darting across roadways and stumbling into traffic with their smartphones held up before them like digital dowsing wands.

Other problems soon emerged, of the kind that became inevitable the moment somebody proposed superimposing a game of imaginary cartoon monsters onto an underlying terrain that may be strongly charged with meaning, memory and sorrow. In its first days, Pokémon Go lured players to a wide array of wildly inappropriate locations like the National September 11th

Memorial and Arlington National Cemetery, where playing any sort of game can only be understood as an act of disrespect.[2] The promise of capturing rare monsters even drew people to places where simply wandering through would place them at terrible risk, like the Truce Village at Panmunjom, in the heavily fortified Demilitarized Zone between North and South Korea.[3] And I doubt that even the most cynical observer ever imagined that a developer would be so irresponsible as to enable game-play superimposed onto the barracks and crematoria of the Auschwitz death camp, but this is just what Pokémon Go did during its first week live.[4] (All of these sites were swiftly deleted from the game by developer Niantic.)

Theorists had discussed the implications of augmented reality for years, and in its first breakout hit just about all of them immediately came to pass: the reality shear, the dissonance of the mundane draped in a virtual shroud of whimsical other-ness, the things that happen when different groups of people are presented with varying versions of what had always been a shared baseline environment. If AR is to be a mode through which we broadly experience the everyday, these are the issues it will compel us to contend with.

Augmented reality, and its close cousin virtual reality (VR), are a little different from the other technologies considered in this book. They are interface techniques—modes of media-tion, rather than anything more fundamental. The difference between the two is largely the degree to which digital graphics dominate the perceptual field. VR is an immersive experience, and accordingly requires the use of a head-mounted appara-tus that isolates its wearer from the rest of the visible world. Once ensconced inside, the user is psychically present in a thor-oughly self-contained, fully rendered environment, and for the most part interacts there with things that do not exist on the outside.

By contrast, AR blends its cues and graphic overlays with the ordinary world as we perceive it, and doesn't require any par-ticularly specialized gear. At the moment, as with Shayla Wiggins and her iPhone, the augmentive layer is most often presented on the screen of a phone or tablet. But it can also be superimposed onto a conventional window, a vehicle windshield, the visor of a helmet, or even a lightweight, face-mounted reticle, as with Google's notorious Project Glass.

AR has its conceptual roots in informational displays developed for military pilots in the early 1960s, when the performance of enemy fighter aircraft first began to overwhelm a human pilot's ability to react to the environment in a sufficiently timely manner. In the fraught regime of jet-age dogfighting, even a momentary dip of the eyes to a dashboard-mounted instrument cluster could mean disaster. The solution was to project information about altitude, airspeed and the status of weapons and other critical aircraft systems onto a transparent pane aligned with the field of vision: a "head-up display."

This technique turned to have applicability in fields beyond aerial combat, where the issue wasn't so much reaction time as visual complexity. One early AR system was intended to help engineers make sense of the gutty tangle of hydraulic lines, wiring and control mechanisms in the fuselage of an airliner under construction; each component in the otherwise-hopeless confusion was overlaid with a visual tag identifying it by name, color-coded according to the assembly it belonged to.[5] Other head-up systems were designed to help people manage situations in which both time and the complexity of the environment were sources of pressure—for example, to aid first responders arriving at the scene of an emergency.[6] One such prototype furnished firefighters with visors onto which structural diagrams of a burning building were projected, along with symbols indicating egress routes, the location of other emergency personnel, and the position of electric wiring, gas lines and other potentially dangerous infrastructural elements.

The necessity of integrating what were then relatively crude and heavy cameras, motion sensors and projectors into a comfortably wearable package limited the success of these early efforts, and this is to say nothing of the challenges posed by the difficulty of establishing a reliable network connection to a mobile unit in the pre-WiFi era. But the conceptual heavy lifting done to support these initial forays produced a readymade discourse, waiting for the day it might be possible to augment the whole world through the use of smaller, lighter, more capable hardware.

That day arrived with the advent of the smartphone. As we've seen, the smartphone handset brings together in a single package several different sensing and presentation technologies, which can be recombined to produce distinctly different ways of engaging networked information. Bundle a camera, accelerometer/gyroscope, and display screen in a single networked handset, and what you have in your hands is something that can sustain at least a rudimentary augmentive overlay. Add GPS functionality and a high-resolution three-dimensional model of the world—either maintained onboard the device, or resident in the cloud—and a viewer can be offered location-specific information, registered with and mapped onto the surrounding environment.

In essence, phone-based AR treats the handset like the transparent pane of a cockpit head-up display: you hold it before you, its forward-facing camera captures the field of view, and an overlay of information is applied on top of it. Turn, and the on-screen view turns with you, tracked (after a momentary stutter) by the grid of overlaid graphics. And those graphics can provide anything the network itself offers, whether identification, annotation, direction or commentary. Here is one of the core premises of AR: that everything the network knows might be brought to bear on someone or -thing standing in front of us, directly there, directly accessible, available to anyone with the wherewithal to sign a two-year smartphone contract and download an app. This is a deeply seductive idea. It offers an aura of omnipotence, positioned as a direct extension of our own senses.

Consider, for example, how AR might be used to address a disorder called prosopagnosia, more commonly known as faceblindness.[7] This condition affects an estimated 2.5 percent of the population, and as the name suggests, it deprives its victims of the ability to recognize faces and associate them with individuals; at the limit, someone suffering with a severe case may be unable to remember what his or her loved ones look like. So central is the ability to recognize others to human socialization, though, that even far milder cases can be the cause of significant discomfort, both for the sufferer and for those they encounter.

Sadly, this is something I can attest to from firsthand experience. Even with a relatively attenuated form of faceblindness, my broad inability to recognize people routinely results in the most excruciating awkwardness. Deprived of contextual cues— the time and location at which I habitually encounter someone, a distinctive hairstyle or mode of dress—I generally find myself no more able to recognize former colleagues or students than I can complete strangers. And as uncomfortable as this can be for me, I can only imagine how humiliating it is for the person on the other end of the encounter. I long ago lost track of the number of times in my life when I would have been grateful for some subtle intercessionary agent, a technological equivalent of the nomenclators of old: something that might drop a glowing outline over the face of someone approaching me and remind me of his or her name, the occasion on which we met last, maybe even what we talked about on that occasion.[8] It would spare both of us from mortification, and shield my counterpart from the inadvertent but real insult implied by my failure to recognize them.

In the abstract, the ambition of using AR in this role is lovely—precisely the kind of sensitive technical deployment I believe in, where technology is used to lower the barriers to socialization, and reduce or eliminate the social discomfort that might otherwise prevent us from knowing one another better. But it's hard to imagine any such thing being accomplished by the act of holding a phone up in front of my face, *between* us, forcing you to wait first for me to do so and then for the entire chain of technical events that must follow in order to fulfill the aim at the heart of the scenario.

The device must acquire an image of your face with the camera, establish the parameters of that face from the image, and upload those parameters to the cloud via the fastest available connection, so they can be compared with a database of facial measurements belonging to known individuals. If a match is found, the corresponding profile must be located, and the appropriate information from that profile piped back down the connection so it may be displayed as an overlay on the screen image.

Too many articulated parts are involved in this interaction, too many dependencies—not least of which is the cooperation of Facebook, Google or some other enterprise with a reasonably robust database of facial biometrics, and that is of course wildly problematic for other reasons. Better I should have confessed my confusion to you in the first place.

If phone-based augmentation performs poorly as social lubricant, what about another role frequently proposed for it, especially by advocates in the cultural heritage sector? The utility and value of this mode of use hinge on the argument that by superimposing images or other vestiges of the past of a place directly over its present, AR effectively endows its users with the ability to see through time.

This might not make much sense at all in a young place, especially not any of those new cities now being built from scratch on greenfield sites. But anyone who lives in a place old enough to have felt the passage of centuries knows that history can all too easily be forgotten by the stones of the city. Whatever perturbations from historical events may still be propagating through the various flows of people, matter, energy and information that make a place, they certainly aren't evident to casual inspection. An augmented view returning the layered past to the present, in such a way as to color our understanding of the things all around us, might well prove to be more emotionally resonant than any conventional monument.

Byzantium, old Edo, Roman Londinium, even New Amsterdam: each of these historical sites is rife with traces we might wish to surface in the city that occupies the same land at present. Neighborhoods overwhelmed by more recent waves of colonization, gentrification or redevelopment, too, offer us opportunities to consider just how we arrived at our moment in time. It would surely be instructive to retrieve some record of the jazz- and espresso-driven Soho of the 1950s and layer it over what stands there at present; the same goes for the South Bronx of 1975. But traversed as it was during the twentieth century by multiple, high-intensity crosscurrents of history, Berlin may present the ultimate terrain on which to contemplate recuperation of the past.

This is a place where pain, guilt and a sense of responsibility contend with the simple desire to get on with things; no city I'm familiar with is more obsessively dedicated to the search for a tenable balance between memory and forgetting. The very core of contemporary Berlin is given over to a series of resonant absences and artificially sustained presences, from the ruins of Gestapo headquarters, now maintained as a museum called Topography of Terror, to the remnants of Checkpoint Charlie. A long walk to the east along leafy Karl-Marx-Allee—between 1949 and 1961, Stalinallee—takes you to the headquarters of the Stasi, the feared secret police of the former East Germany, also open to the public as a museum. But there's nowhere in Berlin where the curious cost of remembering can be more keenly felt than in the field of 2,711 concrete slabs at the corner of Ebertstrasse and Hannah-Arendt-Strasse. This is the Memorial to the Murdered Jews of Europe, devised by architect Peter Eisenman, with early conceptual help from the great sculptor Richard Serra.

Formally, the grim array is the best thing Eisenman has ever set his hand to—here we are most likely perceiving Serra's influence. But as a site of memory, the Monument leaves a great deal to be desired. It's what Michel Foucault called a heterotopia: something set apart from the ordinary operations of the city, physically and semantically, a place of such ponderous gravity that visitors don't quite know what to make of it. On my most recent visit, the canyons between the slabs rang with the laughter of French schoolchildren on a field trip; the children giggled and flirted and shouted to one another as they leapt between the stones, and whatever the designer's intent may have been, any mood of elegy or commemoration was impossible to establish, let alone maintain.

Roughly two miles to the northeast, on the sidewalk in front of a döner stand in Mitte, is a memorial of quite a different sort. Glance down, and you'll see the following words, inscribed into three brass cubes set side by side by side between the cobblestones:

HIER WOHNTE
ELSA GUTTENTAG
GEB. KRAMER
JG. 1883
DEPORTIERT 29.11.1942
ERMORDET IN
AUSCHWITZ

HIER WOHNTE
KURT GUTTENTAG
JG. 1877
DEPORTIERT 29.11.1942
ERMORDET IN
AUSCHWITZ

HIER WOHNTE
ERWIN BUCHWALD
JG. 1892
DEPORTIERT 1.3.1943
ERMORDET IN
AUSCHWITZ

Ermordet in Auschwitz: that is, on specified dates in November of 1942 and March of the next year, the named people living at this address were taken across this very sidewalk and forcibly transported hundreds of miles east by the machinery of their own government, to a country they'd never known and a facility expressly designed to murder them. The looming façades around you were the last thing they ever saw as free people.

It's in the dissonance between the everyday bustle of Mitte and these implacable facts that the true horror resides—and that's precisely what makes the brass cubes a true memorial, indescribably more effective than Eisenman's. The brass cubes, it turns out, are *Stolpersteine,* or "stumbling blocks," a project of artist Gunter Demnig;[9] these are but three of what are now over 32,000 that Demnig has arranged to have placed, in some 700 European cities. The Stolpersteine force us to read this stretch of unremarkable sidewalk in two ways simultaneously: both as a place where ordinary people go placidly about their ordinary business, just as they did in 1942, and as one site of a world-historical, continental-scale ravening.

The stories etched in these stones are the kind of facts about a place that would seem to do well when told via augmented reality. The objection could certainly be raised that I found them so resonant precisely because I don't see them every day, and that their impact would very likely fade with constant exposure; we might call this the evil of banality. But these stones compelled me to see and interpret the mundane things I did in these streets through the revenant past, and altered my consciousness in ways subtler and longer-lasting than anything Eisenman's sepulchral array of slabs was able to achieve. Presenting the same information via AR would admittedly drain the poetry from Demnig's potent metaphor, but it's easy for me to imagine the disorienting, decentering, dis-placing impact of having to engage the world through a soft rain of names, overlaid onto the very places from which their owners were stolen.

But once again, it's hard to imagine this happening via the intercession of a handset. Nor are the qualities that make smartphone-based AR so catastrophically clumsy, in virtually every scenario of use, particularly likely to change over time.

The first of these qualities has to do with the way in which we engage the smartphone's functionality. The smartphone is a platform on which each discrete mode of operation is engaged via a dedicated, single-purpose app; any attempt at augmenting the environment must therefore be actively and consciously invoked, to the exclusion of other useful functionality. When it's used to provide an overlay, the phone cannot simultane-ously be used to send a message, look up an address, buy a cup of coffee, or do any of the other things we now routinely expect of it.

The second reservation is physical. Providing the user with a display surface on which a graphic annotation of the forward view might appear simply isn't what the handset was designed to do. It must be held before the eyes like a pane of glass in order for the augmented overlay to work as intended. It hardly needs to be pointed out that this gesture is not one particularly well suited to the realities of urban experience. It has the doubly unappealing quality of announcing the user's distraction and vulnerability to onlookers, while simultaneously ensuring that the device is held in the weak grip of the extended arm—a grasp from which it may be plucked with relative ease.

Taken together, these two impositions strongly undercut the primary ostensible virtue of an augmented view: its immediacy. The sole genuine justification for AR is the idea that informa-tion is simply *there*, and can be assimilated without thought or effort. And if this sense of effortlessness will never truly be achievable via handset, it is precisely what an emerging class of wearable mediators aims to provide for its users.

The first of this class to reach consumers was the ill-fated Google Glass, which mounted a high-definition, forward-facing camera, a head-up reticle and the microphone required by its natural-language speech recognition interface on a lightweight aluminum frame. While Glass posed any number of aesthetic, practical and social concerns—all of which remain to be convincingly addressed, by Google or anyone else—it does at least give us a way to compare hands-free, head-mounted AR with the handset-based approach. Would either of the augmentation scenarios we explored be improved by moving the informational overlay from the phone to a wearable display?

A system designed to mitigate prosopagnosia by recognizing faces would assuredly be vastly superior when accessed via head-mounted interface. In fact, as things now stand this remains one of the very few credible scenarios in which technical intervention might usefully be brought to bear on relatively close-range interpersonal encounters. The delay and physical awkwardness imposed by having to hold a phone between us goes away, and while there would still be a noticeable saccade or visual stutter as I glanced up to read your details off my display, you might well find this preferable to not being remembered at all.

So maybe here is a valid role for the wearable augmentor—if, that is, we can tolerate the very significant threats to privacy involved, which only begin with Google's ownership of or access to the necessary biometric database. There's also the question of their access to the pattern of my requests, and above all the one fact inescapably inherent to the scenario: that the people I encounter are by definition being identified as being present in a certain time and place, without anyone having lifted a finger to secure their consent to that identification. By any standard, this is a great deal of risk to take on to lubricate social interactions for 2.5 percent of the population.

The Stolpersteine scenario of augmentation, by contrast, fares a little bit better. It's relatively easy to imagine how a "history layer" might usefully, and even resonantly, be superimposed on everything we see. And this suggests something about further uses for augmentive mediators like Glass, for it is by no means just historical information that can be overlaid across the visual field. If our choices are at all times shaped by indistinct currents of traffic and pricing, crime and conviviality, it's easy to understand the appeal of any technology proposing that these dimensions of knowledge be brought to bear on everything we see, whether singly or in combination. The risk of bodily harm, whatever its source, might be rendered as a red wash over the field of vision; point-by-point directions as a bright and unmistakable guideline reaching into the landscape. In fact, *any* pattern of use and activity—so long as its traces were harvested by some data-gathering system, and made available to the network—could be made manifest to us in this way. (In a later section of the book, we'll discuss the very deep challenges involved in producing any one of these bodies of information in a way that doesn't reinforce preexisting patterns of bias and injustice, but for now we need merely note that these are surely present in the datasets that some party will sooner or later attempt to layer over the world via AR.)

Some proposed uses are more ambitious still, pushing past mere annotation of the forward view to the provision of truly novel modes of perception—for example, the ability to "see" radiation at wavelengths beyond the limits of human vision, or even to delete features of the visual environment perceived as undesirable.[10] What, then, keeps wearable augmentation from being the ultimate way for networked selves to receive and act on information?

The consumer-grade augmented reality currently available confronts us with an interlocking series of concerns, ranging from the immediately practical to the existential.

The initial reservations center on the technical difficulties that are involved in articulating an acceptably high-quality experience. Most of the value in AR resides in the proposition that interacting with the world in this way will feel "effortless." But as we've seen, any such effortlessness requires the continuous, smooth interfunctioning of a wild scatter of heterogeneous elements. In order to make good on this promise, a mediating technology needs to fuse a sensitively designed interface with accurate, timely, meaningful and actionable information, and a robust, high-bandwidth connection to the network furnishing that information from any place on Earth.

Unfortunately, the technical infrastructure capable of delivering these elements reliably enough does not yet exist—not anywhere in North America or Western Europe, at any rate, not this year or next. The hard fact is that for a variety of reasons having to do with national electromagnetic-spectrum allocation policy, a lack of perceived business incentives for universal broadband connectivity, and other seemingly intractable circumstances, these issues are nowhere near to being ironed out. This probably doesn't matter very much in the context of a game like Pokémon Go, but would notably degrade the experience of anyone trying to use AR in a more sensitive register.

There are further, deeper concerns as well. In the context of augmentation, the truth value of representations made about the world acquires heightened significance. Merely by superimposing information directly on its object, AR arrogates to itself a peculiar claim to authority, of a more aggressive sort than those implicit in other modes of representation.

Very often, the information that is being furnished so authoritatively will simply be wrong. An overlay can only ever be as good as the data feeding it, after all, and the augurs in this respect are not particularly reassuring. Right now, Google's map of the commercial stretch nearest to my house provides labels for only four of the seven storefront businesses on the block, one of which is inaccurately identified as a shop that closed many years ago. If even Google, with all the resources it has at its disposal, struggles to provide its users with a description of the streetscape that is both comprehensive and correct, how much more daunting will other actors find the same task? It's easy to argue that anyone involved in the provision of augmentive information ought to be held to a high standard of completeness and accuracy, or, at the very least, that some kind of indication should be offered as to the confidence of a proffered identification. But who is in a position to enforce any such standards?

Beyond this lies a series of well-documented problems with visual misregistration and latency, problems that have only been exacerbated by the shift to consumer-grade hardware.[11] At issue is the mediation device's ability to track rapid motions of the head, and smoothly and accurately realign any graphic overlay mapped to the world; any delay in realignment of more than a few tens of milliseconds is conspicuous, and risks causing vertigo, nausea and problems with balance and coordination. The initial release of Glass, at least, wisely shied away from any attempt to superimpose such overlays, but the issue must be reckoned with at some point if usefully augmentive navigational applications are ever to be developed.

A third set of concerns centers on the question of how long such a mediator might comfortably be worn, and what happens after it is taken off. This is of special concern given the prospect that one or another form of wearable AR might become as prominent in the negotiation of everyday life as the smartphone itself. There is, of course, not much in the way of meaningful prognostication that can be made ahead of any mass adoption, but it's not unreasonable to build our expectations on the few things we do know empirically.

Early users of Google Glass reported disorientation upon removing the headset, after as few as fifteen minutes of use. This is a mild disorientation, to be sure, and easily shaken off—from all accounts, the sort of uneasy feeling that attends staring overlong at an optical illusion, and not the more serious nausea and dizziness suffered by a significant percentage of those using VR.[12]

If this represents the outer limit of discomfort experienced by users, it's hard to believe that it would have much impact on either the desirability of the product or people's ability to function after using it. But further hints as to the consequences of long-term use can be gleaned from the testimony of pioneering researcher Steve Mann, who has worn a succession of ever-lighter and more-capable mediation rigs all but continuously since the mid-1980s. His experience warrants a certain degree of caution: Mann, in his own words, "developed a dependence on the apparatus," and has found it difficult to function normally on the few occasions he has been forcibly prevented from accessing his array of devices.[13]

When deprived of his setup for even a short period of time, Mann experiences "profound nausea, dizziness and disorientation";[14] he can neither see clearly nor concentrate, and has difficulty with basic cognitive and motor tasks. He speculates that over many years, his neural wiring has adapted to the continuous flow of sensory information through his equipment. This is not an entirely ridiculous thing to think. At this point, the network of processes that constitutes Steve Mann's brain—that in some real albeit reductive sense constitutes *Steve Mann*—lives partially outside his skull.

The objection could be made that this is always already the case, for all of us: that some nontrivial part of everything that make us what we are lives outside of us, in the world, and that Mann's situation is only different in that much of his outboard being subsists in a single, self-designed apparatus. But if anything, this makes the prospect of becoming physiologically habituated to something like Google Glass still more worrisome. It's precisely because Mann developed and continues to manage his own mediation equipment that he can balance his dependency on it with the relative freedom of action enjoyed by someone who for the most part is able to determine the parameters under which that equipment operates.

If Steve Mann has become a radically hybridized consciousness, in other words, at least he has a legitimate claim to ownership and control over all of the places where that consciousness is instantiated. By contrast, all of the things a commercial product can do for the user rely on the ongoing provision of a service—and if there's anything we know about services, it's that they can be and are routinely discontinued at will, as the provider fails, changes hands, adopts a new business strategy or simply reprioritizes. (Indeed, as we shall see, this is what happened to Google Glass itself.)

A final set of strictly practical reservations have to do with the collective experience of augmentation, or what implications our own choice to be mediated in this way might hold for the experience of others sharing the environment.

For all it may pretend to transparency, literally and metaphorically, any augmentive mediator by definition imposes itself between the wearer and the world. This, of course, is by no means a quality unique to augmented reality. It's something AR has in common with a great many ways we already buffer and mediate what we experience as we move through space, from listening to music to wearing sunglasses. All of these impose a certain distance between us and the full experiential manifold of the environment, either by baffling the traces of it that reach our senses, or by offering us a space in which we can imagine and project an alternative narrative of our actions.

But there's a special asymmetry that haunts our interactions with networked technology, and tends to undermine our psychic investment in the immediate physical landscape; if "cyberspace is where you are when you're on the phone," it's certainly also the "place" you are when you text or tweet someone while walking down the sidewalk.[15] In the past, I've referred to what happens when someone moves through the world while simultaneously engaged in some kind of remote interaction as a condition of "multiple simultaneous adjacency," but of course it's really no such thing: so far, at least, only one mode of spatial experience can be privileged at a given time. And if it's impossible to participate fully in both of these realms at once, one of them must lose out.

Watch what happens when a pedestrian first becomes conscious of receiving a call or a text message, the immediate disruption they cause in the flow of movement as they pause to respond to it. Whether the call is made hands-free or otherwise doesn't really seem to matter; the cognitive and emotional investment we make in it is what counts, and this investment is generally so much greater than that we make in our surroundings that street life clearly suffers as a result.

The risk inherent in this divided attention appears to be showing up in the relevant statistics in the form of an otherwise hard-to-account-for upturn in accidents involving pedestrian fatalities,[16] where such numbers had been falling for years, and of course we can clearly see it at work in the worrisome tally of injuries that began to mount almost immediately after the launch of Pokémon Go. This is a tendency that is only likely to be exacerbated by further augmentive mediation of the everyday, particularly where content of high inherent emotional involvement is concerned.

The sociologist Lyn Lofland argues persuasively that the ordinary flow of movement on big-city sidewalks should be regarded as a collaborative production—a hard-won achievement in "cooperative motility" that requires the most sensitive attention to the subtle signals other pedestrians issue as to their intended course and speed. But is this achievement being eroded by our involvement with technologies that demand to be at the focus of attention, to the exclusion of all else?[17] More broadly, what does our immersion in the interface do to our sense of being in public, that state of being copresent with and available to others that teaches us how to live together, and ultimately furnishes the metropolis with its highest and best justification?

At this moment in time, the maximum enthusiasm for the prospect of wearable augmentation appears to have passed. Its vocal cohort of advocates within the technology community have, for the moment, fallen silent, though remnant expressions of zeal still burble up from time to time. Their fervor can be difficult to comprehend, so long as AR is simply understood to refer to a class of technologies aimed at overlaying the visual field with information about the objects and circumstances in it. It only begins to make sense when we grant AR its proper place in the technological imaginary.

What the discourse around AR shares with other contemporary trans- and posthuman narratives is a frustration with the limits of the flesh, and a frank interest in transcending them through technical means. To advocates, the true appeal of projects like Google's Glass is that they are first steps toward the fulfillment of a deeper promise: that of *becoming-cyborg*. Some of these advocates suggest that ordinary people might learn to mediate the challenges of everyday life via complex informational dashboards; the more fervent dream of a day when their capabilities are enhanced far beyond the merely human by a seamless union of organic consciousness with networked sensing, processing, analytic and storage assets.

Beyond the profound technical and practical challenges involved in achieving any such goal, though, anyone uncommitted to one or another posthuman program may find that they have philosophical reservations with this notion, and what it implies for everyday life. These may be harder to quantify than strictly practical objections, but any advocate of augmentation technologies who is also interested in upholding the notion of the everyday environment as a shared and democratic space will have to come to some reckoning with them.

Anyone who cares about what we might call the full bandwidth of human communication—very much including transmission and reception of those cues vital to mutual understanding, but only present beneath the threshold of conscious perception—ought to be concerned about the risk posed to interpersonal exchanges by augmentive mediation. Wearable devices clearly have the potential to exacerbate existing problems of self-absorption and mutual inconsideration.[18] Although in principle there's no reason such devices couldn't be designed to support or even enrich the sense of intersubjectivity, what we've seen about the technologically mediated pedestrian's unavailability to the street doesn't leave us much room for optimism on this count. The implication is that if the physical environment doesn't fully register to a person so equipped, neither will other people.

Nor is the body by any means the only domain that the would-be posthuman subject may wish to transcend via augmentation. Subject as it is to the corrosive effects of entropy and time, forcing those occupying it to contend with the inconvenient demands of others, the built environment is another. Especially given current levels of investment in physical infrastructure in the United States, there is a very real risk that those who are able to do so will prefer retreat behind a wall of mediation to the difficult work of being fully present in public. At its zenith, this tendency implies both a dereliction of public space, and an almost total abandonment of any notion of a shared public realm.

The most distressing consequences of such a dereliction would be felt by those left behind. What happens when the information necessary to comprehend and operate an environment is not immanent to that environment, but has become decoupled from it? When signs, directions, notifications, alerts and all the other instructions necessary to the fullest use of the city appear only in an augmentive overlay—and, as will inevitably be the case, that overlay is made available to some but not others?[19]

What happens to the unaugmented human under such circumstances? The perils surely extend beyond a mere inability to act on information; past a certain point in time, someone without access to the technology almost always places themselves at jeopardy of being seen as a willful transgressor of norms, even an ethical offender. Anyone forgoing augmentation, for whatever reason, may find that they are perceived as somehow less than a full member of the community, with everything that implies for the right to be and act in public.

The deepest critique of augmented reality is sociologist Anne Galloway's, and it is harder to answer. Galloway suggests that the discourse of computational augmentation, whether consciously or otherwise, "position[s] everyday places and social interactions as somewhat lacking or in need of improvement." Again there's this sense of a zero-sum relationship between AR and a public realm already in considerable peril just about everywhere.

This is conscious, if not in the AR community itself then at least on the part of some of the most prominent developers of commercial virtual-reality gear.[20] One of the primary functions these enthusiasts imagine for VR is to camouflage the inequities and insults of an unjust world, by offering the multitude high-fidelity simulations of the things their betters get to experience for real. This is Oculus Rift developer John Carmack: "Some fraction of the desirable experiences of the wealthy can be synthesized and replicated for a much broader range of people." Here we see articulated—in so many words, and by someone at the center of VR development for many years—the idea that all of the vertiginous inequity we live with is so entrenched and so unchallengeable that all we can do is accede to it, and that the best thing we can do with our technology is use it as a palliative and a pacifier. In a different, perhaps better world, this would be an incendiary statement. But in ours, it was received with barely a batted eyelash.

I have little doubt that there will be creative uses aplenty for VR—richly detailed, gorgeously imagined environments difficult or outright impossible to experience in any other way. I cackled with irrepressible glee, momentarily eight years old again, when in a VR playground called The Lab I stepped through the orbit of Jupiter, picked it up to examine its bands of cloud more closely, and then hurled it below the plane of the ecliptic like a schoolyard basketball. On the shoulder of Iceland's Snæfellsjökull glacier, I tossed sticks for a hyperactive animated robot dog to chase and catch, drawing a joy from its delighted bounding that would surely shock anyone who knows how I generally feel about dogs and robots both. In different ways, on different levels, these brief immersions took me a long way from the room in which I was standing—and while it happened to be a nice room, and I was happy to return to it, I also know that this won't always be the case for everyone. I wouldn't want to deny anyone these experiences, or the still more elaborate and beautifully realized ones to come. But I'm afraid that on a deeper level, Carmack has the truth of the situation.

Maybe the emergence of these systems will spur us to some thought as to what it is we're trying so hard to augment or escape from. Philip K. Dick once defined reality as "that which, when you stop believing in it, doesn't go away," and it's this bedrock quality of universal accessibility—to anyone at all, at any time of his or her choosing—that constitutes reality's primary virtue.[21]

If nothing else, reality is the one platform we all share, a ground we can start from in undertaking the arduous and never-comfortable process of determining what else we might agree upon. To replace this shared space with the million splintered and mutually inconsistent realities of individual augmentation is to give up on the whole pretense that we in any way occupy the same world, and therefore strikes me as being deeply inimical to the broader urban project. A city where the physical environment has ceased to function as a common reference frame is, at the very least, terribly inhospitable soil for democracy, solidarity or simple fellow-feeling.

It may well be that this concern is overblown. There is always the possibility that neither augmented nor virtual reality will amount to very much—that the nausea, disorientation and vertigo they occasion simply cannot be surmounted, or that after a brief period of consideration they are actively rejected by the mainstream audience.

This was the fate of Google Glass. Within days of the first significant nonspecialist publicity around it, Seattle dive bar the 5 Point café became the first commercial establishment known to have enacted a ban on Glass,[22] and this early, weak signal solidified rapidly into a rough consensus that wearing Glass in public constituted a serious *faux pas*. The term most often used to describe users—"Glasshole"—left them with no doubt what others thought of them. By the time Google enlisted couturier Diane von Furstenberg[23] to help design a version that might be more acceptable to the public, and less fraught with overtones of Silicon Valley triumphalism, it was already too late.

Perhaps the AR systems that follow Glass will come to rest in the same cultural-aesthetic purgatory once occupied by Bluetooth headsets, or perhaps, indeed, the paradigm of the face-mounted reticle is permanently dead. But something tells me that none of the objections we've discussed here will prove broadly dissuasive. It is hard to argue against a technology that glimmers with the promise of transcendence. Over anything beyond the immediate near term, some form of wearable augmentive device does seem bound to take a prominent role in mediating the everyday. The question then becomes what kind(s) of shared space will be produced by people endowed with this particular set of capabilities, individually and collectively—and how we might help the unmediated contend with environments unlike any they have known before, enacted for the convenience of the ambiguously transhuman, under circumstances whose depths have yet to be plumbed.

4

Digital fabrication

Towards a new political economy of matter

A roughly cubical object of modest scale, rounded at the corners, sits on a dusty tabletop in the University College London building where I teach one day a week. Faintly smelling of long-chain molecules, it scarcely seems credible that this little box could transform what is meant by "ownership of the means of production." And yet a means of production is precisely what I am looking at. The cubical object is a MakerBot Replicator 2 3D printer, nothing less than a portable manufactory.

No larger than a first-generation Apple Macintosh, the Replicator 2 can be programmed to produce ... just about anything you can imagine, really, as long as it isn't any larger than eleven inches in any dimension, and you don't mind it being made of a slightly greasy polymer. Fed from a spool of thermoplastic filament, the Replicator heats the material until it liquefies, and then deposits it through a precision print head; as the print head sweeps across its stage, the filament emerges in micrometer-scale layers, incrementally building up the desired form.

To be sure, this is an entry-level model, best suited to whimsical trinkets and rough-and-ready prototyping—exactly the sort of things, in other words, that architecture students are likely to produce in the course of their degree work. But 3D printers like the Replicator 2, as well as the computer numerically controlled (CNC) milling machines and laser cutters elsewhere in the building, might just be the most visible sign of a coming revolution: the digital fabrication of all the things we encounter in the world.

We owe the conceptual genesis of the digital fabrication device to the legendary twentieth-century mathematician John von Neumann, who first broached the notion in a thought experiment he entertained as early as the mid-1940s. Von Neumann's *Theory of Self-Reproducing Automata*,[1] published posthumously in 1966, outlined the principles of a "universal constructor" able to pluck resources from its environment and, given enough time, arrange them into anything desired—including, crucially, exact copies of itself. These copies would immediately set about making further copies, underwriting an exponential increase in production capacity.

Von Neumann's constructors existed in an entirely virtual universe of possibility. At the time he imagined them, there wasn't enough computing power in the world to simulate their behavior, let alone physically realize them as anything other than painstakingly inked grids of pen on paper, so-called cellular automata.[2] But with its implication of a continuously and geometrically expanding productivity, his vision of a universal constructor inspired generations of engineers.

Sometime around the turn of the twenty-first century, one of them—a mechanical engineering professor at the University of Leeds named Adrian Bowyer, troubled by the thought of a world riven by material scarcity—finally took von Neumann at his word. Bowyer's take on the von Neumann constructor was a desktop-scale factory, capable of fabricating most of its own components: the replicating rapid prototyper, or RepRap. As originally designed, there were only a few components the "self-copying" RepRap couldn't make for itself: "self-tapping steel screws, brass brushes, lubricating grease, standard electronic chips … a standard plug-in low-voltage power brick, stepper motors," a bill of materials that came to about $250 all told.[3] Given but these few, relatively inexpensive things, RepRap users could print other RepRaps, in principle driving the incremental cost of each new unit every closer to zero and massively expanding the number of units available in the world. True to the von Neumannian model, "the number of them in existence and the wealth they produce can grow exponentially."

Bowyer's vision of a self-replicating future implied not merely an enormous increase in planetary production capacity, but its radical democratization as well. In this conception of things, there may be fairly stark limitations on what can be produced— combine harvesters and pile drivers are out, similarly mobile phones or tablets—but the barriers to entry are lowered to the point that anyone with the requisite will can own the means of production. And because the RepRap's specifications are open, users are free to tinker and improve upon Bowyer's original design, free to contribute those improvements back to the informational commons so everyone can benefit from them. Bowyer hoped that the fabricator itself would become "subject to evolution by artificial selection," as the fruits of constant, iterative enhancement were incorporated into each new generation.

While the RepRap specification did indeed evolve over several generations of largely community-inspired improvement, the massive proliferation of machines Bowyer imagined never came to pass. As with so many other things, it simply turns out to be cheaper to buy conventionally manufactured RepRap parts from China and have them shipped to you from across the world than it does to print them at home, especially once the value of your own time is factored into the equation.[4] The frank TinkerToy aesthetic of the original RepRap, as well, made it something only an inveterate tinkerer would mind looking at every day. It wasn't until designers began to treat the personal fabrication engine as a consumer product that there was any particularly broad uptake. In time, Bowyer's project directly inspired the founders of MakerBot and Ultimaker, and the machines they went on to produce have become the world's most popular 3D printers; by now the number of them in the wild exceeds a hundred thousand.[5]

Digital fabrication appears to be following the developmental curve we're familiar with from the domain of digital computation, where the steady advance of Moore's Law still yields up devices that are more capable, yet cheaper, with every passing year. What this class of technologies offers us, even now, is the relatively low-cost manufacture of artifacts that are simultaneously detailed in their design, complex in their articulation, and one-of-a-kind.

For many of its most passionate enthusiasts, though, digital fabrication was never about a small-scale, narrowly defined commercial success. It was about upending every assumption the culture holds about how things are made, and who gets to make them. For those invested in the original vision of boundless abundance, emotionally as well as intellectually and politically, the central question remains: can you still make the revolution with a printer that costs $2,000?

A revolution is precisely what is in the offing. A slew of recent books argue that the forces unleashed in society when digital fabrication becomes widespread are inherently and powerfully erosive of capitalism as we have known it. These titles, notably Jeremy Rifkin's *The Zero Marginal Cost Society*, Paul Mason's *Postcapitalism*, and Srnicek and Williams's *Inventing the Future*, hold that as fabricator prices continue to fall and the devices become more widely distributed, the cost of producing individual objects approaches zero.[6] As it does, a yawning abyss opens up beneath the commodity form as a crystallization of exchange value, undermining as well any markets that should happen to be based on that form. The thought is clearly abroad in the land—queasily for some, coming on like the rosy fingers of a long-awaited dawn for others—that the general adoption of digital fabrication is incompatible with much of what we understand and experience as the capitalist everyday.

At issue is nothing less than the final defeat of material scarcity. Just what does it mean to us, as individuals and societies? We've lived with scarcity for so long, have so long enshrined it at the very heart of our assumptions about value, choice and necessity, that it's difficult to imagine the contours of a life unmarked by it. It doesn't take any particular clairvoyance, though, to see that the psychology of everyday life, the structure of the economy, and the form of our cities all stand to be utterly transformed in a post-scarcity world.

The ability for any individual to make more or less whatever they want, whenever they wanted it, would sunder the long-established circuit between advertising's provocation of desire and the market's sovereign capacity to fulfill it. While this would by no means necessarily mean an end to consumerism and its familiar arsenal of tools aimed at the manipulation of desire, it would tend to undercut their sustaining logic. As we'll see, too, personal experience with fabrication has important consequences for how we understand ourselves and our own ability to make meaningful change in the world.

In fact, given digital fabrication at scale, the fundamental set of stimuli that underlie *all* economic behavior would be altered quite out of recognition. A command economy seeks to plan ahead of time what things will be needed, and how many of each will be required; a market economy uses prices as signals to determine what should be made and when. An economy based on personal fabrication would undermine the assumptions common to both, by allowing end consumers to fulfill emergent demand more or less directly.

Not the demand for each and every thing, clearly: the process of microchip fabrication, for example, is both so toxic and so dependent on extraordinarily stringent standards of clean-room sterility that it's hard to imagine it ever becoming widely dispersed. But when the specifications for a useful variety of everyday objects can be downloaded for free, the market for a very great deal of what is now designed, packaged and sold evaporates completely. Significant areas of the economy might stand to be reclaimed for the commons.

More profoundly still, a true material abundance would etch away at the very foundations of property itself. In a robust and fully realized world of digital fabrication, you'd make the thing you need, use it for as long as you care to, and throw it in the hopper for decomposition and recycling when you're done with it. What need for any notion of property under such circumstances? Writers like Srnicek and Williams even propose this be accomplished as nearly as possible without the application of human effort, leading to a state of being since described by others—with tongue only partly in cheek—as "Fully Automated Luxury Communism."[7]

As a consequence, we would have to rethink the organization of the built environment. We know that economic forces, and requirements founded in the material conditions of production, shape the organization of human settlements at every scale. Local and precise control over the physical form of things therefore challenges the way we think about the spatial form and social life of cities. To offer just two examples: should local fabrication eliminate extended global supply chains, much of the land we now dedicate to warehousing and distribution could be repurposed, along with the transport capacity now required to move things around. And if we consider that retail is primarily the short-term storage and display for sale of branded goods, the implications of widespread fabrication are equally clear. Should it at all undercut the business model on which retail depends, a good deal of the street frontage our cities now consecrate to that purpose would be freed up to serve other ends. Whether these new uses would attract the continuous, daylong flux of diverse visitors that urban vitality depends on, we can't yet know.[8] But straightforwardly, making things close to where they're needed opens up the possibility of a denser, more compact and efficient way of living in cities. And with clean, city-center workshops sited cheek-by-jowl with living quarters, even urban planning's basic distinction between industrial, commercial and residential zones comes into question.

Furthermore, the bounding constraints on the human

condition would shift, for all of us, in ways we've never before even thought to reckon with. Whether or not our experience of everyday life ever scales the heights foreseen by the most ardent prophets of luxury communism, the ability to produce things locally meaningfully concretizes the "right to an adequate standard of living" enunciated in the Universal Declaration of Human Rights.[9] Put simply, an established practice of distributed fabrication is freedom from want.

We barely have the language to describe what politics looks like when material scarcity no longer sets fundamental bounding constraints on human possibility—and if this is true of politics, then it is still truer of psychology, social organization and spirituality. If "human nature" is a constructed thing, and inseparable from the material circumstances through which it's expressed, then in principle radical changes in those material circumstances ought to result in new natures: fresh chapters in the species-being, entirely novel expressions of what it means to be human.

Little wonder, then, that these technologies should figure so prominently on the fluttering banners of the emerging technological left: you don't get much more world-historical than that. Grounds for optimism, further, are especially welcome in an period when the possibilities for advancement and justice can so easily appear to be squeezed lifeless between neoliberal triumphalism, resurgent authoritarianism and the profound existential challenges posed by our collective misuse of the planet.

But these arguments are based on a number of assumptions that need to be unpacked. What Rifkin, Mason and Srnicek and Williams all celebrate and invest much hope in is an as-yet notional practice of manufacturing that is simultaneously *distributed*, that is to say, locally available, just about everywhere; *on-demand*, able to satisfy needs as and when they emerge; *short-run*, or capable of producing only as many iterations of a thing as are actually needed, without unduly imposing retooling or reconfiguration costs; *materially agnostic*, able to make useful things from a wide variety of base materials, and to fabricate the necessary components for the kind of complex, heterogeneous objects we generally encounter in everyday life; and *circular*, that is, able to recover and make use of waste products generated in the course of production.

And above all, what they are imagining is a material production that is *ultra low-cost*. The unstated premise behind all of these visions of the future isn't merely an economy in which high-precision fabricators themselves are available cheaply. It's one in which all the inputs required to make things with them—specifically, feedstock, energy and specification diagrams—are also available at something very close to zero cost. Without access to these, one doesn't truly own the means of production, only its instruments; with them, but for labor time and amortization of the fabrication engine itself, objects might indeed be had for something close to the cost of the raw material used to make them. But feedstock, energy and specifications all need to be produced by someone, somehow, and the costs involved cannot simply be wished away.

These are the boundary conditions, then, for the emergence of a digital fabrication practice that can't trivially be folded up into the existing capitalist order. Not a single one of them is utterly beyond reach; some, like on-demand and short-run production, are already in hand. But other factors critical to the emergence of ultra low-cost production are proving to be far more elusive. Fabrication devices themselves remain too narrowly useful, too expensive, and far too concentrated in the places on Earth that need them least. They pose major challenges to any notion of sustainability, or efficiency in the use of resources. And given perennial attempts to re-enclose the informational commons with onerous licensing terms and digital rights management software (DRM), access to free specifications for all the things we might desire is something we need to regard as highly contingent.

But if these criteria *can* be satisfied, proposals that would have seemed guilelessly utopian or even science-fictional not so long ago acquire a certain credibility. And if these few stumbling blocks really are all that stands between us and the prospect of an equitably distributed material abundance on Earth, it's incumbent upon us to ask what surmounting them would require.

The first question we need to answer is whether digital fabrication can meaningfully be *distributed*. Rather than being bound up in the highly concentrated factory zones we inherit from the Industrial Revolution, we can now envision a world in which productive capacity moves to the edges of the network, close to where manufactured goods are needed. This would sharply reduce both the monetary and energy costs of logistics, and might even go some distance toward undermining the core-and-periphery paradigm of global economic power.

A truly distributed manufacturing capability would require firstly that there be a great many fabrication engines in the world, and that each individual unit cost very little. As we've seen, this was the crux of Bowyer's original idea: it was axiomatic to him that the very first thing anyone would make with their new RepRap would be yet another, until everyone who wanted one had one to call their own.

In retrospect, this was clearly a fantasy. But perhaps Moore's Law can yet accomplish what exponential replication never had the chance to. Ironically or not, the widespread distribution of digital fabrication began to be realized not when the devices were sold as DIY kits, but when they were offered to the market as finished machine tools, with well-considered enclosures and user interfaces. By mid-2016, a high-resolution desktop SLS printer, the Formlabs Form 2, sold at retail for $3,499, while a capable CNC mill of similar size, Carbide 3D's Nomad 883 Pro, went for $2,599.[10] To be sure, these devices are still too expensive for the great majority of people on Earth, but they're already an order of magnitude cheaper than they were just a year or two ago, placing them well within reach of just about any institution in the developed world that has a use for one, right down to the high-school level.

Indeed, our cities are already dotted with "hacklabs" and "maker spaces," and it's not hard for the truly motivated to get their hands on a 3D printer or a laser cutter for the space of an afternoon. But these are only the first and easiest steps toward a evenly distributed manufacturing base. At present, the great majority of digital fabricators on Earth remain sequestered in limited-access workshops like these, or still harder to get at facilities belonging to universities and private research institutions. Despite their operators' best intentions, many of these spaces still intimidate the people who would most benefit from using them, their very language, branding and framing confronting more than a few would-be users with an insuperable psychic challenge ramp. Any vision of post-scarcity utopia that is predicated on distributed, democratized production would require such sites to be not merely free and formally open but actively welcoming, and that has yet to be achieved just about anywhere.

What about the ability to work with a usefully wide variety of materials? Though 3D printing techniques have been successfully extended to concrete, food-grade edible materials and even living tissue,[11] at the moment a boxfresh Replicator 2 can only print with PLA and ABS plastic. Given the very wide variety of contexts in which we use manufactured objects, though, the range of requirements imposed on them, and the particularly sharp limitations of those materials, we're going to need to do better than that if we're serious about addressing material scarcity with digital fabrication.

What's more, there's a compositional heterogeneity to most of the objects in our daily environment larger than a paperclip. A simple glance around just about any room ought to establish that most of the artifacts we encounter in everyday life are complex assemblages of ceramic and polymer, cloth and wood, glass and metal. To produce anything even as sophisticated as a toaster or a laundry cart, then, implies the need for multiple different digital fabrication engines.

And of course, some assembly is always required, even in an age of on-demand fabrication. The requirements of assembly labor are perhaps the ultimate brake on digital fabrication: you can cut as many precision, one-off bicycle parts as you like, but someone still needs to put them together into a safely working vehicle. That someone needs space and time, and would preferably have some sense of what they're doing.

The obvious answer to these challenges, as well as many of those posed by the need for distribution, is to gather many different kinds of fabrication capability in one place, together with people trained in their use. This is the Fablab approach, advocated by MIT digital-fabrication pioneer Neil Gershenfeld and his Center for Bits and Atoms. A Fablab combines everything from heavy-duty sewing machines to plasma cutters under one roof, and supplements them with onsite instruction and guidance.[12] Gershenfeld has always been clear on the model's constraints, positioning Fablabs as a "means of invention," rather than a way of accomplishing scaled production, but it works beautifully as a proof of concept.[13] Useful, internally complicated things can be and are made at Fablabs around the world, every day of the week.

Today anyone with access to a 3D printer, a laser cutter, a CNC milling machine and sufficient feedstock for each could recreate a great many of the discrete objects that constituted the material fabric of big-city life in Western Europe or North America circa 1965—especially now that sensors, actuators and other mechanisms dependent on conductive circuitry can be printed with relative ease.

Against the long backdrop of human civilization, this certainly counts as a comfortably, even an enviably high standard of living to have access to. But even in this scenario, there are needful things that are well beyond the reach of even reasonably foreseeable distributed fabrication techniques. Making something as simple as a good cast-iron pan, for example, requires access to an induction furnace and the knowledge to use it well, and that's a long, long step beyond downloading and printing simple objects in ABS plastic. If even something as basic as a skillet taxes the capacity of a local workshop provisioned on the Fablab model, how much more so objects made of contemporary materials like glass-filled polymer, foamed aluminum or aerogel?

The field is, however, advancing with particular rapidity.

Though it takes a fair amount of nous to distinguish genuine innovation from wishful thinking or outright hype, there's enough of the former going on that it can be difficult to keep on top of new developments. So I hesitate to state outright that working with a particular material is not possible, or even that it's not likely to be economic. With an active, global community of committed enthusiasts continuously expanding the possibilities of digital fabrication, it's difficult to say with any certitude what may or may not become possible in the near future. Nonetheless, it will continue to take more than one type of fabrication device to produce all the components of anything broadly useful in everyday life, and significant investments of time and effort to assemble those components into something that works. The picture that is beginning to emerge, then, is that the benisons of digital production can be enjoyed most widely and most equitably when fabrication engines of a few different kinds are deployed in neighborhood-scale shared workshops.

Assuming it's achievable at all, though, this world of broadly democratized production capacity seems very hard to square with the needs of sustainability as we presently understand them. "More production in more places" seems to imply "more stuff," and that feels like anathema in an age that has learned to question the insistence on perpetual growth.

The only way widely distributed production might be reconciled with the desire for sustainability would be to ensure that digital fabrication can be made to work as a component of a metabolic process—what the visionary engineers Michael Braungart and William McDonough called a "cradle-to-cradle" industrial ecology, and what is these days more often referred to as a circular economy.[14] Proposals along these lines call for manufacturing processes to consume as much as possible of the waste they produce.

To a degree, we can surely pare down the waste that's generated in the course of ordinary digital production. For depositional fabrication techniques like 3D printing, clever algorithms can be used to determine the optimal form of structural members;

while this approach often lends an uncanny, posthuman aesthetic to machined objects, there's no doubt that it also yields unprecedented strength-to-weight ratios, using the least matter to make the strongest possible component. Similarly, while subtractive methods like CNC milling will always, unavoidably produce some scrap, best-fit algorithms can most efficiently sort the shapes to be cut onto the plane or volume of available material, so that waste is minimized. Such techniques are the essence of a less mass/more data ethic of manufacture.

But part of what makes digital fabrication truly radical is that it's *iterative*. Because single-unit production runs are as economic as any other, successive approximations to a requirement can be fabricated, tried for fit and discarded, as the maker learns what works in a specific case and what does not. This process of thinking-by-making can be extraordinarily fruitful, intellectually and practically, but one of its drawbacks is that it produces any number of failed prototypes and evolutionary dead ends; but for their utility in illustrating the evolution of a thought process, it's hard to regard these as anything but waste. What we're confronted with is not just a world in which many people make many things, it's one in which many people make many *versions* of many things, on their way to the desired outcome.

Among the advocates I've mentioned, some are more aware of these complexities than others. Rifkin, for example, explicitly limits his enthusiasm for digital fabrication to additive methods, on the grounds that "a significant amount of the material" used in subtractive processes "is wasted and never finds its way into the end product." It is true that subtractive methods produce waste: anybody who's ever run a laser cutter is surely familiar with the drifts of offcut that build up, the oddments and ungainly shapes left over after you've cut the forms you need from a sheet of ply. But depositional methods do, too—and not merely a few twists of stray filament but whole objects that fall short of requirements, whose design must be tweaked at the level of the file before trying again. Neither way of doing things can be said to be entirely free from the sin of waste in this regard.

So whether or not these processes ultimately produce less waste on a per-item-produced basis than conventional methods, their efficiency is open to serious question. On a planet with limited resources, digital fabrication cannot make good on its scarcity-ending promise unless most of the waste it *does* generate is recovered locally, reprocessed into feedstock, and directed back into the production stream.

Perhaps mindful of the tendency toward iterative design that went hand-in-hand with its origins in rapid prototyping, this is something the inventors of 3D printing imagined from the outset. At present, the material most often used by printers is the familiar plastic polylactic acid (PLA); made from cornstarch, tapioca roots or sugarcane, its advocates claim that PLA is both biodegradable and indefinitely renewable.[15] My students never need worry that the models they make every semester will wind up stacked in the subsurface strata of some towering, 27th-century landfill, nor choking dolphins as they plunge through mid-ocean gyres.

Often brittle, though, and always unpleasant to the touch, there are distinct limits to what you can (or would want to) do with PLA. Could other kinds of material be recovered? Rifkin expands at length on a "nifty new device the size of a shoe box" called Filabot, "that grinds and melts old household items made out of plastic: buckets, DVDs, bottles, water pipes, sunglasses, milk jugs, and the like," and fuses the result into new filament. It's unclear, though, how such a random assortment of heterogeneous plastics could possibly result in production-grade filament. Some degree of prior discipline in sorting is clearly necessary, and even then it's doubtful that the filament produced would stand up to everything required of it. Degraded at the molecular level by the recovery process, it's unlikely to be useful for anything but non-working parts.

The MIT environmental engineering graduate Sidhant Pai has proposed one novel way of ensuring that the post-consumer content of filament is maximized, informed by some of the harsher social and economic realities of global South production. Working with the SWaCH wastepickers' cooperative in the

Indian city of Pune, Pai founded a social enterprise called Protoprint that intends to produce "Fair Trade, ethically sourced and environmentally sustainable filament from waste."[16] For maximum efficiency, Protoprint's pilot facility is located in one of Pune's garbage dumps, where the raw material of filament— HDPE milk jugs and detergent bottles in their thousands—can be had for the price of plucking it from the fly-bombed mounds.

Schemes like Pai's present us with the specter of slum children prising apart waste plastic components, dumping them in the chipper, and rendering the resulting slurry into reels of fresh filament. Whether you see this as an ingenious practical element of a closed-loop, cradle-to-cradle industrial ecosystem or a nightmare of exploitation and toxic racism is largely a matter of perspective.[17] (It is entirely possible that Protoprint is both of these things at once.) An organization called the Ethical Filament Foundation does promulgate guidelines that are intended to maintain income supports, and some measure of environmental protection, for wastepickers engaged in filament production. But like all such labeling schemes, given the prevailing rules of the market, it only works if people are willing to pay a premium for ease of conscience.

Though finicky to work with, Pai has chosen well in HDPE. When energy expended in the removal chain is accounted for, the plastic is more efficient to produce filament with locally[18] than it would be to turn it into new bottles and jugs through a standard recycling process. Some three years after Pai first announced his partnership with SWaCH, though, Protoprint still does not offer finished product for sale. This makes Pai's claims—that production-grade filament can be made at scale in this way, for example, or that Protoprint's trashpickers earn fifteen times what their unaffiliated peers do—all but impossible to evaluate.

Nevertheless, here is a model for a sustainable, circular economy founded on digital fabrication. We may not be at all comfortable with Pai's vision, or what it implies about our use of things made with HDPE. But millions of human beings, both throughout India and elsewhere around the world, live and work in garbage dumps, and this work recognizes their labor as an irreplaceable element of an extended circuit of digital production. Especially if trashpickers themselves are collectively enabled to make direct use of the filament they produce, building things at will like any of the rest of us would, schemes like Protoprint offer one way to close the loop.

And maybe we can keep more of what we make from hitting the municipal waste stream and winding up in garbage dumps in the first place. At the very least, it makes sense to equip fabrication workshops with some direct, local means of recovery, their 3D printers working side-by-side with the flaking machines and extruders that turn refuse into useful feedstock.[19]

But there's a still more ambitious way of thinking about circularity: we can leverage the deep sinks of energy and human labor that are already embodied in the things around us, via fabricator-enabled processes of repair and adaptive upcycling. How many things, after all, have we ever dragged to the sidewalk on trash day for want of a single lost or broken component? And how many of them might have been saved if we'd been able to make those components cheaply, locally and on a one-off basis? Digital fabrication lets us extend the useful life of household objects, especially when the missing or broken part is expensive, hard to source or no longer produced.

This is already happening in small ways; a Fablab Barcelona workshop with the unfortunate title of Furniture Hacking[20] (and the equally unfortunate pricetag of 100 euros) aims to teach participants how they can use fabricators to restore the things they already own. This technique requires that we take precise three-dimensional scans of damaged artifacts, and then turn these measurements into specification files for the construction of missing parts. Perhaps in this way, we can restore to our lives something like the ethic of repair that was once common to virtually every culture on Earth, in the days before the material conditions of everyday life were founded on mass production, disposability and the consumer economy. This is also an argument for making a much greater proportion of the things we use from free and open specifications: whether we needed a given component for repair or upgrade, finding what we're looking for in the repositories and outputting it at will wouldn't present us with any undue obstacles.

Perhaps a culture of unlimited production seems at odds with the practice of frugality implied by an ethic of repair. But the considered use of digital fabrication techniques enables a way of being in the world the professor of architectural design Nicholas de Monchaux thinks of as "fashioning," in which the things we use emerge from a context of iterative "making, mending and repairing," rather than systematized production at scale.[21] Committing ourselves to the practice of fashioning restores a sense of the relationship between thinking and making to our lives, and perhaps a renewed respect for the complexities of the material world as well. Not nearly everyone will want to live in this way; not everyone will have the time or energy or wherewithal to do so, however much they might want to. But this all points toward a way in which widely distributed digital fabrication can be brought into balance with the needs of ecological survival.

The notion that a distributed practice of digital fabrication would ever, under any circumstances, bring about some kind of challenge to capitalism depends on it being accomplished at extremely low cost, and that in turn requires reliable access to cheap raw materials.

For the moment, desktop 3D printing using MakerBots and Ultimakers remains the most accessible form of depositional fabrication. But the filament these printers make use of doesn't come for free. Depending on its gauge, color and quality, a kilogram of PLA is likely to set you back forty or fifty bucks; ABS is generally a little cheaper. So a printed part weighing 250g can be had for around $10, independent of the costs of power, labor and amortization of the original investment.

For unique components that can be had no other way, this constitutes a real bargain, if not an improbable dispensation of grace. But unless you're already ideologically committed to fabrication, at present printing things will almost always be more

expensive than simply buying them. The high local cost of filament is already limiting the uptake of 3D printing in regions
like sub-Saharan Africa: inevitably shipped from China, subject
to all the exigencies of immature logistics and corruption, a reel
of filament costs three to four times in Nairobi what it might in
London or New York.

This, of course, is precisely the pricing logic Pai's Protoprint
aims to short-circuit: by obviating the necessity of shipping it
across oceans, local sourcing results in filament many times
cheaper, and far sounder energetically and ecologically as well.
But for now, the high price of feedstock tends to suppress the
creative experimentation and broadly iterative approach to
design that digital fabrication thrives on. And given this, it's
hard to see how digital fabrication might threaten standing
models of production unless there are concerted and significant
efforts to lower the cost of feedstock by an order of magnitude,
particularly where 3D printing is concerned.

The final element necessary to ultra low-cost production is
free specification, in which files containing plans for fabrication
devices themselves, as well as objects to be manufactured by
them, are made available from online pattern repositories gov-
erned by the principles of the informational commons.[22]

Those principles are enunciated in the Open Source Hardware
definition,[23] collectively authored by a community of volunteers
in 2010:

> "Open source hardware is hardware whose design is made pub-
> licly available so that anyone can study, modify, distribute, make,
> and sell the design or hardware based on that design ... Open
> source hardware gives people the freedom to control their tech-
> nology while sharing knowledge and encouraging commerce
> through the open exchange of designs."

There's clearly nothing here that's inherently inimical to the
more libertarian forms of capitalism; in fact, while licenses
prohibiting commercial reuse of a pattern certainly exist,
advocates are fond of pointing out that they are explicitly

incompatible with the open source ethos.[24] But aggregating a large number of design patterns that are licensed for zero-cost downloading and use, and rendering them easily searchable, necessarily opens up a more radical prospect.

The pioneering repository of open-source designs is Thingiverse, founded by Zachary Smith in 2008; as of mid-2016, the site offered some 520,000 files, released for free use under the terms of a Creative Commons or General Public License. There is, inevitably, a great deal of noise in the channel, and it's easy to find items on Thingiverse for which no conceivable practical need will ever be articulated. But you can also find working solar-powered Stirling engines and wind turbines, quadcopter drones and robotic manipulator arms, even a goodly number of the *Five Hundred and Seven Mechanical Movements* Victorian-era engineer Henry T. Brown collected in his classic text of the same name.[25]

Beyond Thingiverse, there are initiatives like the OpenDesk project,[26] which offers downloadable specifications for the most commonly needed elements of workplace furniture: tables, chairs, desks, dividers and storage lockers. Or the wildly ambitious Global Village Construction Set, which aims to furnish users with Creative Commons-licensed specifications for the fifty industrial machines they would need to build from scratch "a sustainable civilization with modern comforts," from bakery ovens to cement mixers.[27] Somewhere between *Existenzminimum* and frankly survivalist in its aesthetics, the GVCS envisions communities bootstrapping their way from smaller components to the stuff of collective self-reliance, whether those communities should happen to be rural, informal, poor or otherwise denied access to the full panoply of developed-world production technology.

All of these initiatives call upon an ethos of sharing that is well established in the digital fabrication community. Apart from pioneer Stratasys, which patented the most widely used depositional processes, and has never made any bones about the fact that it is a commercial, profit-seeking entity,[28] it is interesting how much of the early innovation in 3D printing specifically was generated by groups of people who explicitly situated their work in the informational commons, including the RepRap project itself, MakerBot and the community around it, and the original Ultimaker. Just as RepRap eventually abandoned the project of unlimited self-replication, though, its direct descendants ultimately gave up on openness. Similarly, both MakerBot and Ultimaker reinvented themselves as closed ecosystems, alienating a significant proportion of their community in the process, including some of 3D printing's earliest and most prominent developers.[29]

There is excellent reason to believe that this retrenchment will have strongly negative consequences for the future of digital fabrication. The willingness on the part of manufacturers to alienate their own developer community is worrisome enough, because the members of that community have historically contributed technical innovations critical to the fabricator's evolution, and there is every reason to suppose that they would have continued to do so indefinitely, if only they were able to in a way that comported with their values. But the withdrawal of innovation behind a scrim of intellectual property law once it has been consolidated is also a disturbing brake on development, because that law—precisely as it is intended to—keeps fabricator prices artificially high, and their supply constrained.

Just as James Watt refused to license his steam engine, suppressing the development of that technology over the quarter century that elapsed between his first commercial model and the expiry of his patents in 1800, the evolution of digital fabrication has been hobbled by practices aimed at securing a remunerative monopoly.[30] During the period that Stratasys enforced its patents, the practice of 3D printing went more or less nowhere. It wasn't until these patents began to expire, after twenty years of painfully slow progress, that the Cambrian explosion of depositional fabrication devices and things made with them became possible.[31] If we believe that putting this capability into as many hands as possible is a public good worth seeking, then preventing it from being enclosed, packaged and sold as a market commodity is vital.

It's within the maker community itself that we find the fiercest commitment to the values of free specification—and not merely as consumers, but as people actively creating designs to be shared. It was MakerBot co-founder Zachary Smith that complained most prominently when the company announced that from the Replicator 2 forward, its products would no longer be openly specified and licensed; when Thingiverse altered its Terms of Use in 2013, to assert at least formal ownership over the specifications uploaded to it, it was key RepRap designer Josef Průša that called for an "Occupy Thingiverse" movement in response.[32] But for every activist designer motivated by a strong commonist ethos, there's a CEO trying to trademark even the words you use to describe what you're doing—and it's moreover likely to be the case that the CEO can afford better lawyers, or at least more of them.

Much as "capital needs to suppress the skills of computer users in order to uphold the commodity form of information," it needs to suppress circulation of instructions for making them, in order to preserve the commodification of things.[33] Precisely because any practice of free specification that became rooted in the culture would pose such a grave challenge to the many business models predicated on artificial scarcity, there will always be those desperate to limit the degree to which it informs the way significant numbers of things are made.

For now, downloading plans and making the things we use from them remains a marginal pursuit—unthreatening, tolerated as long as it remains confined to the periphery, perhaps even patronizingly praised for its contributions to "innovation." But should any such practice actually start to erode the logic of profit in the core markets of the developed world, it would be certain to come under concerted attack, technically as well as legally. Until specifications for all kinds of useful things are hosted in a decentralized way, so that no one party is meaningfully able to assert control over them, we have to regard access to them as contingent and inherently revocable.

*　　*　　*

Given all this—the inadequate distribution of facilities, the doubtful sustainability of the material-energetic flows involved, and the uncertain intellectual property regime—it feels a trifle premature to be lodging any hope in the notion that digital fabrication might transform the political economy of everyday life. Above all, it's hard to justify making things this way when it remains far more troublesome and expensive to do so than simply buying something comparable at retail. There's a reason you find the same injection-molded knockoff Monobloc chair, for example, or very minor variants thereof, everywhere from Rocinha to Rodeo Drive: by historical standards, it's almost inconceivably cheap. Ordered on Alibaba, shipped from Tianjin, capable of being supplied at velocities upward of 20,000 pieces a month, conventional production and distribution can yield unit costs in bulk as low as $6. And this means that, but for a few true believers, nobody on Earth is going to take the time and trouble to fabricate a chair locally if they can more easily hop in their car, drive to Walmart and pick up a mass-produced Chinese plastic chair for ten bucks.

The question then becomes at what point does the economic calculus shift, and the logic of local fabrication start to make sense? In the abstract, there are a few ways this could happen. Should the price of oil soar, the petrochemical content of the chair might render it prohibitively expensive, or at least uncompetitively so. Maybe the cheap imported chair will be doomed by higher labor costs, should wages in the factories of the global South finally begin to converge on something approximating an ethical minimum. Or perhaps the vulnerabilities of a painfully extended supply chain will make long-distance transportation untenable.

Change in any or all of these areas would, no doubt, go a long way toward making local fabrication a more competitive proposition. But the actual calculus is even more daunting. In order to make sense, a freely licensed, sustainably harvested, locally fabricated chair needs to be economic not when considered against one yet to be produced, *but against the tens of millions of chairs that are already in the world*, any number of which are available more or less for the asking at any given moment. As we've seen, at present, the most radical and energy-efficient choice of all is to reclaim and repurpose, rather than building something new.

All of this suggests that digital fabrication as an economically salient way of living can only truly come into its own under rather heavy manners. But for the time being, in the developed North, just the opposite is true; any purely economic calculus scarcely vindicates the time and effort invested in making things this way. So if digital fabrication cannot be justified on the grounds of economics, it must be justified on the grounds of ideology. And in the main, that means two things: either the ideology of forbidden things, or that of fabrication itself.

The first class of objects we will make with digital fabricators, regardless of the economic incentives or disincentives involved, are those things we desire which cannot be accounted for by conventional indices of value—objects that it would be difficult or impossible for us to acquire in any other way. This might mean things that do not exist yet, for which there is no available template: the kind of objects my students, like all other architecture students everywhere, gin up on the MakerBot, with their improbable geometries and subtle variations. But just as often it will mean producing artifacts that are ordinarily denied to us by virtue of their rarity, in one or another failure of the cornucopian logic of the market.

Some of these things will be wonderful in themselves, or serve eminently desirable ends. We can point at objects like the 3D model of the clitoris that researcher Odile Fillod recently produced,[34] to redress what she perceived as a lack of accurate information about the female body. Made available for anyone to download and print, Fillod's model is a perfect example of the way in which a widespread networked fabrication might, in allowing its users to do an end run around oppressive institutions of control, more fully democratize the acquisition of vital knowledge.

But oppression is in the eye of the beholder. What a great many people in the world seem to want that the market cannot furnish them with is a gun—better yet, a gun that bears no serial numbers, appears in no database, and has absconded in every other way from the possibility of state regulation or control. This desire is particularly concentrated on the libertarian right, where fantasies of resistance to tyranny founded in mass arming of the population remain common currency.[35] And among those trading in such currency is a young "crypto-anarchist" from Arkansas named Cody Wilson, who in 2013 released to the internet plans for a single-shot, 3D-printed pistol he called the Liberator.

It's an ugly thing, the Liberator, even by the aesthetic standards of contemporary handguns. But maybe it should be: a review by New South Wales police found it to be "undetectable, untraceable, cheap and easy to make."[36] They'd downloaded and assembled it themselves, at a total cost of $35 Australian, or roughly 5 percent of the retail price of a new weapon in the same caliber.

The original Liberator was produced of conventional plastic filament, using a leased Stratasys printer; the printer was later forcibly repossessed by the company, for violation of terms of service.[37] In the interests of working with heavier grade of materials, not to mention not being beholden to anyone's licensing agreement, Wilson has since developed an entirely open-source CNC milling machine called Ghost Gunner, "the only affordable, automated package for expanding the rifleman's material and political franchise."[38] The $1,500 Ghost Gunner was specifically designed to machine an AR-15's lower receiver—the component of the assault rifle in which its rifleness is concentrated, and for that reason the component whose production and trade is most heavily regulated. This is an engine specifically intended to allow anyone at all to "manufacture unserialized AR rifles in the comfort and privacy of [their] own home."

For all but the convinced libertarian absolutist, this is a nightmare scenario become the stuff of everyday fact. The most likely outcome of Wilson's work is simply that the everyday world becomes much more dangerous. But here is a first-approximation answer to our question: people will turn to fabrication to provide them with all those things the market cannot, *even when the reason that the market cannot is because of regulation imposed on it for good and sufficient reason.* And this will be true for so long as the technical capability to circumvent that regulation persists, and has not somehow been preempted.

Beyond the desire for forbidden things, there is one further reason why someone might commit to digital fabrication even in the face of a grim economic calculus: the ideological dedication to fabrication itself. For some of its most dedicated enthusiasts, the arguments in favor of digital fabrication are so compelling and so self-evident that they hardly seem to require articulation. And yet they will need to articulate those arguments, patiently and painstakingly, if they wish to convince anyone else of the merits of their cause.

A rather telling story circulates in the maker community, for example, concerning what happened when well-meaning researchers at the Institute of Advanced Architecture Catalunya (IAAC) opened the second in what was to be a series of MIT-supported Fablabs in Barcelona, in the poor neighborhood of Ciutat Meridiana. There are several adding-insult-to-injury elements in this sorry tale. Of all Barcelona's districts, Ciutat Meridiana was perhaps the "most peripheral and most punished by the [2008 economic] crisis"; of all sites in Ciutat Meridiana the researchers could have chosen for their experiment, the one they settled on had previously been a community food bank. And finally, compounding everything, they named their new facility with an optimism that, in retrospect, seems crashingly tonedeaf: they called it Ateneu. (The name literally translates as "Athenaeum," but invokes a long Catalonian tradition of radical social centers.)[39]

In the midst of widespread unemployment and hopelessness, none of this went over particularly well with the local residents. "What's MIT of Massachusetts doing in a neighborhood where people are starving?," one irate local demanded of a reporter for the *El Diario* newspaper. "What we need here are emergency employment schemes, or services like the Food Bank." And with that call to action, members of the Ciutat Meridiana Residents'

Association took matters into their own hands. Working alongside local activists of the 15M movement, they occupied the Fablab, restoring it at least temporarily to service as a community store.⁴⁰

The Meridiana neighbors' action offers a stinging rebuke to what we might call digital vanguardism: the ideological commitment to fabrication for its own sake, coupled to the failure to take adequate soundings of a community's actual needs or desires before proposing it as a universal solution to their social and economic woes. Here people with the best of intentions had gotten too far ahead not merely of the materially productive capabilities of the technology, but how those technologies were understood by the very people they were intended to benefit. Until the residents of Meridiana perceive a direct connection between the things that a 3D printer or a CNC milling machine can do and the wants they experience in their own lives, a Fablab or anything like it is the worst sort of imposition. And this is true in every similarly situated community on Earth.

As evangelical as they often can be, partisans of digital fabrication have done a relatively poor job of communicating what it might offer to anyone beyond those audiences already inclined to be enthused by it; the 3D printed nameplates, lasercut signs and similar tat often produced as proof of what can be done with these techniques certainly don't help press the case.

The 3D-printing kiosk that used to stand in South London's Elephant and Castle Shopping Centre was an excellent example of this tendency: it stood for months, locked up and gathering dust, surrounded by busy stalls catering to the neighborhood's Eastern European, Latin American and African immigrant communities, and offered nothing that any of the shoppers streaming past it might conceivably need. Meanwhile, the bustling quasi-informality of the market in the concrete moat outside suggested that there were a great many people in the immediate vicinity who would be well placed to make excellent use of the capabilities represented by the kiosk, if only someone had bothered to understand their needs and explain how digital fabrication might serve them.

And as it happens, perhaps those needs are not so much the ones that accompany material deprivation, but the ones that arise out of a yet deeper impoverishment in contemporary life. In his book *The Craftsman*, Richard Sennett describes the flood of new material objects into the households of Renaissance Europe[41]—the tide of clothing, tableware, furniture, toys and items for storage that washes up on the shores of the everyday around 1600. As one reads, it's impossible to avoid thinking of our own world, of the 300,000 discrete objects said to be contained in the average North American home. This is our own embarrassment of riches: even objectively poor people in the global North live with an absolute standard of daily material comfort that would have been aspirational for most of history's wealthy. In any raw material sense, we *already* live in a post-scarcity world, even before any particularly elaborate digital fabrication capacity is brought on line. And yet we still seem to suffer from a pervasive sense of want and lack.

And this points out a profound confusion that's seemingly shared by everyone from Bowyer to Srnicek, Williams and the stalwarts of Fully Automated Luxury Communism. Contra Bowyer, wealth is not quite the same as having many things, not even the same as having something whenever you want it. And conversely, poverty is not so much the lack of things as it is dependence on others to furnish the basic needs of life. The essence of what is offered to us by digital fabrication isn't so much the ability to satisfy a material necessity, *but that you be able to do so yourself.* That you can perceive a need—possibly even a need not addressed by any existing artifact—and devise a response to it, locally, experimentally, iteratively.

In the heady rush of enthusiasm for everything implied by these technologies, we need to avoid assuming that digital fabrication will transform the world automatically or magically. As the example of Cody Wilson illustrates, we need to remind ourselves over and over that by no means everyone who picks up this set of capabilities will be interested in using them to unweave kyriarchy.

But neither are the technologies themselves really the point here. In everything I've described here, the act of production is—comparatively, and for all its many rigors—the easy bit. The challenge isn't, at all, to propose the deployment of new fabrication technologies, but to deploy them in modes, configurations and assemblages that might effectively resist capture by existing logics of accumulation and exploitation, and bind them into processes that are generative of lasting and significant shared value. Those interested in seeing digital fabrication used as part of a project of radical transformation will need to invest a great deal of effort into ensuring that the way in which one would go about using it is actively invitational, not merely demystified and formally accessible.

There's a reason why we're still talking about something as dowdy as ownership of the means of production. At every point in history, control over the shape and distribution of matter has been tightly coupled with the shape and distribution of power. The present is no exception. Even now, human dignity is predicated on the satisfaction of material need, on the ability to furnish everyone alive with the made objects that afford us shelter from the elements, comfortably scaled space and some measure of control over our immediate environment.

Our common sense, our values, our very notions of what is and is not possible: we so often treat these things as settled matters of fact, and desperately resist the idea that they're contingent. We seem to have a particularly hard time with the notion that these intimate qualities of self might rest on anything as bathetic and concrete as the way in which we collectively choose to organize the world's productive capacity. And yet scarcity infects our language, molds how we weigh claims on justice and fairness, and conditions our habits of thought. It might sound laughably reductionist to say so, but there is a relationship between the way a society makes and distributes material things and the structure of human affect in that society.

We know what affect looks like in a world in which the scarcity of things is sustained, mediated and satisfied by mechanisms of market; some of us, indeed, know it all too dreadfully well. We're familiar with the endocrine jolt of induced desire, the gnawing obsession with having, the empty pleasure that attaches not to using or even owning something but the sheer act of buying it. We're used to the all-but-postcoital lassitude and tristesse that follow a consummated purchase, to say nothing of the remorse that surrounds a particularly injudicious decision, and we know the arc of want reignited after a refractory period that might be measured in minutes.

In this world we need to have things, or a certain kind of things, or at the very least a certain number of them, to sustain a robust sense of ourselves—more, we need to be seen to have them. The statistics on consumer credit furnish abundant testimony to the psychic salience of our want, the lengths we're willing to go to in order to surround ourselves with objects way past any point at which any of them could be said to be remotely necessary to our survival. And of course the burden of debt that hangs over so many of us constitutes a stunningly effective disciplinary mechanism: people dependent on a paycheck to service credit-card debt that compounds at 24 percent annually don't rock boats at work, or likely much of anywhere else. To whatever degree our addiction to things contributes to that burden, it's part of what breaks us to service and inures us to our complicity in the unspeakable.

Equipped with the technologies of distributed digital fabrication, though, it's possible to imagine short-circuiting all of this. It's possible to imagine that circumstances can be different, and better. It's possible to imagine making more of the things we want or need ourselves, for very little more than the cost of time and materials, and those things replacing many if not most of the material artifacts we now acquire from the market. It's possible for many of us to take concrete and practical steps toward doing this, right now. And as a direct consequence it's possible, if just barely, to imagine some of the baleful magick leaching out of the owning and buying of things.

While I don't believe that industries like advertising will just disappear, or will surrender any time soon their very considerable power to focus our desire on arbitrary objects, we have a far greater chance of bringing just and fruitful configurations of power into existence, and maintaining them over the long term through the new means of production and distribution offered by digital fabrication. But such an infrastructure can only be realized if we know ahead of time what we need, how specifically it serves our values, and what building it will require of us.

What will we be able to make if we do? Not just new things, but new kinds of things—previously unsuspected articulations of matter, limited only by physics and desire. And even in a small way, the chance to live in an environment we've fashioned ourselves, using tools we ourselves have crafted. True to its roots, digital fabrication is helping us work out the shape of the future, one experiment at a time. We remain at the proof-of-concept stage: we now know that in principle, these things can be done. But all the social and intellectual heavy lifting begins now.

5

Cryptocurrency

The computational guarantee of value

All written accounts of the technological development we know as "the blockchain" begin and end the same way. They note its origins in the cryptocurrency called Bitcoin, and go on to explain how Bitcoin's obscure, pseudonymous, possibly even multiple inventor "Satoshi Nakamoto" used it to solve the problems of trust that had foxed all previous attempts at networked digital money. They all make much of the blockchain's potential to transform the way we exchange value, in every context and at every level of society. And they all gesture at the exciting possibilities that lie beyond currency: the world of smart contracts, distributed applications, autonomous organizations and post-human economies, all mediated by "trustless" cryptographic techniques.

Almost all verbal conversations involving the blockchain begin and end the same way, too: in perplexity. This is the first information technology I've encountered in my adult life that's just fundamentally difficult for otherwise intelligent and highly capable people to comprehend. In part, this is due to the very particular framework of assumptions about human nature that drove the blockchain's design, a framework that (we may rejoice) is by no means universally shared. But most of it is down to the almost fractal complexity Bitcoin and its underlying technologies confront us with.

When startlingly new ideas are presented to us, we generally proceed by analogy. We approach understanding crabwise and scuttling, via any number of conceptual placeholders and intermediate metaphors. For the most part, we're able to gloss an emergent technology as something we're more familiar with: for purposes of assimilation, anyway, a car is merely a "horseless carriage," or a pocket nicotine vaporizer an "e-cigarette." Sometimes this gloss is misleading, even badly so—for some of us, evidently, the internet remains a series of tubes—but it gets the job done. We arrive at a mental model and a theory of action that allow us to fit the new thing into our lives, however haphazardly at first. And over time, we are occasionally able to refine it.

But where Bitcoin, the blockchain and related technical developments are concerned, there aren't really any handy metaphors we can bring to bear. The ones that do get pressed into use are, for most of us, counterintuitive.

Consider the dizzying amount of semantic shear in a single sentence of the original paper laying forth the Bitcoin architecture: "We define an electronic coin as a chain of digital signatures." *Coin*, *chain*, *signatures*: the words are all concrete enough, but the way they're being used here confounds whatever it is that they ordinarily signify. Should the reader lack an immersion in the body of shared assumptions that constitutes financial cryptography, meaning skips glancingly across the surface of the words—and that's just the introduction. As a result, it's hard for most of us to get a sense of how these ideas relate to each other or what it is that they are invoking, let alone how a *chain* of *signatures* can become a *coin*. Thus the conceptual fogginess that shrouds the subject of Bitcoin, and the bemused and apologetic tenor of conversation around it.

There's not much clarity to be found in most written accounts, either. At every step of the way, a new primitive seems to crop up—one fundamental term or idea that won't make sense until everything leading up to it has been worked out, but which absolutely must be defined before any of what's already been set down on the page makes the slightest bit of sense. For me, at least, it took more effort to fully internalize the way Bitcoin works than it did to grasp any other idea explored in this book.

That's what concerns me. For all the hype around Bitcoin, it is clear that in its design, important questions about human interaction, collaboration and conviviality are being legislated at the level of technological infrastructure. Its appearance in the world economy gives disproportionately great power to those individuals and institutions that understand how it does what it does, and are best able to operationalize that understanding. At present, only a very tiny number of people truly grasp how Bitcoin and its underlying technologies work to create and mediate the transmission of value. If cryptocurrencies, blockchains and distributed ledgers[1] more generally are to be the crux of the networked, postnational global economy of the remaining century, though, it's vitally important that we, all of us, grasp at least the basic outlines of how they work and what it is they propose to achieve.

At its core, Bitcoin is a digital medium of exchange that has been designed to act like cash in all the ways we might appreciate, and none of the ways we don't. Before 2008, of course, there had been plenty of attempts at developing new forms of digital currency. All the pieces necessary to achieve this ambition seemed to be in place. Just about every adult on Earth carried on their person at all times a computational device eminently suitable for use as a transaction platform. The pioneering Kenyan M-Pesa service had demonstrated the size of the market for mobile payments using a standard handset with texting capabilities, proving that meaningful transfers of value could take place at scale, entirely outside the traditional banking system. A technical standard for "near-field communication," or NFC, had been widely adopted in the mobile-phone industry, allowing anyone with a phone so equipped to make payments with a simple tap. And at retail, merchants were increasingly likely to be equipped with the technical paraphernalia necessary to receive such payments; it had become common to encounter one or more digital point-of-sale terminals orbiting the cash register.

And yet, for most of us in the developed North, the promised utopia of seamless digital cash failed to arrive on time. Almost a decade after most of us had committed our music collections to the aether, at a time when millions of us were happily replacing our painstakingly acquired libraries with e-readers, coins and notes were still the most common form of legal tender we encountered in everyday life. Credit-card companies practically howled in frustration at our recalcitrance, releasing a brace of television commercials aimed at shaming consumers for being so retrograde and inconsiderate as to use cash, while futurists working in the field of financial technology ("fintech") were left to scratch their heads over what went wrong.

Perhaps the futurists would have been less puzzled had they attended more closely to what was going on in the world. It's not such a stretch, after all, to imagine that people might be terrified by the thought of committing their assets to something so intangible, at a time when it felt like the wheels were coming off the entire global economy. With its carnage of foreclosures, evictions, layoffs and bank runs, the acute crisis of 2008 sufficed to prove to many that the core financial institutions of the West couldn't be trusted—and if not the central banks, how much less so a bunch of cowboy startups? Perhaps people simply had more pressing concerns on their mind, and weren't necessarily inclined to take a wild leap into the technological unknown.

Or maybe that's looking at things the wrong way around. Maybe a time of cratering confidence in existing institutions is precisely the correct moment at which to propose something fundamentally new. Enter "Satoshi Nakamoto."[2]

Nakamoto's was the sole name on a nine-page paper describing the proposed design of a new digital currency, first posted to the Cryptography mailing list on Halloween 2008, and in one or two other places around the internet soon thereafter.[3] There is still very little we can say about "him" for sure, even whether he wasn't actually a team of close collaborators producing work under a collective pseudonym. Orthographic, lexical and stylistic cues drawn from his relatively small corpus of verified communication do strongly suggest that whoever he was, he was almost certainly a native speaker of British (or possibly Commonwealth) English. But other than that, and despite sporadic and fruitless investigations in the mass media, his identity remains a total cipher to this day.

From the rather modest way in which he first characterized his innovation ("a peer-to-peer electronic cash system"), we can reasonably infer that Satoshi wasn't proposing something intended to function as a long-term store of value, nor even as a unit of account in its own right. But it was clearly very carefully designed to work as an effective medium of exchange,[4] between parties who would presumably continue to hold the bulk of their assets in some other currency. Perhaps we could think of Bitcoin in this sense as analogous to a trade pidgin or auxiliary language: the Esperanto of currencies.

As Satoshi described it, Bitcoin was to be a cryptocurrency— that is to say, a purely digital currency, founded on computational code breaking. It aimed to fold into its audacious design all of the desirable qualities of both cash transactions and electronic transfers, without any of the drawbacks associated with either. As we'll see, none of the features he described were precisely new to the tight global community of financial-cryptography enthusiasts, but even they would agree that he combined them in strikingly novel ways.

The original Bitcoin specification has to be regarded as a dazzling display of intellectual bravura, still more so if actually pulled off by a single person. It rather elegantly proposed that well-understood cryptographic techniques could be used to resolve, all at once, a cluster of problems that had beset all the electronic cash schemes that came before.

At its most abstract, any digital transaction is nothing more than an entry in a database somewhere, specifying the time at which a given amount left one account and was deposited in another. In the context of fintech, such a database is referred to as a "ledger," a pleasing word that summons to mind a universe of baize desktops and steel-nibbed pens, all watched over by a corps of eyeshaded accountants.

However resonant the word itself may be, though, there's an unavoidable fact about ledgers, and that is that they have to be held by someone in particular. The critical vulnerability of all pre-Bitcoin digital cash schemes was that they required parties to a transaction to repose their trust in an intermediary institution, who they'd rely upon to maintain the ledger and update it every time value was passed across the network. That intermediary institution—the "mint," in fintech jargon—would be the sole arbiter of the legitimacy of a given transaction.

This was a hugely undesirable design feature, for a great many reasons. First, the mint would have access to a distressing amount of information about the identity of contracting parties and their patterns of interaction with one another. Especially for those preeminently concerned with safeguarding their privacy —and the fintech subculture is richly supplied with such people—this is *prima facie* philosophically abrasive.

As a consequence, there is tremendous fear that whoever controls the mint would have the power to prevent some transactions from taking place entirely, for whatever arbitrary reasons they chose.[5] The notion that the governing body of a mint might take it upon themselves to choke off payments to parties that have fallen into disfavor for political or other reasons isn't just a theoretical possibility, either. The effective 2010 blockade on contributions to WikiLeaks that was imposed by Bank of America, Visa, MasterCard, PayPal and Western Union is the most prominent example of this sort of thing, but it's far from the only one.[6]

Conversely, by deleting debits from their accounts from the ledger, the mint could effectively enable favored parties to use the same money *more* than once, and nobody else would be any the wiser. This was a deep design issue the fintech cognoscenti referred to as "the double-spending problem," and it had vexed all previous digital currencies.

Finally, the mint and its ledger would constitute that thing a conscientious engineer most devoutly hopes to avoid in the design of a complex system: a "single point of failure." A single, centralized ledger recording every transaction would constitute both an acute technical vulnerability and an overwhelmingly attractive target for attempts at exploitation; its corruption for any reason would bring the whole network of exchange crashing down.

These issues were all well understood by members of the fintech community, who devised a variety of ways to circumvent or resolve them. Some of these tactics were cleverer than others; a few, notably the ones underlying Adam Back's proposed Hashcash[7] currency and those devised by cryptographic pioneer David Chaum,[8] even came glancingly close to Bitcoin's final grand assembly of design ideas, a decade or more before Satoshi posted his paper. But none satisfactorily addressed the final and perhaps most deeply cutting of all digital cash's limitations, which it shares with most other forms of money: any sum of value denominated in a given currency is still tied to the performance of the institution responsible for issuing it ... and that institution is generally a nation-state.

For most of us, this never really presents us with cause for concern. For those of a certain ideological cast, though, the mere fact that we depend on institutions of government to underwrite the worth of the cash in our pockets is a searingly painful, permanent reminder of their, and our, unfreedom. To these people, not all of them on the anarchocapitalist and libertarian right, any truck with money in its conventional form necessarily means subjection to the despised strictures of the State.

Even for the rest of us, the fact that the value of currency depends so sensitively on the perceived performance of a state undoubtedly has a certain salience. If it's never an issue for most of us, most of the time, it becomes one with a vengeance when the national economy we live in collapses, when that economy is mismanaged to an extent that global markets are moved to impose discipline, or when it is simply run in a way those markets don't happen to approve of. Such forcible restructuring generally involves a devaluation of the currency, as Argentines learned during the period in 2001–2002 when the peso lost close to 70 percent of its value. Worse still is when a central bank attempts to buy its way out of crisis by issuing new currency, radically diluting the value of the amount already in circulation. This is what led to the proverbial wheelbarrows of marks we associate with Weimar Germany, the 1946 appearance of Hungarian pengő notes with a denomination of 100 million, the 98 percent *daily* inflation rate experienced by Zimbabweans in late 2008 or, still more recently, the precipitous 93 percent depreciation of the Venezuelan bolívar that took place over a matter of months in 2015.[9]

By these lights, even the best-designed digital currency isn't good enough, as long as its value remains pegged to the decisions of any nation state. And if it's foolish to repose one's trust in the governance of a nation state, isn't it more foolish yet to let a currency's valorization ride on the whims of virtually unaccountable institutional actors like the IMF? This certainly seems like something you'd want to avoid if you were going to redesign money from scratch.

But what if the value of a currency could be founded on something other than hapless trust—something as coolly objective, rational, incorruptible and extrahistorical as mathematics itself? What if that same technique that let you do so could all at once eliminate any requirement for a central mint, resolve the double-spending problem, and provide for irreversible transactions? And what if it could achieve all this while preserving, if not quite the anonymity of participants, something very nearly as acceptable—stable pseudonymity?

This was Satoshi's masterstroke. One of Bitcoin's fundamental innovations was that its architecture bypassed reliance on any centralized mint or reconciliation ledger. It replaced trust with cryptographic proof of validity, proposing that transactions could be authenticated, and a currency's value maintained, by an emergent process of consensus among a globally distributed network of peers.

It's everything promised by the possibility of distributed consensus that's key to understanding why the advent of Bitcoin has ignited so much interest. Armed with the technology at its core, we would no longer need to rely on institutions like governments or banks to guarantee the commitments we make to one another, whether public or private. One shared, public record, jointly maintained by the global network, would suffice to record all transactions, all contracts, and all votes, and do so safely, incorruptibly and in a way that preserves the privacy of all parties.

How does this work? The following account is greatly simplified—I've gone to some lengths to shield you from the implementation details of SHA-256 hashing, Merkle roots and so on—but it's accurate in schematic. I hope it gives you a reasonably good feel for what's going on, and for why it has its partisans and enthusiasts so excited.

Every individual Bitcoin and every Bitcoin user has a unique identifier. This is its cryptographic *signature*, a mathematically verifiable proof of identity. Any given Bitcoin will always be associated with the signature of the user who holds it at that moment, and by stepping backward through time, we can also see the entire chain of custody that coin has passed through, from the moment it was first brought into being.

A Bitcoin transaction, like a transaction of value in any other digital currency, consists of a message that a given amount is being transferred from my account (or "wallet") to yours. Every time a transaction takes place, it's timestamped, then cryptographically signed by both parties. This message is then run through a specialized calculation called a *hashing algorithm*, and what comes out the other end is a string of known and unvarying length—a cipher 256 bits long.

This is the transaction's *hash value*, and it is utterly unique. It functions as a reliable, unforgeable fingerprint for that set of facts. Changing even a single bit of the information compiled into a transaction will result in an entirely different hash value, so it's a simple matter for anyone equipped with the algorithm to authenticate that a given combination of time, actors and transferred amount will produce that (and only that) particular string.

Instead of being recorded in a single reconciliation ledger owned by one particular party, though, as an ordinary electronic interbank transfer would be, this transaction is propagated across the entire global network of Bitcoin users. Every node independently does the work of inspecting the history of previous transactions in order to verify the one now before it, and ensure its compliance with criteria for validity that are rigorously specified by the Bitcoin protocol. For example, to prevent a double spend, the protocol stipulates that only the earliest transaction involving a given coin is legitimate; any attempt by the same party to spend it again will be rejected by the network. Similarly, if rather more obviously, nobody can spend a coin they didn't own in the first place.

As a result, the precise path of ownership traced out by every individual coin as it moves through history is known. At any time they want to, any member of the network who wants to can download and refer to their very own local copy of that history—the full ledger of all Bitcoin transactions, ever.[10] And this makes checking to ensure that a particular exchange is valid a surprisingly straightforward process.

When every node agrees that the transaction submitted for consideration is valid, it is bound to the previous verified transaction, and these are hashed together. Such verified, but as yet unconfirmed, transactions are then aggregated into a candidate *block* that is, in its turn, also propagated across the network. Again, every node on the network works independently, competing to be the one that first completes the calculations that will result in confirmation of a candidate block. The block that results from this process is then appended to an ever-growing stack of such records. At last we have arrived at the *blockchain*.

The same technique that guarantees individual transactions is now marshaled to secure the blockchain against tampering. Just as all the parties to every transaction are timestamped and hashed together to produce a unique fingerprint, so is each block. Because each successive block's hash value is generated with the signature of the one immediately preceding it in time, it folds into itself the details of every block of Bitcoin transactions ever executed, tailing all the way back to the very first, the so-called Genesis Block.

And again, because every participant in the network holds their own local copy of the blockchain, at no point is there the slightest need for transactions to be checked against any central registry or clearinghouse. The entire network works to maintain and protect the blockchain: its shared, public, *distributed ledger*.

Once a block has been confirmed by the network and added to the blockchain, all of the transactions bundled into it are considered to have been *settled*; from this point forward, they are a part of the permanent record. For very low-value transactions, this is where the story ends; a single-pass confirmation is sufficient to ensure that they probably won't be overturned. (The Bitcoin documentation describes such one-confirmation transactions as "safe if you trust the person paying you.")[11]

Because the validity of the entire chain is computationally reverified every time a new block is added to it, though, any given transaction gets exponentially more reliable over time. Most wallet applications will therefore show a transaction as unconfirmed until the block in which it was included is six blocks deep in the blockchain. This number reflects the nominal 0.1 percent risk that a transaction will be overturned after its *bona fides* have been recalculated five additional times, a calculation which in turn is based on an assumption that a forger controls no more than 10 percent of the network's available processing power.

Parties to high-value transactions may well want to wait, therefore, until many more block-confirmation cycles have elapsed. Newly created coins, for example, aren't recognized by the Bitcoin protocol until the transaction creating them has been folded a full 100 blocks deep. At this point the odds are astronomically high that no recalculation of the blockchain will displace them, and even the biggest transaction can truly be considered irrevocably settled, irreversible and effectively permanent. As my wallet, yours, and all other Bitcoin applications consult the blockchain to establish the current distribution of coins, they will all reflect the same account balance. Whatever coin we control can now be spent like any other currency.

The complex, decentralized process by which a block of transaction histories is validated and added to the permanent record is called *mining*, and it's the single aspect of Bitcoin's mechanics that most seems to confound efforts at comprehension.

Let's start by recognizing that only a subset of machines on the Bitcoin network participate in mining. Each miner is presented with the task of gathering from the network all of the loose transactions that have taken place since the last block was confirmed, aggregating them into blocks, and performing the calculations that will result in confirmation.

Any mining node can submit a candidate block for validation, and as we've seen, the decision as to whether or not a given block should be confirmed is made individually by each one. Coupled to the distributed topography of the Bitcoin network, this means that multiple potentially valid chains will be floating around at any one tick of the clock. Yet somehow the entire network of miners reliably converges on a single history, a single ledger and a single canonical blockchain, as a firm consensus as to its soundness and reliability emerges among them.

Here is where the confusion arises. So often a word like "consensus" means different things to different groups of people. In horizontalist politics, "consensus" is generally understood to mean a decision rule that requires unanimous or near-unanimous agreement to a proposal before it can be adopted by a group—and if not full agreement, then at least an absence of active dissent.

But computational consensus works a little differently. At any given moment, there may exist in the network two or more candidate strings, each a block or two long, each waiting for final confirmation and incorporation into the canonical blockchain. This isn't necessarily indicative of an attempt at forgery; it's simply a property of the network's varied physical topography, and the uneven length of the paths messages take as they travel across it. Whether the discrepancy arises from forgery or a simple delay in transmission, though, the result is the same: some nodes will reflect one version of history, some another.

But because it is so critical that the blockchain reflect one and only one chronological sequence of transactions, only one of these versions of history can be adopted. In particular, the potential for a successful double-spend exists as long as such multiple orderings of transaction history are allowed to persist. How are these conflicts resolved?

There is no ballot, per se. Where such a fork occurs, a mining node will maintain local copies of all of the candidate additions to the blockchain, and then "vote" among them according to a simple heuristic. It will work on validating the longest of the options available to it—implicitly, the one that has already had more of the network's processing capacity dedicated to assuring its reliability than any other.

If, while the node is working, another miner somewhere else on the network succeeds in confirming a block to the sequence it happens to have selected, nothing changes. The current string remains the longest, and the node will simply begin working on a new block that further extends it. But if a block is confirmed to another sequence among those held in local memory, and that sequence now becomes the longest, it is compelled to switch its efforts.

Dissent may persist for a while, but it will expire gradually, as one candidate sequence crosses the threshold past which the likelihood that it can be challenged dwindles toward zero. All mining nodes eventually converge on this single longest chain, which becomes canonical once all its onetime competitors have fallen by the wayside.

This certainly seems like a simple enough decision rule. But why the longest? What's the correlation between the length of a candidate sequence and the likelihood that all the records it contains are legitimate?

We've already noted that any mining node can submit a candidate block for validation. In order to deter bad actors from cluttering up the network with attempts at forgery, though, a cost is imposed on this participation. All would-be miners are required to solve a problem of known complexity before submitting a block for confirmation, essentially by running random numbers through an equation until a specified value is matched. This calculation is called *proof-of-work*, it is based on the unique hash value associated with the transactions in each block, and it's deliberately designed to tax computational resources by consuming as much electricity as possible. The difficulty of the proof-of-work problem is continually adjusted by the Bitcoin protocol itself, and is calibrated so that a successful solution will be found, on average, every ten minutes, no matter how many nodes are participating in the calculation.

Achieving a valid proof-of-work for a specified hash and the block it represents is expensive, both computationally and energetically, and as a result imposes a financial cost upon whoever manages the node responsible. While early on in its history, it was feasible to mine Bitcoin on an ordinary desktop or laptop, such everyday machines were quickly outpaced by specialized mining rigs built on microprocessors known as application-specific integrated circuits, or ASICs. (The architecture of ASICs is optimized for brute-force calculation, but they nevertheless run so hot that mining at scale long ago decamped to places like Iceland, where energy costs are relatively low and the climate furnishes a built-in source of cooling.) None of this comes cheap, and that's even before factoring in the amortized cost of hardware.

But if it's so costly to participate in the process of validation, why would anyone rational ever do so? This is where the considerable elegance of Satoshi's design really manifests itself: to incentivize undertaking the burdensome proof-of-work calculations, the first miner to submit a valid proof-of-work for a given block is rewarded with freshly minted coin. At time of writing this bounty was set at 25 BTC, worth just north of $11,000 at today's exchange rates—a not-inconsiderable amount of money standing to be won every ten minutes, and, for the successful miner, a handsome return on their investment.

To put it in the most concrete possible terms, you need to spend electricity on computation to have a chance of earning that 25 BTC; the more computing cycles you are able to dedicate to the challenge, the better your chance of being the one who's able to solve the proof-of-work problem, confirm a block of transactions before anyone else does, and be awarded the bounty for that block. This is the provision of the Bitcoin protocol that simultaneously incentivizes distributed work, and deters attempts at forgery: *doing the gruntwork of validating previous transactions is the only way new Bitcoin gets made.*[12]

This move kills quite a few birds with a single cryptographic stone. It neatly circumvents the problem of a mint arbitrarily diluting the value of existing currency by flooding the market with new coinage: we know the exact schedule on which new coins will be minted, and by what rules. It eliminates any need for a trusted intermediary to reconcile transactions: not through recourse to any central clearinghouse, but by consulting the local copy of a shared record that is annealed with all the others every time a block is confirmed. And it cunningly allows the network to insulate itself against forgery via proof-of-work, the very mechanism of artificial scarcity that underwrites Bitcoin's value in the first place.

What happens if someone *does* try to spend a given coin twice, erase the record of a payment, or otherwise tamper with consensus history? Understand what forgery means in this context: that someone is attempting to inject a record that *cannot be found anywhere else in the ledger*, that does not and cannot be made to agree with a collective history that has been computationally confirmed and reconfirmed, thousands or millions of times over. Because the transactions represented by the forgery cannot be reconciled with the ledger, the candidate block will fail the basic checks specified in the Bitcoin protocol, and will neither be validated nor propagated by any other non-colluding node. So crucially, the forgers themselves will remain the only party that will begin calculating a proof-of-work based on this specific hash value.

But meanwhile, there will be many, many more copies of whatever legitimate blocks *have* been validated and propagated across the network. Because all of the network's other nodes are working on a calculation generated from the same hash value, the cumulative amount of processing power dedicated to discovering a solution will be vastly greater than the amount a forger can bring to bear. Barring what has historically been the unlikely situation in which the forger controls a majority of the nodes on the network, a miner that is working on its own to discover a proof-of-work for a problem generated by an entirely different hash will be at a terrible disadvantage. One of the many miners working on a legitimate solution is overwhelmingly likely to complete their calculations first, arrive at a valid proof-of-work and confirm their block.

Even if a forger does manage to land on a proof-of-work solution and broadcast its candidate block to the network, it is still vertiginously unlikely that the version of transaction history it proposes will ever be bound into the canonical blockchain the necessary six layers deep. Other mining nodes will only accept the candidate, and use its unique hash as the seed for a new block, if they can independently reconfirm the validity of all the transactions bundled into it. This, of course, they cannot do; meanwhile, in the same ten-minute interval, probability strongly favors the confirmation of a competing, legitimate block. In the time it takes for the corrupted string to propagate, the lawful string will have grown by yet another block.

And as we know, here a positive-feedback loop kicks in: miners converge on the chain that is the longest, which by this logic will always be the one that has the highest number of proof-of-work calculations associated with it. At this point the bogus transaction fork is "orphaned": rejected by the collective as simply discordant with what is now an agreed version of history, it falls away like a dry husk and is forgotten. All effort and energy expended on proof-of-work for blocks in the orphaned sequence is lost, while none of the bounties associated with confirming the blocks in it will ever be paid out.

Remember that even would-be forgers themselves are

confronted with this calculus. A mining node can choose to dedicate processing cycles toward confirming whatever block its owner wishes, but if a miner wishes to have any chance of earning a bounty on it, that block must eventually wind up being bound into the main-sequence blockchain, and surviving a trial of strength repeated one hundred times over. Bad actors are, in effect, forced to choose between burning all their resources on a quixotic attempt at forgery that's all but mathematically certain to fail—incurring a significant cost, but earning no reward whatsoever—and dedicating those same resources to confirmation of a competing, legitimate block, earning at least some chance of eventually being awarded the bounty for it. Every participant in the network is therefore strongly incentivized to enforce the purity of the one true ledger.

And there it is: the emergence of distributed consensus, and with it a functioning, usable cryptocurrency. Bitcoin is like a black box crammed full of oddly shaped moving parts that don't seem to make any sense, which mesh together in all sorts of disturbingly non-Euclidean ways—and yet do exactly what they're supposed to do.

However improbable it may be, Bitcoin works according to the terms set forth for it by its shadowy creator. But how well does it work as money? Which is to say: how well does it function practically as a medium of exchange, as a unit of account and as a store of value?

As a unit of account, relatively few products and services are natively denominated in BTC—the kind of thing you'd have found for sale on the Silk Road exchange, perhaps, or elsewhere on the darknet—and I've never yet met anyone who intuitively reckons prices this way. People who use Bitcoin therefore need to consult realtime apps like ZeroBlock to measure their holdings against the US dollar or the euro to see how much they are worth; often such a ticker is the first and most prominent thing you see on enthusiast websites.

Nor has the currency worked particularly well as a stable and reliable store of value, dismaying those many investors who want it to sustain or appreciate in worth. While a slow, steady upward trend can be discerned, during the epoch in which it has been at all widely held Bitcoin been reasonably volatile, trading as high as $1,230.69 to the BTC and as low as $164.49. This rather complicates Satoshi's original conception, which was that his currency would be permanently deflation-ary: though that number is high, there are only a finite number of Bitcoins that can or ever will be mined, and their creation gets progressively more difficult.

On the surface, Bitcoin's deflationary quality seems to make it an ideal investment vehicle: in a vacuum, any amount of it you're able to earn, buy or mine now would only ever increase in value. Like any other financial token ever devised by humanity, though, from cowrie shells and gold ingots to Tubman twenties, the worth of Bitcoin rests on a psychological sleight-of-hand: even if its supply is artificially constrained, even if the authentic-ity of each coin is guaranteed by an airtight process of collective computational verification, the currency is still only as valuable as other people think it is.

This game of perceptions has over time played hob with Bitcoin's valuation. Speculation is rife, exchange hacks (and even total collapses)[13] are unnervingly frequent, persistent discord among the Bitcoin core developers does little to dampen perceptions of the currency's essential instability, and inevita-bly there are those who hoard whatever BTC they've mined for the future, rather than exchanging them for goods and services in the present. Of course, this last fact is only a "problem" if you primarily conceive of Bitcoin as a currency, rather than as a commodity. But it exposes a basic tension between the ways in which the currency is understood by the very people who hold it, and undoubtedly renders it far too volatile for conservative investors to consider holding as a long-term repository of value.

Even as a medium of exchange, in practical terms Bitcoin has never been all that useful. And this does demand at least some explication: of all the ways in which money manifests itself in our lives, exchange is the one Bitcoin was explicitly designed for, and seems most suited to.

Why is Bitcoin's failure to gain traction as a medium of daily exchange so surprising? Firstly, and entirely by design, the currency welcomes those who find themselves locked out of other ways of exchanging value over the global network. This includes the billions of people on Earth who derive all or part of their livelihood from participation in the informal economy; the so-called "unbanked," those 2.5 billion of us who lack access to conventional financial services; and, of course providers of goods or services that would be overtly illegal in one or more jurisdictions.

All of these people can securely transact in Bitcoin, given only a network connection and access to a smartphone or other device on which they can safely store a wallet application. One of the beauties of distributed consensus is that no one can censor the ledger, or prevent someone else from adding a legitimate transaction to it. This means there's no way, other than moral suasion, of enforcing boycotts or blockades on transaction with disfavored parties. In principle, then, Bitcoin ought to have a built-in constituency among those who, for one reason or another, cannot participate in other modes of digital value exchange. And with World Bank and ILO estimates placing the size of the informal economy at anywhere up to 72 percent of total economic output, depending on region, this implies a very large number of highly motivated potential users.

Moreover, because of the relatively low transaction costs it imposes—nothing like the considerable overhead banks and credit-card issuers must dedicate to detecting fraud, assessing the merits of chargeback attempts and so on—the Bitcoin network can in principle economically process much smaller amounts than other payment systems. Some, indeed, thought of it as a key enabling infrastructure for an economy based on micropayments, minuscule charges that would be levied every time a song is played or a news article downloaded.[14] One would think that a mode of payment capable of supporting entirely new business models might attract no small amount of interest, especially at a time when "content creators" and the media more broadly are under extraordinary, even existential financial pressure.

With all these advantages, then, why hasn't Bitcoin become the universal economic solvent its most fervent fans so clearly want it to be?

To begin with, Bitcoin suffers from relatively high latency. Because all the different local versions of the blockchain are only "eventually consistent" with one another, it takes on the order of ten minutes for even low-value transactions to settle, and up to an hour for larger ones. Though this certainly compares favorably to other modes of digital value transfer, it simply cannot compete with cash, which remains a mainstay of face-to-face transactions precisely because, as a bearer instrument, it "clears" immediately.

There are real drawbacks to using Bitcoin for bigger-ticket purchases, as well. Despite boosters' wide-eyed claims that you can actually pay for hotel rooms and international flights with Bitcoin, it's by no means the most straightforward thing to do. Technically, you can accomplish these things, with a little effort: UATP, the network that processes payments for virtually all of the planet's airlines, announced in February 2015 that they were preparing to accept Bitcoin.[15] But well over a year later, it's still impossible to book flights directly with the major carriers and paying with the currency. So for the moment, anyone wanting to swap BTC for travel arrangements is forced to use a service like BTCTrip—i.e., precisely the kind of obscure, not-particularly-confidence-inspiring intermediary the whole business of distributed consensus was supposed to route around in the first place. A similar situation obtains for the hospitality industry: among major booking sites, only Expedia allows users to pay with Bitcoin, and even then only on the US version of its website.

And as far as everyday life is concerned, Bitcoin—far and away the best-known and most widely accepted of all crypto-currencies—remains virtually invisible. Here its adoption has clearly been hamstrung by two factors: setting up a wallet isn't particularly straightforward, and the process of acquiring BTC to put in it is downright arcane.

The array of wallets available immediately confronts the novice user with a bewildering thicket of choices, the implications of which won't be clear until they've used the application for a while. The Bitcoin Project itself lists no fewer than twelve options, all of which have different features, run on different platforms, offer different levels of security, and in general display all the variability in design quality you'd expect of a field open to developers of every stripe. It's not so much that downloading and setting up any one of these is an especially confusing process, as that the initial choice itself can feel a little overwhelming, particularly for those of us who don't happen to be conversant in the jargon of cryptocurrency.

That accomplished, one is still faced with the necessity of getting hold of some BTC to spend. With mining long ago become the province of those who control immense pools of computing power, there are relatively few ways of acquiring Bitcoin remaining to ordinary people who want to transact in the currency:

You could accept Bitcoin yourself, in exchange for whatever products or services you happen to offer. (For example, if you find that you're particularly enjoying this book, you're entirely welcome to send a BTC-denominated gratuity to my wallet at 1CaMGXfRCdfUVb1FFWfDR8h8Qzbzm5w2FA.)

You could buy from an exchange: one among dozens of colorfully named registries like CEX.IO, BTC-e or OKCoin, any of which will be happy to take your state-backed fiat currency, take a smallish cut on the conversion, and send BTC to whatever wallet address you furnish. You may have to use the exchange's own-brand wallet, you may have to wait until your offer to buy is accepted by someone willing to sell at that price, but you can generally convert any amount of currency you please to Bitcoin. (The fact that people are actually doing so at scale at every hour of the day is attested to by a fascinating site called Fiatleak, on which you can see torrents of value gushing out of national currencies in real time—chiefly, at any time I've ever consulted it, the Chinese yuan.)

If you were dead set on exchanging fiat cash for BTC physically, you could perhaps avail yourself of one of the planet's few Bitcoin ATMs, most of which were located in hipster enclaves like

London's Shoreditch. But describing their coverage as "sparse" would be generous in the extreme; as of the end of 2015, there were a grand total of eight such machines deployed in all of New York City, for example, including two deep in what was then the decidedly unhipsterish, mostly Hasidic neighborhood of Crown Heights.

Let's stipulate that with a little trial and error, you are eventually able to fill your wallet with whatever amount of BTC you desire. You would still have to locate merchants who might be willing to accept them. Frustratingly, you will very likely find that there's just about nowhere around that does—that it's virtually impossible to use your new wallet to, say, ring up a packet of gum at the corner bodega.

What you *are* offered instead is a website which, rather plaintively, helps holders of Bitcoin "find places to use 'em."[16] This is a problem which surely has never confronted holders of dollars, Euros, pounds Sterling, or other currencies in good standing. Only in wartime or cases of state failure do large amounts of people generally worry about finding vendors willing to take their money. So while the scarcity of vendors is most likely inevitable at this stage in the adoption of any currency, the mental images evoked by the hunt for a place to spend your Bitcoin do not furnish a particularly good advertisement for it.

All of this leaves Bitcoin a distinctly minor, even a declining, factor in everyday exchanges of value.[17] Globally, its transaction velocity peaked at just over three per second in March 2016. Compare Visa, which on the average day supports 3,000 times as many exchanges per second as Bitcoin, or even PayPal, which by the end of 2014 was supporting something on the order of 112 transactions per second, and we can see just what a long road Bitcoin will have to travel before it can make good on any of its pretensions to planetary relevance.[18]

Together, these problems have no doubt gone some way toward sabotaging Bitcoin's utility as a mass platform for the everyday exchange of value. But they are nevertheless problems of a kind that can be solved, and for that matter there are any number of parties, from basement hackers to Goldman Sachs-funded startups, lining up to solve them.

There are, however, other and more severe drawbacks to Bitcoin *qua* Bitcoin, and these aren't nearly as amenable to resolution. For all the glittering technical brilliance of Satoshi's design, these aren't so much brakes on adoption or further expansion as they are early portents of doom—likely both Bitcoin's own, and that of any cryptocurrency or distributed-ledger scheme founded on the same intellectual kit of parts.

The first of these concerns the privacy of parties to a transaction: while breathless, early coverage often touted Bitcoin as "anonymous," this simply isn't so, at least not in any way that should be relied upon by anybody who's at all vulnerable. It is true that there is nothing in the protocol, its clients or their operation that directly ties a transaction to any one person. But sending or receiving Bitcoin requires a wallet application, that application has to live on some specific computational device, and we know that it gets easier with every passing day to associate devices with named and otherwise identified individuals.

The experts assure us that due to the way they sequester encrypted data, smartphones in particular are tolerably safe. But when the string identifying your Bitcoin wallet resides alongside your own encoded fingerprints, on a phone that bears a unique IMEI number, you are inherently at risk of being connected to whatever pattern of transactions you've left behind in the blockchain.[19]

And even without access to the physical device, or anything it may contain, parties to transactions may find that their identities can be pinpointed with surprising ease. As early as 2011, for example, security researchers were able to cross-reference forum posts, Twitter handles and the blockchain's own record of public transaction data to determine the identity of "anonymous" donors to WikiLeaks.[20]

The sources of potentially identifying information are legion, and not all that easy for a user to clamp down on. The blockchain itself, of course, retains everything, and shares it on demand with anyone who asks. By their very nature, exchanges and wallet providers have access to still-greater stores of compromising data, making them necessary but worrisome points of friction for the privacy-minded. And when it comes time to turn BTC into some currency with potency in the workaday world, via some commercial exit point, the identities of the individuals or institutions involved become highly vulnerable to exposure.

In order to prevent a new address from being "tainted" by the persistent traces of past transactions, then, Bitcoin's official documentation recommends that users rely on each address only once, and generate a fresh one each time they undertake a transaction.[21] This isn't as clumsy as it sounds, but it does nevertheless present users with yet another cognitive burden, and it's easy to imagine this step being forgotten, overlooked or simply not bothered with at a critical moment, with all the consequences that implies for the eventual revelation of identity. In short, as is so often the case, an engineer has designed a privacy-conserving system of considerable internal coherence, rigor and refinement, that nevertheless becomes radically compromised at the very moment it encounters the legacy systems, habits and practices of everyday life.

Amplifying these risks, and a surfeit of others as well, is the undeniable fact that the once-dispersed Bitcoin network has in recent years undergone a fairly radical degree of recentralization. Professional miners have always dramatically shifted the odds of landing confirmation bounties in their favor, by assembling immense pools of processing power. But with ASIC hardware having become thoroughly commodified, the mere fact that one is able to marshal large amounts of computational capital is no longer even remotely a guarantee of meaningful return on investment.[22] The only competitive advantage remaining to a prospective miner is energy arbitrage: the ability to locate their operations where electricity is cheapest, and cooling costs are lowest.

Taken together, this brutal economic calculus, and the scale of investment that's now required to set up a mining operation that has even the slightest chance of turning a profit, bring a strongly centripetal force to bear on the shape of the network.

The resulting sharp concentration of mining power leaves the shared ledger, transaction privacy, and even the specifications of the protocol itself subject to the whims of a very few operators.

In particular, with power over the network now resting in the hands of a very small number of actors, one of the gravest weaknesses of Satoshi's original design suddenly looks a great deal more vulnerable to exploitation. This is its susceptibility to something called a "51-percent attack," the property that, if some party ever accumulated more than half of the network's total processing power, they could assume control of the ledger, and modify it in a variety of ways.[23] During whatever period that they were able to maintain their numeric supremacy, this party could double-spend to their heart's content, as well as prevent anyone else from successfully confirming a block: bad enough, surely. But more seriously by far, the credibility of the propositions on which Bitcoin's reliability is predicated would be shattered, once and for all time.

Safety from a 51-percent attack has always relied entirely on a decentralized network, and the dispersal of processing power that went with it, because under these circumstances it actually is prohibitively difficult to assemble even a fraction of the computational resources required to mount the attack, even given the known assets of entities like the NSA. Bitcoin's advocates have always touted the network's dispersal as key to its safety.

At the time of writing, though, two massive Chinese mining operations, AntPool and DiscusFish/F2 Pool, controlled between them just over 51 percent of the network's total mining power. In theory, the benefits they could derive from legitimate mining outweigh any that might be yielded by exploitation of the network's weakness, and this is supposed to furnish them with a strong incentive to protect the status quo. But should they for whatever reason decide to collude with one another, they could execute a successful, and devastating, attack at any time.

The 51-percent vulnerability has been there since the very beginning, coiled up and waiting in every transaction executed and every block confirmed, from the Genesis Block onward. The fact that it existed at all was tolerable, maybe, so long as processing power was widely distributed. And yet it remains, unpatched and incapable of *being* patched, even into an era in which that power has become concentrated in just a few hands. The reliability of the entire network therefore teeters on the fact that it simply hasn't been exploited yet. It is inconceivable that anything so dangerously exposed to the risk of permanent, irreversible corruption could ever be allowed to furnish the world economy's payments infrastructure and backbone.

And yet the real Achilles heel of any vision of everyday life predicated on Bitcoin or the blockchain technology at its core is not this, or any of the other limitations we've discussed. It is, rather, a factor that only began to tell once the Bitcoin network had grown past a certain threshold of scale, and therefore aggregate processing power: the failure to account for the thermodynamic cost of distributed consensus based on proof-of-work.

Computation, after all, isn't some species of magic: every last bit that's flipped in a server somewhere is work, in the strict physical sense.[24] Like all other forms of work, it requires the application of energy, and generates waste in the form of heat. And as we've seen, in the Bitcoin protocol, proof-of-work is deliberately designed to eat processor cycles. This is to say it deliberately burns energy—and what's worse, burns it on a calculation without any intrinsic meaning, value or utility.[25]

How much energy are we talking about? A Bloomberg Business writer estimated in early 2013 that Bitcoin mining then used some 982 megawatt hours per day, globally, at a time when the currency remained the all-but-exclusive preserve of a deeply marginal technolibertarian class.[26] By 2015, the British government was citing estimates that the Bitcoin network consumed on a daily basis an amount of energy "in excess of 1GW [and] comparable to the electricity use of Ireland."

And how much heat? Remember, we're not even considering whatever warming is associated with generating the power consumed by computing devices, but the direct waste heat produced by the network's own, furious proof-of-work calculations. The thermal buildup is so noticeable in the immediate environs of mining that there have been serious attempts to heat houses in wintertime using ASIC rigs, dedicating whatever amount of Bitcoin was successfully mined in the process to offset the cost of doing so. If its global contribution is presently all but lost in the background warming, it's clear that at scale the entire Bitcoin network could be entirely powered by clean, renewable solar and wind power, and it would still generate problematic quantities of heat.

Some back-of-envelope calculations extrapolated from the specifications of the Antminer S5, a reasonably typical commodity ASIC unit, will at least give us an idea of the order of magnitude we ought to be imagining. The 590-watt S5 yields 1,155 gigahashes (or proof-of-work calculations) per second; powered by household current, it generates just over 2,000 BTUs per hour. The Bitcoin network *in toto*, meanwhile, currently runs about 1.4 billion GH/s. So even accounting for the more efficient processing architecture presumably relied upon by the largest mining pools, the global calculation of proof-of-work is already in aggregate producing something on the order of 20,000 MBTUs every hour, every last joule of which gets dumped into the atmosphere somehow. And this at three transactions per second, some 1/3,000th of the scale of a fully global, truly ubiquitous value exchange network.

So tight are the margins between the network's production of heat and its production of value that one knowledgeable skeptic described Bitcoin as primarily a "decentralized waste heat creator."[27] (The same skeptic observes that there's little rational expectation that this situation might improve with the advent of more energy-efficient mining hardware, "because the number of such installations rises to the profitability limit.") Perhaps it is possible to harness the waste produced by mining for domestic or industrial heating, even power generation, or somehow redesign proof-of-work calculations so they at least served a public good, like mapping the folding of proteins.

But as things stand, the stark, uncomfortable truth is that Bitcoin mining only makes economic sense if it treats the atmosphere as a giant heatsink, and the global climate as the biggest externality of all time. The implications for any proof-of-work-based system deployed at scale aren't merely sobering; they ought to be permanently prohibitive.

For all these reasons, then, you may have noticed that your paycheck does not happen to be denominated in BTC (or any other cryptocurrency, for that matter), nor the price of your monthly phone bill, nor that of this book. If Bitcoin is too hard to acquire, too hard to spend and too volatile to hold, if it's too leaky to trust with your identity and too dangerous to mine at scale—and as we've seen, it certainly is all of these things—then why are we still talking about it? Why hasn't it been cast into the recycling bin of history?

As money, it probably has been. Even the enthusiasts and true believers have started to reckon with its many limitations, tiptoeing warily right up to the cusp of confessing its failure. Confronted with empirical evidence of the network's concentration, or the declining interest in accepting Bitcoin at retail, they've started to bruit about instead the notion that electronic cash was never *really* the point at all, that the genuinely disruptive innovation is blockchain applications. (Depending on what exactly they mean by "blockchain," they may even be right.) Most of the remaining Bitcoin-specific buzz you hear is merely the sound of giant institutions hedging their bets—and if they can eke a tenth of a point here or there in the meantime, by moving private bank liabilities or other debt obligations across the blockchain, so much the better.

Yet for all the hype, for all the inequities it reproduces, and all the qualities that prevent it from working at scale as intended, there is something permanently valuable in Bitcoin. It turns out that the coordination of parties unknown to one another, who don't necessarily trust one another—who would be, in fact, very well advised to not trust one another in the slightest—is a standing Hard Problem, something that has long bedeviled a great many disciplines and communities of interest.

We can think of institutions like governments and banks and systems of jurisprudence as technologies intended to address this class of challenges—the best-fit approximations to an answer that we've been able to arrive at, after a few thousand years of working the problem together. And if these institutions are potentially displaced by the newly available technology of the blockchain, then by analogy so is any relation that's previously required the participation of a trust-mediating or risk-buffering third party.

When you start looking for these relations, of course, they're everywhere in our lives. They shape the contours of the world we are cast into at birth, and we move in their shadows throughout our lives. We have perforce been constrained to approach the questions of our existence through whatever apertures they offer us. But now we are faced with a new set of possibilities. The blockchain, as it transpired, had greater salience as a figure of thought than it did as a working technology; the details of its specific implementation in Bitcoin turned out to be far less important than what it suggested about the ways in which the efforts of a globally dispersed group of people might be yoked together in a common effort.

So however Bitcoin fares in the world—and my own feeling is that its utility *per se* is at or very close to an end—there was a persistently useful contribution at its core. Abstracted from the question of value exchange, the blockchain offers us a tool of surprisingly broad utility that we didn't know we needed, and didn't even have the language to properly describe, until it was dropped in our laps.

If the blockchain can be extracted from Bitcoin, perhaps the idea of a networked, self-sustaining framework for the development of consensus can be further elaborated, beyond the constraints imposed by the blockchain itself. Freed, in particular, of the impossible thermodynamics of proof-of-work, the provocative notion of a robust, programmable and widely available trust infrastructure becomes credible. In principle, this infrastructure is something we might use to organize ourselves in entirely new ways, opening up approaches to collaboration that none of our previous institutions could have supported. And just as clearly, its advent would present profound implications for the way we assemble ourselves into groups at any scale beyond the strictly local, and with any degree of structure beyond the most ad hoc and informal.

What any of this might mean for the political economy of everyday life anywhere on Earth is as yet far from clear. As with the other technologies we've considered so far, we will need to sift the options presented to us with the most exceeding care, ask pointed questions about the arrangements and distributions of power they afford, and make acute judgments as to how and under what circumstances we will allow them to structure our reality. But the post-Satoshi explosion of interest in technologies of distributed consensus has catalyzed an intellectual ferment that is still working itself out, bringing startling new ideas about organization, coordination and cooperation to the table.

6

Blockchain beyond Bitcoin

A trellis for posthuman institutions

There may well come a time in the future when cryptocurrencies like Bitcoin become broadly relevant to our lives, but for better or worse that time is not yet upon us. Amid clear signs of a speculative asset bubble, by late 2015 a convergence of factors—the domination of mining by a very few large Chinese pools, the fading interest in accepting Bitcoin at retail and the drifting of institutional attention toward newer, shinier technologies—made it evident that the promised utopia of universal, frictionless digital transaction would have to be deferred.

This posed something of a gut check for the community of experts, think tanks, startups and media outlets that had grown up overnight in the wake of Bitcoin's appearance. Observers were treated to the unedifying spectacle of would-be thought leaders—many who had recently hyped the currency for its limitless potential—waving away the contentions they had made just a month or two previously. You could almost hear the gears grind as the conventional wisdom pivoted; the new line was that the enabling technology of the blockchain itself was more interesting, and far more worthy of sustained investigation, than anything as naff as a mere decentralized global currency. The insight took hold that the emergent techniques of sharing and securing data at Bitcoin's core might have disruptive applications far beyond the financial sphere.

Bitcoin might be a dead letter as a method for the exchange of value at any meaningful scale, in other words, but it functioned beautifully as a proof of concept. Consider the intellectual kit of parts that Satoshi assembled to build his currency: a means for the cryptographic verification of identity, a universal ledger with the properties of transparency and persistence, and a procedure for the consolidation of agreement among parties, all founded on a diffuse, decentralized, serverless architecture that is very difficult to eradicate, or even hinder, by any means short of dismantling the network itself. Liberated from the specific context of Bitcoin, this is a powerfully general vocabulary, and it can be used to build all kinds of useful things.

The new applications aimed beyond transactions of value, squarely at the far larger domain of information brokerage in all its forms. A cluster of startups appeared, promising to replace all the unwieldy baggage of corporate and governmental databases—the word suddenly seemed fusty and old-fashioned —with a universal, distributed data-storage infrastructure based on the blockchain. This new infrastructure would be programmable, capable of actively disposing of the assets it tallied. It would live on the network itself, in principle placing it beyond the reach of meddlesome bureaucrats and the regulations they ginned up amongst themselves. It would replace paper agreements with contracts written directly in code that afforded no ambiguity of interpretation, and executed with literally inhuman precision.

In this light, it suddenly made sense to talk about the secure, verifiable and transparent movement of any fiduciary token whatsoever—assets and liabilities, agreements and obligations, wagers and votes, tickets and claims—across the blockchain from one party to another. This prospect opened up extraordinary possibilities for the world of administration, which in large part consists of little more than keeping track of such positions as the information encoding them is moved through, across and between organizations. More profoundly yet, it presented new ways of thinking about organization itself—about what it means to associate with others, how joint intention might be harnessed, and parties unknown to one another yoked in effective collaboration, across all the usual barriers of space and time.

As a consequence of this post-Bitcoin explosion of activity, we now find ourselves having to reckon with a sprawling conceptual menagerie, populated by exotica like "distributed applications," "smart contracts" and "autonomous organizations." Some see in these tools the advent of a "digital consensus space" in which startling new forms of coordination and governance might emerge, in which the activity of leaderless horizontal organizations might be supported at global scale. Others see a reinvention of government itself, as the state masters powerful new tools for the verification of identity, the certification of compliance and the distribution of benefits. At the outside, glimmering faintly like a distant constellation, some even glimpse the makings of a fully posthuman economy. And all of this mediated by "trustless" techniques, unfolding in absolute, cryptographically guaranteed safety.

Just what is being proposed, though? How did we get from Bitcoin to a "programmable trust infrastructure"? How might such a thing be useful? Who devised these tools, and why?

It sometimes seems that every age gets the technological icons it deserves, and if so it would be hard to invent a character more pungently appropriate to our own than Vitalik Buterin. Though an identifiable, individual, flesh-and-blood human being, Buterin is in every other way almost as much of a cipher as the mysterious Satoshi Nakamoto. We know a few biographical facts; we know too that he is evidently a fierce believer in the decentralization of power. But otherwise he is a blank. So little personal information about him is available that it's all but impossible to get a sense of who he is, or what values he might cherish beyond this one core conviction.[1]

Born in Russia in 1994, Buterin was just shy of twenty when he dropped out of Ontario's Waterloo University, spurred by a $100,000 grant from the foundation of libertarian venture capitalist Peter Thiel. As a co-founder of and primary contributor to *Bitcoin Magazine*, he had immersed himself in the body of theory developing around the blockchain, mastered its abstruse concepts, and in so doing, become convinced that Satoshi's design was profoundly limited. Now, Thiel's stipend in hand, he was free to pursue the intuition that he could improve upon that design.

In November 2013, Buterin published a white paper describing a protocol intended to rectify all the flaws and shortcomings he saw in Bitcoin. Fusing comprehensive technical understanding and a clear vision to a series of crisply articulated value propositions, it swiftly attracted a number of accomplished developers in the cryptocurrency space, and together they more or less immediately set to work on building out the set of tools described in it. The successful launch of a framework called Ethereum just a few months later would demote "the" (implicitly Bitcoin) blockchain to merely "a" blockchain, just one alternative among many.

While there has been a groundswell of competing initiatives in the post- or para-Bitcoin space, with cryptic names like Juno and Sawtooth Lake, I have chosen to center the discussion that follows on Ethereum. It remains preeminent among these second-generation blockchain efforts, is now rapidly approaching the size of the Bitcoin network, and seems likely to remain salient when other streams of activity have dried up or come to nothing.[2] More importantly, though, Buterin and the substantial community he has attracted to his initiative have generated most of the domain's fundamentally new ideas, and have otherwise proven adept at translating those already in circulation into their own highly particular idiom. If Deleuze and Guattari held that the fundamental task of a philosopher is the creation of new concepts, indeed, it's not entirely ridiculous to think of Buterin's work in this way.[3] However we may evaluate them practically or ethically, the explosion of post-Satoshi development has populated the world with new and challenging objects of thought, and the community around Ethereum has been especially fruitful in this regard.

Ethereum does offer its own token of value—a cryptocurrency called Ether[4]—and people do mine and trade in Ether directly, just as they might Bitcoin. But what the network does with it is quite a bit subtler and more interesting than the mere transfer of value between human beings. Buterin had conceived Ethereum from the outset as a single, massively distributed computing engine sprawled across the global network, in which all processing is paid for in increments of Ether. In this model, computing power aggregated from that of individual machines becomes immanent to the network itself. This architecture allows Ethereum to serve as a platform for networked applications that run on a decentralized, peer-to-peer basis, rather than the more conventional client-server model. With such distributed applications (or, cloyingly, "dapps") there is no central server, no one physical place where the program resides, and therefore no single point of failure. This isn't particularly efficient, but it does confer at least one significant advantage for applications that skirt the law, like file-sharing: when functionality is smeared out across the entire network, no one jurisdiction can suppress it, however much they might want to.

Its protean quality can sometimes obscure just what it is that Ethereum promises to bring to the table. Is it best understood as an alternative to the Bitcoin blockchain, a flexible, powerful, general-purpose distributed computing infrastructure, or an environment for running applications that cannot be easily suppressed? The straightforward answer is that it aims to be all of these things, all at once, and its development team has demonstrated at least some progress toward each goal. But however much one or another of these propositions might appeal to some pie-slice of its target audience, none of them is quite as compelling to the community gathered around Ethereum as its power to act conditionally.

This ability to trigger events should certain contingencies arise is something the Bitcoin blockchain could not do, and Buterin had designed it into his creation from the start. You can store data of any nature on the Ethereum blockchain, and it will be validated, agreed upon and permanently accessible to anyone who asks for it, just as records of Bitcoin transactions are accessible to anyone querying the Bitcoin blockchain. But you can also perform logical operations with Ethereum—any operation that a general-purpose computer would be capable of handling. And one of the things this allows a programmer to do is specify conditional triggers for certain events: *if this happens, then do that.* Or, put slightly differently: *when these conditions are met, execute the following set of instructions.*

This is the core of an idea that had been floating around cryptological, fintech and libertarian circles for more than two decades, but had lacked any practical enabling infrastructure until Buterin came along with his programmable blockchain: the so-called "smart contract."

First proposed by the pioneering cryptographer Nick Szabo in the mid-1990s, a smart contract not merely *records* the terms of an agreement between parties in an autonomous chunk of code, but *enacts* it as well.[5] What gives a smart contract its teeth is that its compliance mechanism is woven into the network itself; enforcement of its terms is direct, intrinsic and incontestable. A scenario Szabo offered a 2001 conference for hardcore technolibertarians is illustrative in this regard: smart contracts would solve "the problem of trust by being self-executing. For example, the key to a car sold on credit might only operate if the monthly payments have been made."[6]

In 2001, this could still plausibly be dismissed as a rather unpleasant thought experiment, but by 2014 all the pieces to accomplish it had been assembled. What Szabo had imagined, Buterin now set out to build. He had glossed the idea as "cryptographic 'boxes' that contain value and only unlock it if certain conditions are met," and Ethereum offered him a set of tools with which to make them. Convinced adherents saw in the smart contract the foundation of a transhuman economy in which people, machines, organizations and other entities could enter into agreements as or more binding as any ever validated by a body of law. The rest of us struggled to figure out what it all might mean.

As a paralegal, many years ago, I was taught that a contract is a voluntary, legally binding agreement between two or more competent parties, in which a good or performance of service is exchanged for some valuable consideration. (That last bit is critical: no consideration, no contract.) Cornell Law School's definition is more elegantly minimal: "an agreement creating obligations enforceable by law." An important aspect of both these definitions is that a third party—the law—is implicitly invoked by all contracts, invited to supervise the performance of obligation, and if necessary, punish parties that fail to make good on their commitments. This understanding of a contract as a binding agreement between parties has withstood the passage of centuries and many, many trials of strength. Nevertheless, there are a few inherent limitations to the form.

First, generally speaking, "law" here means the law of a state. This poses little enough problem for most of us, but it is of course *a priori* ideologically distasteful to those who think of state order as an illegitimate imposition on the affairs of free individuals. Secondly, more pragmatically, the enforcement of contracts involves a great deal of managerial and bureaucratic overhead, and these costs mean that the contract mechanism is ordinarily reserved for situations of a certain heft.

A third complication relates to the way that truth is formally constructed in our world. The terms of an employment contract, for example, may specify the date on which employment is to begin, the rate at which an employee's wages are to be paid, the interval at which they can expect payment and so on. In order to have binding legal force, these terms need to be enunciated in a document, and even now that document must be printed on paper and physically signed by the parties to it, whereupon both parties keep a countersigned copy as proof of the terms they have committed themselves to. Should all physical copies of a signed contract somehow be destroyed, of course, no record of agreement to its terms will exist, and it will effectively become unenforceable.

In the contemporary world, however, whatever terms are established on paper and agreed to by signature must now be translated into functional code running on some digital information-processing system. It is this that determines how much money gets deposited in the employee's bank account, what level of insurance coverage they are entitled to, what medical procedures they are pre-authorized for—in short, all the million ways in which the operations of code acting on data shape our daily experience. But however precise they might be, these instructions for the manipulation of data are necessarily an approximation of what the contract specifies in natural language. Depending on the limitations of the various databases involved, there will likely be some slippage involved in this act of translation, things that don't quite make it across the divide intact. And this in turn means that the material performance of the contract will from time to time be at variance with what it actually calls for—occasionally, actionably so.

As implemented on Ethereum, the smart contract addresses all of these formal limitations. Just as the blockchain eliminates the need for a trusted intermediary in transactions of value, so the smart contract eliminates the need for one in enforcement of a promise to perform. Consider Buterin's working definition of a smart contract: "a mechanism involving digital assets and two or more parties, where some or all of the parties put assets in and assets are automatically redistributed among those parties according to a formula based on certain data that is not known at the time the contract is initiated." In other words, this is structurally more like a bet than it is a conventional contract—in effect, a bet that a specified outcome will come to pass, with a neutral and reliably disinterested third party, the blockchain itself, holding the funds wagered in escrow until that time.

That the definition specifies "digital assets" turns out to be pivotal. The law, such as we have known it, is a purely extrinsic phenomenon.[7] It cannot prevent actions from taking place; at most, it can only discourage us from choosing to undertake them. By contrast, what makes a smart contract is not simply that its obligations are recorded on the blockchain for all to see, but that they are exacted in Ether (or, more generically, whatever cryptocurrency is used by the environment in which the smart contract is running).

Just as Bitcoin lowers transaction overhead to the point that micropayments become practical, so too do smart contracts lower the cost of enacting binding agreements between two or more entities, whether they happen to be "machines, companies or people." In fact, because the overhead imposed is so minimal, it becomes feasible to deploy contracts in contexts where they wouldn't have been remotely economic before.

And just as the form of a Bitcoin transaction is identical with its content, the terms of a smart contract are articulated unambiguously, in the same code that governs its execution. There is a precise, 1:1 relationship between what it specifies and what it actually does, and those specifications can be retrieved from the blockchain for reference at any time.

If the atomic unit of the Bitcoin blockchain is transactions, then, that of the Ethereum blockchain is contracts. This "simplest form of decentralized automation" is key to everything else Ethereum does or proposes to do. Armed with this mechanism, it is capable of binding previously unaffiliated peers in a meshwork of obligation, whether those peers are human, organizational or machinic.

As clever as the notion of a smart contract is, it in turn remains subject to real drawbacks. In particular, it reinforces a sharp conceptual boundary between the ecosystem where Ether circulates, and in which it has force and meaning, and the material world beyond. The relevance of a smart contract will therefore hinge vitally on the degree to which any jurisdiction ever accepts its terms as legally binding, or, conversely, that to which the cryptocurrency involved has any liquidity in the broader world.

An excellent example of this weakness when applied to extrinsic affairs is the prenuptial agreement Sayalee Kaluskar and Gaurang Torvekar committed to the Ethereum blockchain in June 2016.[8] The covenants of this agreement—the world's first to be published in this manner, but surely not its last—specify among other things that both "parties should spend at least 100 minutes every 10 days" on a date night. As published to the blockchain, this contract is clearly meaningless. It's not equipped with any mechanism to tally the number of minutes actually devoted to date night, there is no penalty specified for failure to meet the terms, and even if there were, the contract would have no means of enforcing that penalty unless the accounts to be docked were denominated in Ether. This gesture is therefore not actually a true smart contract at all, merely a bog-standard agreement between two people solemnized by its having been written to a public blockchain. For all that Kaluskar and Torvekar's prenup was (we can devoutly hope) not intended to be taken entirely seriously, it's helpful nonetheless in making this distinction clear.

One can also see that there will be a certain two-edged quality to the smart contract's societal implications. On the one hand, the surety of a public, verifiable and intrinsically enforceable contract might afford at least some protection for precarious labor in our time of compulsory flexibility.[9] But the context in which smart contracts are supposed to operate is that of a globally networked, open market, in which atomized workers bid on jobs. Any such arrangement would bring each bidder into direct competition with any number of others from all over the world, surely exerting the sharpest downward pressure on wages and fees. Buterin himself even illustrates this, presumably inadvertently, in the smart-contract scenario he offers as an example, in which a freelance designer is offered $500 (!) to build a website.

And all of this, again, is supposed to operate in a decentralized manner, beyond the reach of any terrestrial jurisdiction's minimum-wage laws or other regulations. Whatever Buterin's intentions, then, or Szabo's, or those of anyone currently working to design and build out the smart contracts infrastructure, the effect of a market bound by such agreements is the brutal dilution of any bargaining power labor may still lay claim to. The great cyberneticist Stafford Beer taught us that the "purpose of a system is what it does," and if smart contracts work not to protect but to undermine working people, we must conclude that on some level this is what they are for.[10]

Nor are workers the only ones who might find the rug pulled out from under them in a world of smart contracts. Think of Kickstarter, for example. The crowdfunding site asks sponsors to pledge a sum of money toward a project (i.e. it is a box that contains value), and disburses that sum to the project originators only if the aggregate amount amassed in this way exceeds a preset threshold (and that box unlocks when certain conditions have been met). Kickstarter takes a cut for providing the platform on which pledges are aggregated and then paid out. But a well-designed smart contract framework would handle that whole process on a peer-to-peer basis, and do it for a relative pittance of Ether—a few pennies, against a few percentage points.[11] A world of functioning smart contracts, then, holds existential peril for those intermediary enterprises like Kickstarter whose whole business model can effectively be boiled down to a single conditional statement.

The complexity of the challenges we face spirals upward when smart contracts are applied to the physical world, via the intercession of networked objects. Some developers understand the blockchain not primarily as an end in its own right, but as an enabling payment and security infrastructure for capturing the value from situations and settings there's no efficient way to monetize at present—something capable of "fractionalizing" industries, "liquifying" markets, and siphoning from the world that fraction of gain that has to date remained beyond the reach of the so-called sharing economy. In this vision, it is through the blockchain that the internet of things will acquire the ability to exchange access permission for payment, and via the internet of things that gradients of access will be inscribed on the physical world.

Specifically, this means that the smart contract's property of intrinsic enforcement need not be limited to exchanges of digital assets, or debts denominated in cryptocurrency like Ether, but can be extended to whatever tangible artifacts can be joined to the network. A rudimentary version of this proposition is already being trialled by a German startup called Slock.it (tagline: "the future infrastructure of the Sharing Economy").

Slock.it claims that its devices will function as a bridge between the blockchain and objects in the physical world, affording those objects "an identity, the ability to receive payments and the capability to enter complex agreements." Their first product is a networked lock, that releases if and only if the terms of its contract are met. Here's where everything implied by intrinsic enforcement comes into its own, in the real world of apartments, storage lockers, conference rooms and cars: applied to such physical spaces, the smart contract functions as a potent gatekeeping mechanism, supporting ever-finer gradients of payment and remote access control. It's easy to imagine such a module being retrofitted to doors and gates, replacing the code locks which have sprouted like fungus all over certain high-demand districts in recent years—the telltale sign of a property being rented on AirBnb.

What we now know as the sharing economy, then, only begins to suggest what is possible in a world where the smart contract is grafted onto the pervasive fabric of sensing and actuation we think of as the internet of things. By giving blockchain-mediated smart contracts tangible real-world impact, Slock.it's "smart locks" make something that might otherwise remain an abstraction concrete and easy to understand. But they also shed light on what this is all for, in the minds of the people currently working hardest to make it a reality.

Incumbent actors, too, perceive the greatest promise in the blockchain. At present, governments and large financial institutions appear to believe that they can contain the technology, breaking it to harness as simply another tool for service delivery in the established modes.

At least, that is what they are willing to say in public. US Federal Reserve Board chair Janet Yellen reportedly told a June 2016 conference of the planet's central bank managers that they should be "accelerating" their efforts toward adoption of blockchain technologies.[12] The Canadian government announced at the same event that it was working to develop a ledger-backed version of its dollar, called CAD-Coin.[13] The British government goes still further, specifically proposing that "public regulatory influence ... be exerted through" a layering of ledger-based techniques and law, "rather than exclusively through legal code as at present."[14] (There's even a term for this type of bureaucratized statecraft via the execution of computational rules: "regtech.")

The prospect that the state and its capacity to supervise and regulate could all wind up being reinforced by the blockchain is, of course, anathema to many of its more ideologically motivated partisans. For the moment, though, there appears to be little enough they can do to keep the technology from being adopted by forces they're elementally opposed to, and turned to ends they despise.

The blockchain and many of the concepts that orbit it may well have been devised and developed by a coterie of renegade libertarian thinkers, who themselves held decentralization as a virtue and individual privacy as a matter of unswerving principle. They did so, however, in a world in which the state and similarly scaled actors yet wielded substantial power, and retained the means to protect the wellsprings of that power. It was inevitable that incumbents would mobilize the resources to study the emergent threat, understand its implications in depth and circumvent them early in their evolutionary history. What we see now is precisely that mobilization.

The essence of this institutional interest in the blockchain is the efficiency, verifiability and incorruptibility it promises to bring to the information gathering and processing techniques all large-scale organizations rely upon.

At this moment in history—as has increasingly been the case, since the rise of statistical techniques of government in the 19th century—large, complex organizations represent the state of the world via the structured collection, storage and retrieval of data. Another way to say this: that which is operationally true in our world is that set of facts whose truth value is recorded in at least one database belonging to a party with the ability to set the parameters of a situation. And most irritatingly, each one of the organizations we truck with over the course of our lives maintains its own database, and therefore, quite literally, its own version of the world.

Anyone who owns a car, for example, will at various points in their experience interact with the DMV, an insurance provider, and very likely one or more mechanics. If they bought their car new, they will have taken delivery from a dealer. If they financed their purchase, they will have submitted paperwork to a loan provider. And each one of these parties, with dominion over a slightly different facet of reality, will record information salient to their understanding of the car and its owner in a storage and retrieval system—a database.

Because these databases were developed by different engineers, sold by different vendors, offered to market at different times, and deployed in different cultures and contexts, no two of them behave in quite the same way. Perhaps in one, the make and model of a car are specified by a pulldown menu, which was populated in the year the database software was purchased. If that software was last updated in, say, 2010—and that is not at all an impossible prospect—the database will have no way of representing a Tesla. Perhaps another system offers a free text field in which to record a vehicle's manufacturer, but the text that can be entered into that field is limited to 20 characters—apologies to those trying to register an International Harvester Scout. There is always some degree of slippage between the ways in which any two organizations choose to represent a situation of mutual interest.

Library science handles this issue with the notion of authority control—shared, inter-institutional guidelines which specify the structure and organization of information about the identity of things. The agencies of any one government, as well, tend to use common data standards—in principle, anyway. But generally speaking, the commercial world lacks such measures. And so the slippage persists.

At the interfaces between different databases—which is to say, any time information passes from one company, agency, or even department into another—these different standards for the representation of information must somehow be reconciled. And even in our nominally digital era, these acts of reconciliation are still mostly conducted on slips of paper.[15] Your utility bills certify that you reside at a given address, so you bring them to the bank as *bona fides* when you first open an account. Your birth certificate establishes the validity of your claim to citizenship, so you bring it with you when applying for a passport. And so it is, at different times and in different contexts, with your marriage certificate, your diploma, your visa, your honorable discharge from the military or your record of immunization. The effective truth value of these slips of paper is underwritten by an official stamp, the signature of a witness, a notarization; we ourselves are mobilized to carry them from counter to counter and clerk to clerk, and we ourselves are responsible for their prudential stewardship at the times when they're not actively being invoked.

And then someone, very often someone paid minimum wage, will have to manually enter whatever details they retrieve from the slips of paper you've brought them into their own organization's information-processing machinery, with all the transpositions, misspellings, elisions and omissions you'd expect to result from such a clunky process. (God help you if your circumstances require that salient details be transliterated from Arabic or Korean into roman characters.)

Whether we're quite aware of it or not, this is the thing that underlies a very great part of the missed opportunities, wasted effort, frustration, delay and error we experience in everyday life. It's the reason why your parcel was sent to the wrong flat, why hospital patients receive the wrong dosage of a medication, and why thoroughly innocent people who happen to share their name with a onetime hijacker get added to no-fly lists.[16] The individual stories of people trapped in the mis-meshing teeth of institutional data-processing systems often have a bitterly Kafkaesque flavor to them, but the commercial impact is surreal, too; one frequently cited 2002 estimate places the annual cost to business of bad data beyond $600 billion, in the US alone.[17] All this chaos, confusion and waste is caused because the information that conditions our ability to act in the world is scattered across hundreds or thousands of individual databases, none of which entirely agree, all of which contain a slightly varying representation of the underlying reality.

We can think of these systems and their rules as regimes of truth, if you're feeling Foucauldian, and the truth they make is badly, fundamentally fractured. But what is the blockchain other than a single shared database, and a set of agreed procedures for the production of a single truth?

Where so much of the original enthusiasm for Bitcoin had a raffishly antinomian quality, the greater part of the interest in new blockchain applications is corporate, governmental and institutional, and this insight helps to explain why.[18] Such complex organizations are currently compelled to make enormous outlays on systems that improve data quality, they are often exposed to significant liability for data errors they fail to prevent, and above all they bear the impact of these circumstances directly on the bottom line. As a "trusted framework for identity and data sharing," the blockchain promises to solve these problems all at once.

One scenario along these lines is that proposed by Simon Taylor, VP for Blockchain R&D at Barclays Bank, in a white paper on distributed-ledger applications prepared for the British government.[19] Taylor imagines all of our personal information stored on a common blockchain, duly encrypted. Any legitimate actor, public or private—the HR department, the post office, your bank, the police—could query the same unimpeachable source of information, retrieve from it only what they were permitted to, and leave behind a trace of their access. Each of us would have read/write access to our own record; should we find erroneous information, we would have to make but one correction, and it would then propagate across the files of every institution with access to the ledger.

Where the data undergirding our lives is now maintained on a thousand separate systems, and vital knowledge so often falls into the cracks between them, Taylor sees a single common and shared truth, referred to equally and with equal transparency by all parties. His immediate audience may care for little beyond the promise of streamlined operations, efficiency gains and lowered overheads, but we should be clear: should any scheme of this sort actually be realized, it would strike to the very constitution of the contemporary world. No institution would remain unchanged by it.

This is how a very small group of ideologues—so bright in such a very particular way, so certain of their own brilliance— brought forth upon the world something that may yet wind up achieving the opposite of most everything they intended for it. Despite the insurgent glamor that clings to it still, blockchain technology enables the realization of some very long-standing desires on the part of very powerful institutions. The most likely outcome is simply that it will be captured and recuperated. We need to prepare ourselves for the eventuality that its advent will only accelerate existing tendencies and consolidate existing distributions of power in the world.

But there is another, more felicitous set of possibilities. For many of its most energetic developers and advocates, what is central to the blockchain's appeal is that it appears to enable modes of large-scale collective action that bear very little resemblance to government as we've known it. Much of the current activity along these lines—and, indeed, most remaining hope for liberatory implementations of the blockchain—is dedicated to something called the distributed autonomous organization, or DAO.

Many of the blockchain applications we've discussed so far are not actually all that novel. But the DAO is that genuine rarity: a new thing upon the Earth, something that really could not have been conceptualized before the techniques underlying it were in place. Ethereum's official documentation describes it as a way to "automate direct interaction between peers or facilitate coordinated group action across a network." But that doesn't really shed much light. Amidst all the motivational ambiguity, definitional idiosyncrasy and sheer unnecessary complexity so endemic to this space, then, our task is to understand what a DAO is, how it works and what it might allow us to do.

Life on Earth, of course, constantly confronts us with tasks and ambitions that are far beyond the capability of any one person to achieve on their own, and for this reason we have always formed ourselves into groups. The Bitcoin blockchain, in constructing the world as a set of decisions made by thoroughly atomized individual actors, had no formal way of recognizing this desire, let alone implementing it. It produces a strictly and narrowly functional "consensus" solely dedicated to the task of validating transactions, but it can not oversee truly collective behavior.

By their very nature, though, second-generation, programmable blockchains like the one at the heart of Ethereum are ideally suited to handling most all the tasks imposed by management of a formal group, such as the low-level logistical and housekeeping details that eat up so much of any coordinator's time and energy. What's more, any group harnessed via a shared ledger—even a relatively informal, *ad hoc* gathering—might find itself equipped with the ability to collect and dispose of whatever assets were tabulated by that blockchain. Bound only by code, such a group could receive investment, marshal property, disburse benefits, and in general act in the world with as much potency as any other kind of assembly.

Similar ideas had cropped up across the broader community working on second-generation blockchain technology, and circulated under a variety of names—autonomous corporations, decentralized autonomous ventures, and the like. Perhaps with an eye toward a future in which such ideas might find more general application, though, it was the ubiquitous Vitalik Buterin who called it by the name which appears to have stuck: distributed autonomous organization.

As Buterin saw matters, any group of people consists of a set of decisions: decisions about who is a member of the group, and who is not; decisions about how to allocate resources; decisions about what courses of action the group wishes to commit itself to. In order to construct a group that would have some independent reality on the network, then, each one of these decisions would have to be translated into terms legible to the Ethereum blockchain. The members of a group would be represented by individual accounts in Ether, and the bylaws and provisions of an association between them by a complex mesh of smart contracts.

Here we can see how the basic outlines of a blockchain-legible group were progressively built up from pieces of kit that were lying around free for the taking, as it were, after earlier rounds of innovation. Beyond that, though, Buterin argued that a DAO would fuse many of the most desirable properties of three other kinds of entity that could be encoded in a blockchain: autonomous agents, distributed applications and decentralized organizations.

From the autonomous agent, Buterin took the idea of self-executing code that acts whether or not a single human being who is aware of its existence and operation yet draws breath. His DAO operates without human intervention, continuously and all but imperceptibly pursuing advantage on its members' behalf, according to whatever guidelines they'd encoded into it. It resides outside of any one terrestrial jurisdiction, making it robust and very hard to suppress, and poses particular conceptual difficulties for state organizations that might be interested in regulating its conduct.

By "decentralized organization," Buterin meant something quite specific, beyond any way in which the term might ordinarily be understood: a group of human beings whose agreements are specified in code and coordinated via blockchain. Decision-making authority is diffused across such an organization via the use of multiple-signature technology, which requires a predetermined number of parties to sign off on a course of action before it can be enacted;[20] Buterin now proposed to use this as a model for a still more flexible kind of transhuman assembly, in which one or more of the parties involved in steering a group might themselves consist of code.

Combine these qualities, and we wind up with something Buterin describes as "an entity which lives on the internet and exists autonomously, but also heavily relies on hiring individuals to perform certain tasks that the [software] itself cannot do." This is the DAO.

Nowhere does Buterin constrain what form this entity can assume. It could, in particular, take the aspect of a corporation, and do all the things a corporation can do: own property, employ people, offer goods and services for sale, issue ownership shares, and so on. But, importantly, it doesn't have to. It could serve, rather, as the coordination mechanism of any group of people bound by common purpose, whatever that purpose might be, however widely scattered they might find themselves.

Here we have, in outline, a decentralized association with global reach, able to dispose of real-world assets, transparently and persistently accountable, in which decision-making power truly vests in the hands of its members—a powerfully appealing set of properties to yoke together in a single organizational form, and capable of being applied to just about any domain of endeavor.

But neither Buterin nor the team around him set out with the intention of designing a general organizational form suitable to the complexities of 21st-century culture. The question they proceeded from was specific, forthright and entirely explicit: "How can revenue be generated within a purely decentralized environment?"[21] So let's take them at their word, and start by considering how the DAO might work in its original intended role, as an investment vehicle. How would this work?

While formally open to anyone, a DAO presents would-be investors with barriers to entry only a little less onerous than those of participation in the traditional equities market. One invests in a DAO by purchasing "vote tokens" denominated in whatever cryptocurrency the organization runs on, in most cases Ether, and this means going through all the steps of down-loading and setting up a suitable wallet.

Once purchased, tokens allow the investor to share in profits realized by the DAO, also denominated in cryptocurrency, and they carry voting rights to a degree proportional to the magnitude of the investment. The tokens themselves would fluctuate in value on the open market, in principle appreciating like any other equity should the DAO's ventures meet with success. (If tokens sound an awful lot like shares of stock, you're not wrong. Terrified of exposing the whole scheme to regulation, though, this plain equivalence is something the theorists involved have taken the greatest pains to deny.)

The DAO, then, is first and foremost a way of reinventing the company form, outside the strictures of state incorporation and regulation. But there is a catch here. In the DAO, we see the same pattern that we did in Bitcoin's provisions for privacy: a technology brilliantly designed to be disruptive falters at its point of interface with everyday practice. Just like an "anonymous" Bitcoin user finding their privacy compromised the moment they try to turn their BTC into dollars or pounds, the investors in a DAO will have to reckon with the way power works in the world.

Historically, the joint-stock company emerged as a technology to distribute risk. The earliest joint-stock enterprises, such as the Dutch East India Company, the Virginia Company and the South Sea Company, were set up to underwrite transoceanic colonization projects, ventures that by their nature both required heavy capitalization and involved an unpredictable (but certainly high) risk of failure. By purchasing shares of stock, any investor who wanted to could buy into these companies, in whatever amount they could afford. This diluted the upside reward, perhaps, but it also diffused any individual investor's exposure to failure, to the extent that even a collapse of the entire project could readily enough be borne. It was also very likely the only way certain ventures could be entertained at all, as nobody in that world had the wherewithal to fund a colony singlehandedly, crowned heads not excepted. We can think of such firms, then, as history's first examples of organized crowdfunding.

The tale we are told is that the dissipative structure of the joint-stock firm is what unlocked hitherto-underutilized capital, triggered the explosive growth of the European empires, and allowed those societies equipped with the technology to achieve effective hegemony over vast swathes of the globe in a relatively short period of time. Enthusiasts of the DAO clearly mean for it to be the next step in this evolutionary process—something empowered to trade autonomously on their behalf in friction-less networked markets, able to adjust its investment strategies adaptively in response to emergent circumstances, and ultimately outperform merely human competitors.

But the joint-stock organizational form also has another, very significant feature, which is that it buffers its principals and other investors from individual liability for debts incurred by the company. The venture may fail, but its members are shielded from the risk of personal bankruptcy. It's this protection that DAO investors, in their wish to decouple themselves and their enterprises from the law of the state, are failing to avail themselves of. Stripped of the law's protection, principals become liable "jointly and severally," which is to say that they are fully responsible as individuals for any financial obligations taken on by the venture.

And that inevitably means that the question of an enforcement mechanism crops up as well. It may be trivially easy for all parties to verify that someone has shirked their obligations under a blockchain-mediated smart contract. But what are the penalties for being in breach in this way? Who is to enforce these agreements, and how? As we know, a DAO can only organically enforce contracts that are purely specified in terms of networked events and networked currencies—Bitcoin or Ether, for example. Any- and everything else it or its investors might want to do in the world will require human enablers—so-called Contractors or "service providers"—and that will generally mean contracts of the non-smart variety. Common sense suggests that any breach of these contracts would be handled in the ordinary way, via ordinary courts of law, however ironic it might be for the state jurisprudential complex to weigh disputes originating on a system explicitly set up to circumvent government oversight.

Right now a DAO is coupled to a formal legal entity, which will serve as its avatar in the human nomosphere.[22] Its operators set up a conventional company, incorporated in the ordinary way, that corresponds to the particulars of the DAO in every respect. But the relation between the two is artificial, arbitrary—whimsical, even. What impinges on the one does not necessarily affect the other in any way. So the interesting problem for theorists in this space isn't so much how one might arrive at networked consensus without the state, but how one might arrive at networked *law* without the state—a *lex cryptographia*[23] as transparent, equally applicable and accessible to agreed modification as any other operation of the ledger, and as just and far-seeing as the wisest human jurisprudence.

The most motivated ideologues of the DAO have pressed on ahead, even without the benefit of such a law, and we'll shortly see what price they paid for their ambition. The lack of clarity on basic points of governance and regulatory compliance almost certainly dooms their attempts to use the DAO as a revenue-generating investment vehicle. But curiously, it doesn't necessarily undermine the form's utility for a different cohort of users, motivated by an entirely separate set of values.

A distributed autonomous organization, even in the form proposed by Buterin, promises to solve standing hard problems in the praxis of democracy. It gives organizers the ability to form associations rapidly, and equips them with clear, binding and incorruptible decision processes. It allows members to float proposals, raise points for discussion among their peers, and ensure that there is adequate time for deliberation before a question is called to a vote. It seems well-suited to address some of the limits and frustrations of the Occupy-style general assembly as a decision-making forum, chiefly its requirement that everyone sharing an interest be physically co-present at once in order to have their voice counted.

Here, then, is another use of the DAO: the decentralised, non-hierarchical organization of political movements. Interest in such possibilities is one of the main reasons why left-leaning horizontalists and others invested in participatory democracy are likely to find themselves aligned with the otherwise strange bedfellows of the mostly anarchocapitalist blockchain crowd.

A tool with these properties would appear to be a scalable infrastructure for doing democracy. Little enough surprise, then, that the DAO should feature prominently in table talk at gatherings of the technically proficient left, in Europe and North America both. And what enthusiasts of this ilk appear to be responding to is the vision of a world in which effective power is distributed across a federation of light, mobile, nonhierarchical decision-making frameworks unsanctioned by any apparatus of state, each one of which has just enough substance to act concretely in and on the world. In this oddball investment vehicle, some of the most dedicated community activists I've ever met glimpse the makings of an operating system for a planetary anarchism.

But the provisions at the very heart of the DAO may be difficult to reconcile with the values and commitments of any left politics worthy of the name. Consider Ethereum's description of a DAO's origin: "The way this particular democracy works is that it has an Owner which works like an administrator, CEO or a President. The Owner can add (or remove) voting members to the organization."[24] It's the original Owner of a DAO, then, that sets its binding decision rules, and retains the capacity to change that rule whenever it desires. This is certainly a novel and interesting definition of a democracy. And in fact it's owners all the way down.

Remember too that a DAO requires that members buy shares in it in order to participate. This requirement is imposed by the Ethereum framework itself: a DAO is woven of smart contracts, and like all such contracts running under Ethereum, pays a sum of Ether to the network node that executes it. This may well be refreshingly honest in the materialist sense, emphasizing that everything that takes place inside history has a cost, and that this cost must be borne by some party. It incentivizes the contribution of processing cycles by all of the nodes of a distributed network, and does so without exposing users to an exploitive business model based on data capture and targeted advertising. But it's curiously at odds with our time-honored understanding that political participation should be accessible to all. It's hard to imagine members of the Brazilian Landless Workers' Movement, or Slum- and Shack Dwellers International, finding much comfort in a democracy they need to buy into in order to have a voice.

Though the attempt to build equal and democratic relations on a platform originally designed to advance the ends of capital investment often feels like a category error, I think it's worth asking if the DAO's capabilities can be lifted whole out of the matrix of their origins, and rerouted to some entirely different destination. Perhaps, as Buterin and others insist, this organizing tool can indeed give rise to exciting new forms of mutuality, in what is otherwise so often a world of atomized, sovereign, armored individuals. But it must be said that the auspices are not particularly good.

The reason why comes down, yet again, to the central importance placed on relations of property and ownership in the theory woven around the DAO. This, for example, is how Buterin conceptualizes human sociation: "In general, a human organization can be defined as combination of two things: a set of property, and a protocol for a set of individuals, which may or may not be divided into certain classes with different conditions for entering or leaving the set, to interact with each other including rules for under what circumstances the individuals may use certain parts of the property."

Here is where the danger of trying to reconstruct the furniture of the world from first principles becomes clearest. Because as it happens, that's not at all how a great many human organizations are defined.

Consider contemporary movements like 15M, Occupy, or Black Lives Matter, each of which has surely been able to make some increment of change occur in the world without property or a formal membership register; consider all of the many groups, as various as ACT UP and Alcoholics Anonymous, that have historically been able to operate effectively without recourse to these things. Any conceptual schema that treats the effectiveness of a social formation as being primarily founded in the property it owns is going to have a very hard time accounting for the success of such movements. And running in parallel with the DAO's misplaced emphasis on property rights is a similar fascination—"obsession" is not too strong a word—with markets.

Again, as with the smart contracts whose functionality they are based on, a DAO makes a market where there was none before. A crystal-clear example of this tendency is SweepTheStreets, a notional DAO described by Slock.it's Stephan Tual. Tual explicitly imagines SweepTheStreets as a group of people "living in the same neighborhood and wanting their streets swept clean of pesky autumn leaves."[25] But instead of proposing that they accomplish this end via some analogue of the Norwegian *dugnad*—a semi-annual event where neighbors voluntarily come together, collectively clean their street and reward themselves with a hearty potluck—Tual has them yoked together by a DAO that "would require the services of many different Contractors. One (a reseller) could be hired to source brooms to a certain specification, another (a project management firm) to coordinate the sweeping of the streets, and 15 others (individuals) to do the actual street sweeping." He appears to mean this seriously. It is striking that whenever their imaginations are given free reign, the market is the sole paradigm the prime architects of the DAO reach for, even in the most trivial scenario.

Fairly or not, the unyielding emphasis on contract and markets feels to me like a shibboleth of the libertarian right, and not something necessary to the organization of decentralized groups. If you already believe that on some level all public affairs are transactional exchanges of quid for quo, this aspect of the DAO won't present you with any particular problem. But for many, the market is an organizing principle every bit as obnoxious, every bit as pervasive and every bit as powerful as the state, and for those of us who hold such beliefs, there's no particular succor to be found in the DAO.

As it happens, there is a progressive social tendency entirely consistent with the fundamental framework of property and the market offered by the DAO: the cooperative movement. A cooperative is an association chartered to provide a product or service, much like any other company. What sets cooperatives apart from more conventional enterprises is that they are entirely owned by the people who work for them—their members— and that their policies and growth strategies are steered by the membership itself, via some kind of democratic decision-making process. All the benefits and rights attendant on the ownership of capital are distributed equally within the organization.

Though participants are often drawn to the cooperative movement by a concern for basic tenets of fairness and economic justice, there's nothing in it that conflicts with private ownership, property rights or the market as a mechanism of resource allocation. It seems possible, then, to instantiate a cooperative as a DAO without doing too much conceptual violence to the principles on which it is founded.

The advent of the DAO may therefore constitute good news for those invested in the cooperative form, or who have otherwise made their peace with the market. But they are hardly a means of achieving postcapitalism, and anyone who aspires to build a space outside state and market both is bound to find them unsatisfying.

In recent decades, such aspirations have found a home in the global community dedicated to the commons. Where market logics generally seek to collectivize risk and privatize gain, adherents to the principles of the commons believe that the greatest degree of sustainable benefit is derived from resources when they are held jointly, and managed democratically for the good of all. In their concern for the wise management of shared resources, they invoke a tradition of far longer standing, one that the economist Elinor Ostrom won a Nobel Prize for studying.

Ostrom's lifework focused on communal institutions for the management of open but inherently rivalrous goods like fisheries, agricultural land or forests. What she discovered was that communities all over the planet had spontaneously developed techniques that allowed them to manage such resources "with reasonable degrees of success over long periods of time," and that these techniques bore no resemblance to the mechanisms of market or state her training had led her to expect.[26] Still more surprisingly, she found a strong degree of commonality among the practices the more consistently successful groups had evolved to support their stewardship of resources, however different the contexts they were working in and however scattered they may have been in space and time. From this body of overlap, Ostrom abstracted eight principles of effective governance.

Given their success in such a wide variety of contexts, it makes sense to ask how easily these principles, and the other structures and practices fundamental to Ostrom's understanding of commoning, might be encoded in a DAO. And equally, given the immediate applicability to the many local struggles for self-definition now being waged around the planet, it makes sense to ask whether the understanding of the commons reflected in contemporary participatory-democratic movements might be similarly inscribed. And what we learn when we undertake this challenge, even as a thought experiment, is that the DAO—at least as Buterin and his colleagues now describe—it-is poorly suited to either context.

It's not merely the strong emphasis on property and the differential enunciation of property rights we find throughout the DAO body of discourse that spells trouble for this ambition, though that surely doesn't help. It's that the smart contracts on which DAOs are built, by their very nature, render decisions in the present on situations that were conceptualized at some arbitrary point in the past. In other words, a smart contract intervenes in a state of affairs that may have evolved in ways that were not foreseen by the parties to it at the time they agreed to be bound by its terms, and does so irreversibly. This is potentially disastrous for all sorts of endeavors—imagine a smart contract locking America's most beloved celebrity into a 20-year endorsement deal, only for that celebrity to be revealed halfway through as a rapist dozens of times over—but it poses particular difficulty when modeling situations that unfold dynamically in real time, as the negotiations at the heart of any commons tend to.

This quality of being bound in time can only undermine the supple management of common-pool resources. The very first of Ostrom's principles calls for "well-defined boundaries" between the members of a group entrusted with the stewardship of a resource and those without such a responsibility, as around the resource of interest itself. With its highly formalized procedures for buy-in and voting participation, and its ability to encode geofencing in a smart contract, the DAO would seem ideally suited to the establishment of distinctions along these lines. And so it is. But a body of empirical work undertaken since Ostrom's original publication suggests that in practice, rights of access and physical boundaries in a commoning community are almost always subject to negotiation, and in general remain far more fluid than the implacable, binary worldview encoded by a block-chain.[27] It's unclear how a DAO entrusted with the management of a common-pool resource would handle the entire range of easily foreseeable situations such a community might face—a nonmember allowed temporary access to a common good, but only under supervision, or a short-term and informal exchange of prerogatives among members of two adjacent collectives.

Even beyond the question of lock-in, the highly formal quality of the relations inscribed in a DAO makes it completely unsuitable for situations characterized by a shallow gradient of commitment, where participants might prefer to maintain some ambiguity about the nature and degree of their involvement. It turns out that one of the defining characteristics of a commons, in the contemporary political sense, is precisely its lack of a hard boundary, its disinclination to present the newcomer with barriers to entry. National Technical University of Athens professor Stavros Stavrides, author of a well-regarded book on the experience of spatial commoning, argues that it is the funda-mental openness and porosity of any true common space—its invitational quality—that enables it to survive as such over time.[28] To seal off opportunities for participation is to invite metabolic death. And yet sealing off such opportunities is what a DAO does in a dozen tiny ways, by requiring participants to invest Ether, insisting on interpreting all exchanges as formal contractual obligations, and in general failing to accommodate the suppleness and idiosyncrasy of the arrangements we make to support collective endeavors.

And of course it verges on the perverse to describe a DAO as "nonhierarchical" or "leaderless" in the mode of contemporary social movements. To say the least, this is a problematic way of framing something which has a originating Owner, whose Owner can change the rules of participation at any time.[29] A DAO built for commoning would require a comprehensive redesign of the origination process, so that participants could embark on a common endeavor without arrogating definitional control to any one party among them.

It seems absurd to spell all these things out—somewhat like pointing out all the reasons why a tire iron planted in soil is unlikely to flower, no matter how much sunlight and water are lavished on it. But activists on the participatory left are just as easily captivated by technological hype as anyone else, especially when that hype is couched in superficially appealing language. We want to believe in the possibilities of a technology that claims to give people powerful new tools for collective action, unsupervised by the state. We find ourselves enticed by the idea that in reconstituting themselves as a DAO, neighborhood assemblies and affinity groups might intervene in the world as concretely, effectively and enduringly as any private enterprise or government body.

And it may yet be so. But it will not be as a commons—not in any sense in which that term is currently understood. The recapitulation of Ostrom's principles, and their point-by-point reconstruction on the blockchain, isn't really the issue. The virtue of the commons as a mode of thought and action isn't simply that it provides for the scaled management of pooled resources, but that it spurs us to envision a way of life founded in interdependence, mutuality and shared responsibility for the outcomes experienced by others. Any situation organized in this way offers us a way to get outside of ourselves, a scaffolding for the development of intersubjectivity. I'm not at all sure that, whatever their other benefits, distributed organizations based on the blockchain will ever be able to work in quite the same way.

Fortunately for those who are trying to think through these matters with anything like empirical rigor, the properties that distributed autonomous organizations display as they operate in the world are no longer exclusively a matter of conjecture. In April 2016, Buterin and his closest colleagues founded an entity they simply, if somewhat confusingly, called The DAO, giving us a real-world instance to study and hopefully learn from.

Upon its founding, The DAO was immediately capitalized with a sale of Ether worth somewhere between $50 and $150 million, becoming far and away the largest venture ever launched on crowdfunding. Specifically set up to function as a distributed venture capital fund, The DAO proposed to disburse Ether to whatever projects its voting members considered worthwhile. It was clearly intended as a proof-of-concept, establishing Ethereum's own suitability as a platform for such vehicles. Beyond that, though, it wasn't immediately obvious what other ends it might have been chartered to achieve, or what philosophy guided its choice of investment strategies.

The DAO's first two investments had a predictable all-in-the-family quality to them: the German smart-property startup Slock.it, and a French concern called Mobotiq, which rather ambitiously took on the dual challenge of engineering an autonomous passenger vehicle and, at the same time, designing a blockchain-based service framework for its rental and use. Whether The DAO's membership invested in these specific ventures from legitimate belief in their upside potential, or for obvious reasons of propinquity and affinity, is of course open to question. In fact, anyone but the most casual observer cannot help but notice that precisely zero degrees of separation divide the Ethereum Project, The DAO as a nominally independent entity, and Slock.it management.

Though it would be entirely reasonable to conclude from this pattern of circumstances that The DAO's named Curators had something to do with its launch, it was in fact initiated by an Ether address belonging to a currently unidentified party. (According to Slock.it CTO and Ethereum Project lead tester Christoph Jentzsch, one of the core developers of the Solidity software The DAO runs on, the Curators themselves "actually don't know who started it.")[30]

This raises more general alarms concerning the structure of DAO governance. Because of the the way in which any DAO is structured, it is difficult to discern the otherwise undeclared coincidences of interest between formally discrete entities. Counter to the premise of total transparency, in fact, a DAO acts to diffuse and obscure accountability for the things it does. So long as pseudonymous participation is allowed by the bylaws of a DAO, we have no real way of assessing the beneficial ownership of that organization. We can inspect the blockchain at any time we please, identify the tokenized signatures of all its voting members. But we have no idea if that token denotes an individual, a group entity, or a chunk of code recursively delegated by some other DAO or autonomous process. With ownership screened behind a cryptographic baffle, the relationship between individuals, groups and entities in the world of DAOs is murky at best.

This, of course, is a quality the DAO inherits from the blockchain, with its permanent friction between the imperatives of privacy and transparency, and we even might argue that a certain degree of opacity is one of its core premises as an organizational infrastructure. It nevertheless deprives would-be analysts of a useful tool for understanding the origin, nature and intended consequences of the propositions we're being offered. So tangled and obscure, indeed, are the links of ownership in a DAO that we are presented with the curious possibility of an autonomous association that owns itself, makes decisions based on algorithmic weightings it independently evolved, and acts in the world to advance its own interests such as it alone perceives them.

This prospect may give futurists a definite frisson, but it's going to have trouble meeting the test of any merely human jurisprudence. Nor is "We actually don't know who started it" an explanation likely to satisfy a magistrate interested in assuring an organization's regulatory compliance.

This is one of the reasons why skepticism about The DAO has run deep from the very beginning. Within days of its launch, the venture was criticized for the dubious quality of its initial investments, mocked for its naivete, pilloried as a Ponzi scheme, and characterized as "the first scam where the participants scam themselves."[31] After just a month up and running, a group of the experts most familiar with its codebase (including one of its own Curators, Ethereum researcher Vlad Zamfir) had developed reservations so pronounced that they called for a moratorium on submitting funding proposals to The DAO.[32]

But it was already too late for precautionary action. Overnight on June 16th–17th, 2016, The DAO was attacked, in just one of the ways the skeptics had predicted: an unknown party used the provisions of The DAO's own code to spawn a "child DAO," and siphon into it a quantity of Ether worth roughly $72.5 million. That valuation plummeted, of course, as word of the exploit spread and the market price of Ether plunged from $19.42 to $11.32, but it nevertheless represented a solid third of the investment garnered by The DAO during its much-vaunted crowdfunding round. News of the attack reverberated far beyond the cozy cryptocurrency community, receiving coverage from *The New York Times*, the BBC and the *Financial Times*— and that coverage was predictably scathing, blasting everything from the personalities involved to the fitness for purpose of the very language The DAO was written in.[33]

Sentiment in the Ethereum community immediately split into two factions. One wanted the Ethereum board to "hard-fork" the code running The DAO, seal off the child DAO containing the pilfered Ether, and make them whole. (This was Buterin's own proposed solution.) The other hewed to libertarian orthodoxy —how, they wanted to know, would that course of action make The DAO different than the slave-morality-soaked institutions of state they so despised? Let the losers live with the consequences of their freely chosen actions, "a 30 percent haircut for their lack of due diligence."[34]

A cryptographically signed statement from a party claiming to be responsible appeared the next day, pointedly characterizing their exploit as legitimate "participation" in The DAO, and expressing disappointment at those who would characterize it as theft.[35] And certainly this interpretation chimes with that of Cornell cryptocurrency expert Emin Gün Sirer: "The 'code was its own documentation,' as people say. It was its own fine print. The hacker read the fine print better than most, better than the developers themselves."[36] As it happens, the signature failed verification, leaving onlookers none the wiser as to who was responsible for the exploit, or what their actual motivation might have been. There is even the distinct possibility that the entire event was engineered to allow the attacker or attackers to profit by shorting Ether. But Sirer's point stood.

Whether his interpretation would prevail is something that would ordinarily be adjudicated in a court of law, in a process of binding arbitration, or via some other agreed framework for conflict resolution. Either out of hubris, carelessness or ideological conviction, though, the Curators of The DAO failed to specify a venue for the settlement of disputes, an utterly routine clause common to all soundly written contracts.

For all their swagger and soaring rhetoric, everyone connected with The DAO suddenly looked culpably credulous. It was evident that nobody involved in the project understood the very first thing about human nature, or had bothered to consult the several-thousand-year record of collective attempts to compensate for that nature—an available history tailing back far deeper into time than any blockchain.

In short, this is what it looks like when very bright people outsmart themselves. Hopefully those chastened by the failure will think more carefully before embracing the many other poorly considered ideas in the space. What remains to be seen is whether the abject, humiliating collapse of The DAO undermines the credibility of the distributed autonomous organization as a concept, the broader Ethereum project, or indeed that of Buterin himself.

The crucial point, though, is that there is no turning back. These techniques are now on the table. At some point in the not-too-distant future, they or some descendent based on them will be used effectively in the coordination of group activity, giving rise to collectivities we can't quite now conceive of.

Yes, it is possible to imagine (say) the street vendors of Guangdong linked by their partnership in a nameless DAO that invests on their behalf, leases space for their stalls at algorithmically optimized spot rates, and orders the expendables they burn through at bulk prices they couldn't swing on their own. We are equally free to envision the weaving women of rural Balochistan organizing themselves into a networked cooperative, hiving off dozens of self-directing enterprises and raining plenty upon their villages. Or a global collective of human journalists and autonomous search agents working stories together, linked in a comradely fashion by a collaboration platform that lets them render findings vital to the public interest permanently visible. We might even join Bitcoin core developer Mike Hearn in dreaming a transhuman future in which sovereign autonomous vehicles own themselves, lease themselves to users, and transact with a marketized grid for the power they need.[37]

It's not unreasonable to be intrigued by these possibilities, whatever your own politics. But if the collapse of The DAO holds any lesson for us, it's that any envelope of potentials in which these things are possible must also necessarily contain monsters. If Ethereum's vision proves out in any way, we need to prepare for densely layered Ponzi schemes whose true beneficiaries are ultimately obscured by cryptographic means, for vampiric rent-extraction syndicates and fully autonomous nonhuman grifters. We may well wonder, when beset with these horrors, why anyone ever believed this was a future worth investing in and bringing to fruition.

And for those of us who are motivated by commitment to a specifically participatory politics of the commons, it's not at all clear that any blockchain-based infrastructure can support the kind of flexible assemblies we imagine. I myself come from an intellectual tradition that insists that any appearance of the word "potential" needs to be greeted with skepticism. There is no such thing as potential, in this view: there are merely states of a system that have historically been enacted, and those that have not yet been enacted. The only way to assess whether a system is capable of assuming a given state is to do the work of enacting it.

This was never more relevant than in the discussion around blockchain technologies. Many thinkers on the horizontal and participatory left, including not a few I hold tremendous respect for, argue that these techniques give ordinary people a way to organize themselves democratically at scale, outside the state. But these discussions are always couched in terms of their potential: what *might* happen, what *could* be achieved. Nobody has yet shown that a distributed autonomous organization *has* done so, among any group of people, anywhere on Earth. All that has been accomplished in this space so far has been the creation of a venture fund—and even that fell apart, in the most predictable way, after a mere six weeks.

So until some propensity to support collectives, cooperatives and communes is demonstrated, I think those of us who share this set of values are best advised to sit in their skepticism. To do so with optimism and charity, certainly, and to make good-faith efforts to weigh the evidence we are offered fairly. But for now it strikes me as being unlikely that the things done with and by a DAO can ever entirely escape the matrix of assumptions built into the form by its inventors. I strongly suspect that, in the end, the libertarian roots of these technologies will tell— that they portend not the democratization of governance but its full privatization, in a world where only those with the bent of mind to understand the arcana of cryptofinance have the means to prevail. Nobody would be more delighted than I, though, were I to be proved wrong on this count. The only true test of these new collectivities, whatever form they wind up taking and whatever architecture they are eventually built on, will be what they are seen to do.

Beyond that, in any full flourishing of the DAO we find ourselves presented with the makings of a machinic economy capable of absconding entirely from its human objects, or at least making do without them to a still greater degree than is presently the case. We can see value functions peeling off, lifting up and away from merely human valuations of resources. This is the final transvaluation of all values, accomplished by autonomous, self-executing code running on a distributed global mesh of processing devices. It's not the Singularity rapturously awaited by the geeks, but it may as well be, for all it leaves of the Earth and the earthly. At that point, to be human is to belong to a lumpen biomass denied even whatever paltry dignity attends serfdom. The blogger Anne Amnesia calls this human residue "the unnecessariat," and the phrase captures something essential to our understanding of an autonomous economy.[38] We, you and I, are simply not needed by the fully realized posthuman. We're merely supernumerary, surplus to requirements. Unworthy even of contempt, and due at best only an indifferent maintenance, we become something to be cast behind in their maximum reach outward.

This is the context in which we need to interpret the rhetoric about autonomous agents and organizations. They are conscious steps toward a trans- or even entirely posthuman ordering of the world, not because their designers imagine autonomous technologies working alongside human beings in fruitful, comradely relation, but because they conceive of humanity as something to be transcended. Quite simply, this is who these people are and what they actually believe—what, to their credit, they've never made any bones about believing. Given their demonstrated ability to sustain purposive activity across three decades, they have to be regarded as consistent, disciplined, highly capable, and absolutely dedicated to developing themselves the tools and infrastructures they think will bring about their preferred order of being most swiftly. This doesn't at all mean that they will achieve their desires. But one of the things history teaches us is that when people who intend to change the world in this way publish their plans and describe their motivations, we might want to consider taking them at their word.

7

Automation

The annihilation of work

By the first decade of the twenty-first century, the average technologically augmented individual had effectively become superhuman. By and large, however, those of us who have undergone this transformation don't stop to wonder or even notice that this is the case, unless the temporary failure of our augmentive systems brings us up short. So long as everything stays up and running, we communicate instantaneously and on demand with anyone, more or less anywhere on Earth. We traverse the planet physically in a matter of hours. We enjoy near-universal access to a medium that connects virtually everyone we've ever met or ever will meet, and furnishes us beyond that with immediate access to most of the things anyone has ever spoken, written, painted, sung or committed to the screen—if not by any means all of the knowledge ever developed by the species, then certainly a very respectable fraction of it. Within the bounds imposed by our current understanding of material science, we can design and build just about anything it is possible to imagine.

Yet for all the impressive scope and reach of our power, we still face stark, seemingly fundamental limits of materiality and mortality. Life still presents us with the broadest array of tasks we're not very good at—those we can only do for so long before tiring, those we quail at, and those that place us in physical or psychological danger. None of those tasks are getting any easier, and none of them are disappearing any time soon. And overhead arcs the distant but certain promise of mortality. In a very real sense, we are all of us pressed for time.

Some of us are willing to accept this state of affairs as a given, and possibly even as a tutor. But others are not. Out of this unwillingness, these people have set out to devise technical systems that are more capable than we are ourselves, along any axis or dimension of evaluation you might care to mention: systems that are stronger and faster than we are; that have finer perception and greater endurance; that never, ever succumb to boredom, fatigue or disgust; and that are capable of operating without human oversight or guidance, indefinitely. We are, of course, talking about using robots and automated systems to replace human labor.

The great twentieth-century economist John Maynard Keynes had foreseen much of this early on, coining the expression "technological unemployment" sometime around 1928.[1] He saw, with almost clairvoyant perspicacity, that societies might eventually automate away the jobs much of their labor force depended on, and his insight is borne out in recent United States government estimates that an American worker making less than $20 an hour now has an 83 percent chance of losing their job to automation.[2] But what Keynes concluded—that the eclipse of human labor by technical systems would necessarily compel a turn toward a full-leisure society—has not come to pass, not even remotely.

And what neither Keynes nor any other economist reckoned with, until very recently, was the thought that the process of automation would hardly stop when it had replaced manual and clerical labor. If automation was initially brought to bear on tasks that were one or more of the "four Ds"—dull, dirty, difficult or dangerous—the advent of sophisticated machine-learning algorithms means that professional and managerial work now comes into range. We need to be clear that automated systems might replace any one of us in our jobs, however nominally executive or "creative" those jobs might be.[3]

We should be careful not to overstate how fast this process might take place. Nor should we make the mistake of imagining it as some impersonal, ahistorical transformation, beyond anyone's control; like any other such process, its progress turns upon identifiable actors, acting from discernible motivations, intervening at material sites. But it's just as crucial that we not underestimate the speed, force or thoroughness with which this is taking place. We now stand at a juncture where there is no pursuit that cannot in principle be undertaken by an automated system, and we need to come to terms with what that might mean for the economy, the ways in which we organize our societies, and our own psyches. However disturbingly crude they remain, to whatever extent they are all too evidently the fruit of their creators' biases, neuroses and projections, these systems are nevertheless poised to assume responsibility for much of the work that furnishes us with a livelihood, an identity and a sense of self. And they are getting better at what they do with every passing day.

What I wish to argue is that whether they are brought together consciously or otherwise, large-scale data analysis, algorithmic management, machine-learning techniques, automation and robotics constitute a coherent set of techniques for the production of an experience I call the posthuman everyday. This is a milieu in which the rhythms we contend with, the ordinary spaces we occupy, and the material and energetic flows we support are all shaped not so much by our own needs but those of the systems that nominally serve us, and in which human perception, scale and desire are no longer the primary yardsticks of value.

This posthuman turn will profoundly reshape the environment in which we live and act. But it will also compel political change, driving realignments of belief and commitment along a set of novel axes. Our ability to think clearly about what kind of a deal we wish to pursue with these technologies—what place we wish for them to occupy in our economies, our societies and our lives, and ultimately what kind of everyday we ourselves wish to occupy—will depend on what we know about how each of them works, and how they may come to be fused in something powerful, purposive and self-directing.

As is so often the case, the language around these subjects can be daunting, but none of this complexity need stand in the way of understanding the basic propositions on offer. Before immersing ourselves in it, though, it's worth asking a question whose answers evidently strike advocates as being so obvious and so self-evident that they hardly warrant discussion: Why do so many of us seem to want to replace ourselves so very badly?

Reflexively, most of those who are now working to develop automated systems would probably prefer to speak of supplementing, rather than replacing, human beings in all the myriad roles we now fill. They paint pictures of hybridized teams working in varying degrees of comradely harmony, toward ends that are exclusively those specified by the human partner. If asked what motivates them in their drive toward the post-human, they'd very likely say they intend no such thing at all.

Instead, there's a very good chance they would offer a selection from among the following justifications, some of which are all but self-contradictory, and others of which are far more defensible. Assuming that none of them actually nurture a suppressed craving for the twilight of the species and a will to extinction, these are the justifications people offer when they undertake the development of learning algorithms, or the fully autonomous systems based on them:

We shouldn't underestimate, firstly, the force of desire that drives not a few researchers in robotics and artificial intelligence—the magnitude of the intellectual challenge. Any ascent to human-level intelligence by a technical system would by definition rank as one of the towering achievements of human history. Its designers could be assured of being remembered and celebrated alongside the titans of science and industry, for however much longer the species subsisted. While that prospect might not drive you or me toward this work, it's manifestly not without its power to seduce.

Nor do I think we should underestimate the degree to which some are invested in the development of autonomous systems for commercial reasons—purely, that is, as a business play, and not because they have any other personal, intellectual or ideological commitment to the idea. As long as there is money to be made in the field, there are those who will be willing to dedicate themselves to it, body and soul, whatever it might portend for the future.

We can be sure, then, that some cohort of the people working in this field will confessedly not actually care much about what automation is, what it means, or what might happen to result from its development. But others are very explicit in what they want from this set of technologies.

I don't think it's overly cynical to suggest that we might want to discount any professed concern for relieving human beings of dirty, dangerous or degrading jobs. Even in our era of acute sensitivities, employers seem to have little compunction about exposing workers to virtually any level of drudgery or peril, as long as their labor can be had cheap enough, and the consequences of catastrophe made tolerable enough.[4] The problem, from an employer's perspective, isn't so much that their workers' dignity must somehow be protected, but that even the minimal steps necessary to do so are becoming increasingly expensive. So one clear motivating factor behind research into automation is the creation of a *cheaper* and far less fractious labor force—one that never demands overtime, never agitates for higher wages or better benefits, never sues on grounds of discrimination, never files for workers' compensation,[5] and never complains about the conditions to which it is exposed.

Blue-collar wages may be stagnating globally, but automation costs are falling.[6] A used palletizing robot in good condition, capable of going 50,000 hours between overhauls (or just over eight years of three-shift operation), may cost $15,000 or less on the open market; while for the time being it may require an operator (at some $36,000 a year), even that outlay compares very favorably to the wages that would otherwise be paid out to a full-scale crew of human workers over that eight-year period. (As we shall see, that operator's job is itself in jeopardy: most of what he or she does is already within reach of rapidly developing machine vision systems and control algorithms.)

A slightly different calculus of cheapness drives much of the interest in military robotics: a *concern for the relative price of human life*, or at least those human lives that are designated as friendly. For decades, strategists have nurtured ideas about swarms of "fast, cheap, out of control" cybernetic combat systems, capable of occupying contested terrain, degrading an enemy's will to resist, and ultimately destroying that enemy's ability to wage war.[7] The remotely piloted vehicles we think of as "drones" are a gesture in this direction; more or less disposable for all their expense, they can be shot down or blown to pieces even as an operator reposes in air-conditioned comfort 8,000 miles away. But they're merely an incremental step toward more fully autonomous combat systems that would allow a state to pursue its territorial ambitions all without exposing (its own) human combatants to risk.

There are contexts in which the appeal to *safeguarding life and limb* actually does furnish a reasonable, even an ethically compelling, case for automation. In the United States alone, more than 30,000 people are killed in motor-vehicle crashes every year;[8] more than nine in every ten of those crashes were caused, at least in part, by driver error.[9] Though the number of fatalities is slowly falling over the decades, as regulation tightens and safety technology improves, this remains by any standard a heartbreakingly high price to pay for our desire for unlimited mobility. Given the scale of the risks involved, not least to insurers,[10] we can readily enough imagine a time when it is illegal to operate a vehicle, tool or other potentially destructive device manually, if the option exists of surrendering control to an algorithm bound to be more competent than we are ourselves.

There are, of course, other contexts where the vagaries of human discretion may produce intolerable effects. We know, for example—many of us know all too well—that our public institutions are pervaded by pernicious, systemic bias, and that this bias not infrequently has lethal consequences for anyone on the wrong side of it. This is, in some bleak sense, an opportunity for the vendors and advocates of algorithmic systems, which are commonly promoted as being neutral, rational, objective and scientific. Often with the noblest of intentions, they aim to restore probity to processes of public administration by supplanting imperfect human discretion with a synthetic judgment that is invariably figured as *free from the contaminating influence of prejudice.*

Our inability to act without bias is not the only way in which we fall short of the standards we set for ourselves, or which are routinely expected of us at work. As they develop over time, every industry, every profession and every domain of human endeavor will demand tolerances, sustained efforts or throughput velocities that are simply unachievable by human means. This might mean the ability to sift through large evidentiary productions without losing focus or succumbing to boredom. It could entail the capacity to maintain watchful awareness at a fence or border crossing deep in the night, without becoming distracted or sleepy; or, given the pace that capital already expects from human workers, it might involve the acuity to correctly identify contaminated chickens on a production line churning by at 175 birds per minute. Algorithmic systems will be pressed into service in all of these cases, and any number of contexts beyond where the demands of performance tax human strength, endurance, sensory discernment or motor coordination, simply because they are seen as being *more reliable.*

Another way in which nominally autonomous systems are thought of as being "better" than human beings is that they are *more obedient.*

Consider the lessons of a chastening post-World War II study conducted by the US Army, which found that few soldiers bothered to aim when firing their weapons in combat, or for that matter seemed to have any particular taste for killing at all, even when faced with a clear and highly motivated enemy. Since this finding, enormous sums have been invested in research aimed at ensuring that a military unit might actually bring kinetic force to bear on its intended target. Much of this research has focused on indoctrination and other methods of inculcating troops with the instinct to kill, and much of it has been successful.[11]

But in recent years the thrust of this effort has moved toward removing human beings from the decision loop entirely, along with any feelings of fear, compassion or mercy that might compromise the will to act at the decisive moment. Already well advanced in the doctrine of remotely piloted aerial warfare, with its air-conditioned control trailers and rhetoric of near-bloodless "precision strike,"[12] work proceeds toward the development of fully autonomous combat vehicles in China, Israel, Pakistan, Russia, South Korea, Turkey, the United Kingdom and the United States.[13] Though such systems are blessedly far removed from everyday experience for most of us, the long, sordid and well-documented history of "blowback," along with the increasing material and psychic militarization of policing,[14] suggests the strong possibility that techniques originally developed in and for distant theaters of war will eventually find their way into domestic life.

Finally, beyond arguments from cheapness, safety, reliability or obedience, I have no doubt that a few advocates for automation are driven by a sincere and passionate belief that automation is the surest way of achieving a *more equitable* future. Some on the left—accelerationists such as Alex Williams and Nick Srnicek and the proponents of Fully Automated Luxury Communism prominent among them—have argued that the ends of economic justice in our time are best served by maximum automation and the elimination of work.[15] Thinkers of this stripe argue that the soonest possible supplantation of human labor by cybernetic means is something close to an absolute ethical imperative.

In some ways, left accelerationism is just a contemporary gloss applied to the visions of total leisure that were developed by the generations immediately preceding, in a few distinct currents. Forerunners like Constant Nieuwenhuys, the French Situationists, and the radical Italian architectural practice Superstudio explored the spatial dimensions of post-work society between the late 1950s and mid-1970s, developing conceptions of what urban environments might look like when more broadly arranged around self-actualization and play, while it was left to second-wave feminist thought to explore the social dimensions of full automation. Shulamith Firestone organizes much of the later argument of her 1970 *The Dialectic of Sex* on "machines that ... surpass man in original thinking or problem-solving," "the abolition of the labor force itself under a cybernetic socialism, the radical restructuring of the economy to make 'work,' i.e. wage labor, no longer necessary," and ultimately the creation of a society in which "both adults and children could indulge in serious 'play' as much as they wanted."[16] And automated production, of course, furnishes Valerie Solanas one of the hinges of her *SCUM Manifesto*, with its ever-resonant demand to "overthrow the government, eliminate the money system, institute complete automation and destroy the male sex."[17]

But for that last, these themes have recently reemerged to be picked up and developed in the contemporary accelerationist discourse, after a long interval during which utopian thought on the left seemed more captivated by the possibilities of networks than by any catalyzed by automation per se. As the accelerationists would have it, the advanced econometric modeling, algorithmic planning and networked digital fabrication we now have access to finally make it possible for someone to "do one thing today and another tomorrow" as Marx foresaw—to binge-watch in the morning, write fanfic in the afternoon, make reaction GIFs in the evening and criticize after dinner, just as she has a mind. The problematic before us then actually would become the Keynesian (or Olympian) one of learning to live "wisely and agreeably and well" under conditions of absolute and universal freedom from want.

In the end, what is it that people want from these technologies? As near as I can tell, a few want just exactly what some have always wanted from other human beings: a cheap, reliable, docile labor force. Others, though, are seeking something less tangible: sense, meaning, order, a ward against uncertainty.

They're looking for something that might help them master the combinatorial explosion of possibility on a planet where nine billion people are continually knitting their own world-lines; for just a little reassurance, in a world populated by so many conscious actors that it often feels like it's spinning out of anyone's control. These are impulses I think most of us can relate to, and intuitively react to with some sympathy. And it's this class of desires that I think we should keep in mind as we explore the mechanics of machine learning, automated pattern recognition and decision-making. For all the arrogance, the reductionism and the more than occasional wrongheadedness that crop up in this development effort, I believe it is founded in a set of responses to the world that most all of us have experienced at one time or another. If nothing else, to consider automation with any seriousness is to be presented with a long, poignant and richly elaborated index of our deepest longings and fears.

Sometime in the early months of 2015, a curious map started to circulate through my social-media networks.[18] Generated by the data-graphics specialist Quoctrung Bui for National Public Radio, it charted the most commonly held job in each of the fifty United States during the period 1978–2014.

For Nevada, this job was "retail clerk," Washington State and Virginia "software developer," and North Dakota "farmer." Just about everywhere else in the United States, though, the most common occupation over this span of time was that of "truck driver." It was in seeing that job title lettered over every corner of the map that I really began to understand what automation is going to do to the American economy—and by extension, every other national economy on Earth at a similar stage of development.

In some ways, perhaps, the NPR map was a little misleading. Due to a quirk in the way the US government classifies jobs, long-haul truckers, delivery personnel and farm-equipment operators are shoehorned into the single category "truck, delivery and tractor drivers"; Bui had chosen to apply the label "truck driver" to this category, collapsing still further whatever distinctions may have nestled within it. But his animation of the map, and the year-by-year job tables he helpfully included, left no doubt that the phenomenon was and is real. The occupation has only become more dominant over time, displacing farmer, factory worker and machine operator as the number-one job— and, by extension, presumably the chief source of household income—in state after state.

As it happens, though the congelation of long-haul trucking, mechanized farming and urban logistics into a single job category obscures as much as it clarifies, it may not matter for our purposes. Trucking, farming and logistics are all seething sites of research into automation, and none will likely survive very long as distinctly human fields of endeavor.

"Driverless" cars like those being developed by Google and Uber may dominate the mainstream media coverage, but the spare, highway-bound performance regime of long-haul trucking is far more amenable to automation than the stop-and-start, high-complexity environment of city and suburban driving, as Tesla's July 2016 announcement of plans for an autonomous semi recognizes.[19] Meanwhile, logistics has already shed most of the human labor force it once supported, with Jeff Bezos's Amazon pioneering the development of robotic warehousing and fulfillment.[20] Research has already moved on to attack the challenges of delivery by swarming drone as well as autonomous ground vehicle.

So when a worthy body like the Pew Research Center convenes a panel of experts[21] and just over half of them argue that automation will create more jobs than it displaces between now and 2025, I'm forced to wonder if anyone involved has spent much time contemplating the pastel contrasts of Quoctrung Bui's map.[22] What is now the most commonly held job in twenty-nine of the fifty states will surely number among the very first to be automated. Autonomous trucking alone is going to land on the American economy (and the American worker) with devastating force.

The usual rattling off of statistics doesn't really tell us very much, but it can at least help sketch in the outlines of what it is we face: of 702 detailed job categories in the United States, Carl Benedikt Frey and Michael A. Osborne of the University of Oxford found that 47 percent of them were vulnerable to near-term advances in machine learning and mobile robotics.[23] Among developing countries, this rises to 69 percent in India, 77 percent in China and an astonishing 85 percent in Ethiopia.[24] (Again, these figures refer to the percentage of job *categories* that are susceptible to replacement, not of workers in employment.) Meanwhile, against the oft-cited hope that technology would generate more jobs than it eliminated, Frey found that fewer than 0.5 percent of the US workforce have found employment in the high-technology industries that have emerged since the turn of the century. A World Economic Forum estimate that some five million jobs would be lost to automation by 2020 has to be regarded as a stark outlier, if not a gross error, especially since Bank of England Chief Economist Andy Haldane reckons that 15 million jobs would disappear over the same timeframe in the United Kingdom alone.[25]

I'm not qualified to discuss, in any but the broadest terms, what will happen to the shape and structure of national economies in the aftermath of pervasive automation. What I can speak to, however, is what the working environment will look and feel like for those of us who do manage to remain in employment.

We often tend to visualize automation in heroic terms, as if limned in the hues of a cybernetic Socialist Realism: we imagine ranks of mighty robot tractors furrowing the grain in parallel bands ten miles across, or enormous darkened warehouses where relentless manipulators pick, pack and ship in silence. As far as industry is concerned, though—and in this instance it really is their perspective that weighs heaviest and counts most—automation also means far less elaborate technologies, like the touchscreen ordering kiosks McDonald's began introducing into its locations in the fall of 2014. In fact, automation means *anything* that reduces the need for human workers, whether it's a picking-and-packing robot, a wearable biometric monitor, a mobile-phone app or the redesign of a business process.

Like McDonald's CEO Steve Easterbrook, some executives insist that bringing service-sector automation on line won't eliminate jobs, but merely allow them to deploy their employees in more "value-added" roles.[26] Former McDonald's head of US operations Ed Rensi argues just the opposite; as part of a campaign against efforts to increase the US minimum wage to $15 an hour, he noted that "it's cheaper to buy a $35,000 robotic arm than it is to hire an employee who's inefficient, making $15 an hour bagging french fries."[27] Whichever of these two perspectives does prevail—and the pitiless logic of shareholder value strongly bolsters Rensi's position—it is clear that whatever human participants do remain in the waged labor force are in for a particularly rough ride in the years to come.

This shrunken workforce will be asked to do more, for lower wages, at a yet higher pace. Amazon is again the leading indicator here.[28] Its warehouse workers are hired on fixed, short-term contracts, through a deniable outsourcing agency, and precluded from raises, benefits, opportunities for advancement or the meaningful prospect of permanent employment. They work under conditions of "rationalized" oversight in the form of performance metrics that are calibrated in real time. Any degree of discretion or autonomy they might have retained is ruthlessly pared away by efficiency algorithm. The point couldn't be made much more clearly: these facilities are places that no one sane would choose to be if they had any other option at all.

And this is only the most obvious sort of technological intervention in the workplace. We barely have words for what happens when an algorithm breaks down jobs into tasks that are simple enough that they don't call for any particular expertise—just about anybody will suffice to perform them— and outsources them to a global network of individuals made precarious and therefore willing to work for very little. Naturally, this newly intensified Fordist production regime sees its workers paid by the minute, without security of tenure, a guaranteed weekly minimum or any other form of benefit, and this too is automation.

Most of the blue-collar workers that do manage to retain employment will find themselves "below the API"—that is, subject to having their shifts scheduled by optimization algorithm, on little or no notice, for periods potentially incommensurate with their needs for sleep and restoration, their family life, or their other obligations.[29] (In the UK and elsewhere the practice is tolerated, the terms of such employment may be specified by so-called zero-hour contracts, which offer no guaranteed minimum of shifts.) Former US secretary of labor Robert Reich recoils from the prospect of work under these conditions: "Can you imagine if this turns into [an economy] where everyone is doing piecework at all odd hours, and no one knows when the next job will come, and how much it will pay? What kind of private lives can we possibly have, what kind of relationships, what kind of families?"

Under such circumstances, the workplace itself becomes an arena for every kind of performance monitoring and calibration. Every checkout interaction at the Target chain, for example, is rated Green, Yellow or Red by an automated system, according to whether or not the clerk hit targets for speed and accuracy, and these ratings are used to determine employee compensation. Target worker "Tessa" explained in a blog post that the company "keeps a running average of your scores for the week, month, and year. They expect over 88 percent of your transactions to make the speed cut, and your score reflects on possible raises, promotions, and sometimes even who remains as an employee."[30] (An alternate—and in truth, almost equally credible—possibility is raised by a Target employee commenting at another site: "No one cares about it at the store level, it's just to get people at Corporate to feel that your store is productive.")[31]

Since June 2016, sales associates at every Container Store location have been required to wear "enterprise wearables" made by a startup called Theatro.[32] These are devices that track employee location and provide real-time feedback regarding their interactions with shoppers. The company uses the accompanying analytic suite to "identify top performers" (and, by implication, those at the bottom as well), and plan schedules and distribute assignments in the store accordingly.

Theatro's devices are less elaborate than a Hitachi wearable called Business Microscope, which aims to capture, quantify and make inferences from several dimensions of employee behavior.[33] As grim as call-center work is, a Hitachi press release brags about their ability to render it more dystopian yet via the use of this tool—improving performance metrics not by reducing employees' workload, but by compelling them to be more physically active during their allotted break periods.[34]

Hitachi's wearables, in turn, are less capable than the badges offered by Cambridge, MA, startup Sociometric Solutions, which are "equipped with two microphones, a location sensor and an accelerometer" and are capable of registering "tone of voice, posture and body language, as well as who spoke to whom for how long."[35] As with all of these devices, the aim is to continuously monitor (and eventually regulate) employee behavior.

Whether furnished by a large and globally established enterprise like Hitachi, or a startup along the lines of Sociometric Solutions or Theatro, employers will have their choice of devices that allow them to track worker performance and attitude, along an ever-increasing number of axes and in constantly improving resolution. It's also worth pointing out, in turn, that in every generation of product, such specialized employee monitors are notably less capable than consumer-grade biometric wearables like the Fitbit Charge or Apple's Watch; smaller, or cannier, enterprises may simply choose to capture data from the devices their employees are already voluntarily wearing. In either case, the disciplinary regime specific to the workplace becomes instead an all-but-placeless control regime, an "ambient factory" where decisions once thought to be purely personal—sleep cycles, nutritional patterns, exercise habits— become subject to employer monitoring and intervention.[36]

Wearables work in synchrony with workstation systems to furnish bosses with a comprehensive overview of employee behavior. At KFC, Wendy's and the RiteAid drugstore chain, workers at the point of sale log into their workstations bio-metrically via the Crossmatch u.are.u suite of hardware and software. Crossmatch touts this system as preventing "tardy arrivals, 'buddy punching,' 'lollygagging,' extended breaks and early departures, inventory shrink, unauthorized discounts and returns, and fraudulent gift card transactions;"[37] anyone who's ever worked retail will understand this list as an almost perfect, point-for-point recitation of the tacit measures employees have always taken to compensate themselves for having to put up with abusive bosses, shitty pay and intolerable working conditions. For that matter, "buddy punching"—the act of clocking in a friend who's late for work, possibly because they've had to take a child to daycare or a sick parent to the doctor—is just the kind of small act of solidarity that might save someone their job in the harsh, zero-tolerance climate of contemporary work. But these are the tactics such oversight systems are expressly designed to eliminate.

As the capacity to detect and characterize emotional states has grown, these reasonably traditional, Taylorist notions of time-and-motion efficiency have been supplemented by a concern for the worker's affective performance.[38] Japan's Keikyu Corporation, for example, began measuring the quality of its frontline employees' smiles in 2009, scanning their "eye movements, lip curves and wrinkles," and rating them on a 0-100 scale.[39]

As intrusive as this may seem, smiling is at least something under an employee's conscious control, which cannot be said for all of the measurements of "body posture, facial expressions, physiology, semantics [and] who a person talks to and when" that the management consultancy Accenture recommends to ensure employees are "exhibiting effective social behaviors."[40] Such subconscious tells are picked up by the People Analytics suite the "emotion-aware sentiment analysis company" Kanjoya offers, which uses unstructured voice and text data to calibrate an employee's "Attrition Risk" and "Workplace Value," in addition to the expected "Performance."

The concern for retention implies something that a review of similar sentiment analysis systems makes entirely explicit: the demand that inner states be measured and used to determine the conditions of labor now applies to the white-collar workforce every bit as much as it does to checkout clerks or line workers. As well, in a theme that we'll be taking up repeatedly, what is salient is not so much whether these tools actually perform as advertised, but whether users can be induced to believe that they do. The prejudicial findings of such "HR analytics," i.e. that a given employee is unreliable, costly or a litigation risk, may be acted upon even if the algorithm that produced them is garbage and the data little better than noise.

Though top executives may, for the time being, manage to wriggle free from algorithmic performance evaluation, it seems highly likely that employment at all other levels will become increasingly contingent on a continuously iterated double articulation of assessment and selection that leaves no room whatsoever for the distracted, the halfway-competent, the deliberately shirking or simply the different.

Everything that wearables and workstation systems do for the shop floor, the call center and the checkout counter, analytic suites like BetterWorks do for the management echelon.[41] The same anomaly detection subroutines that identify when a customer service representative's average call length or escalation rate has climbed past the permissible value can trivially discover when someone is away from their desk too long, taking over-frequent bathroom breaks or gossiping with friends in other departments (never mind that such interdepartmental contacts are how organizations break through groupthink and actually innovate).[42]

As employee monitoring (and self-monitoring) inexorably advances across the enterprise, the data it generates won't simply evaporate. It will pile up in drifts, with measurements characterizing every last aspect of job performance in exquisitely high resolution rapidly accumulating in the corporate servers. It will, of course, make a tempting target for theft and exploitation— and if the past is any guide, the obligation to exert some kind of fiduciary responsibility over this cache won't be felt nearly as urgently as it should be.[43]

But something else happens as well, whenever a volume of data this large is gathered: feature extraction becomes easier, the development of training sets more straightforward, unsupervised learning a very real possibility. And this brings us full circle to the training of algorithmic systems, and their eventual deployment in replacement of human workers.

These disciplinary techniques will no doubt continue to be relied upon into the indefinite future, and they will continue to be responsible for their share of misery. But they are not the processes that are relentlessly and progressively reducing the scope of human labor.

Behind the wheel, the learning algorithm and the multispectral sensor do for the human driver, moving vehicles across the land more swiftly, more reliably, and more safely than the most responsible flesh-and-blood operator, whether they are charged with the transportation of freight or of passengers.

In the warehouse and the loading dock, the standardized container, the RFID tag, the autonomous pallet sled, and the development of sprawling big-box distribution centers that are very little other than enormous robotic systems in themselves— all these things sooner or later settle a quietus onto the prospect of unskilled employment in the fulfillment and logistics sector.

At retail, "seamless" point-of-sale processes and the displacement of responsibility onto the shopper themselves via self-checkout slash the number of personnel it takes to run a storefront operation, though some staff will always be required to smooth out the inevitable fiascos; perhaps a few high-end boutiques performatively, conspicuously retain a significant floor presence.

In customer service, appalling "cognitive agents" take the place of front-line staff.[44] Equipped with speech recognition and natural-language processing capabilities, with synthetic virtual faces that unhesitatingly fold in every last kind of problematic assumption about gender and ethnicity, they're so cheap that it's hard to imagine demanding, hard-to-train human staff holding out against them for very long.

Even in so-called high-touch fields like childcare and home-health assistance, jobs that might be done and done well by people with no other qualification, face the prospect of elimination. Xenophobia and racism subtly, if predictably, shape the possibilities here: in sector after sector, from healthcare to farming,[45] a Japan that is rapidly shrinking and aging would rather invest in developing advanced (and often specifically humanoid) robotics than admit an immigrant labor force of any significant size. There are always choices, and this is the one that Japanese society has made—but the techniques and conventions that are developed as a consequence of this choice will find purchase far beyond its shores.

In the military, in sex work, in eldercare, in one domain after another where you'd think the law or good taste or common sense might prevent someone from proposing the automation of a historically human function, the effort proceeds apace. If we can judge fairly from the statistics we're offered, or the things that CEOs say in unguarded moments, automation is already sweeping across the economy at its foundations, taking up entry-level jobs and popping them one by one like blisters in a strip of bubble wrap. The presumption that was until very recently not merely tenable but persuasive—that even the otherwise-untrained had something unique and definitive to offer on the job, whether that thing was cognitive or affective or empathic—begins to yield before the cold equations of capital. Something new looms into view.

One of the very few points on which I am likely to agree with former US secretary of the treasury Larry Summers is his reminder that "[n]o one should speak with certainty about these matters, because there are challenges in the statistics, and there are conflicts in the data."[46] It would be easy to overstate the impact of automation on entry-level employment, especially in the near term.

But as someone profoundly skeptical of the claims that are so often and so breathlessly made about technology—as someone who knows from personal experience full well how hard it is not so much to develop, but to deploy, integrate and make use of technological systems—what I've seen in the course of research for this book has convinced me that automation is an existential mid-term threat to the livelihood of the most vulnerable workers. Capability is advancing more quickly than most realize, or are prepared to accept.

The dirty, dull, dangerous and demeaning jobs will be the first to be automated, and these remain, for better or worse, precisely the reservoir of opportunity for unskilled, undocumented or otherwise marginalized participants in the workforce.

What this does to the culture of work, and to labor's already imperiled ability to make demands and specify the conditions under which it produces value, deserves treatment at book length. For the present purposes, it seems safe to conclude that between algorithmic management and regulation, and the more than usually exploitative relations that we can see resulting from it,[47] hard times are coming for those who have nothing to offer the economy but their muscle, their heart or their sex. I don't doubt that those who benefit from any such state of affairs will be able to focus the rage of the permanently disemployed on immigrants and other convenient scapegoats, but eventually they too will be compelled to seek some sort of *modus vivendi*.

The tacit assumption that has held sway in the developed world for most of the past century, and which has only deepened its hold since women began to enter the workforce in great numbers around 1950, is that whatever their degree of skill or education, the vast majority of adults will eventually be able to find employment in the formal economy. And this fact structures virtually everything about everyday experience, not merely economically, but materially, psychically and socially.

It's the logic beneath the twice-daily surge we call the commute; the factor shaping the great commuter hubs of the world; the reason why there is such a thing as "rush hour" at all. It shapes the width of sidewalks, drives the content of daytime television and underwrites the viability of businesses whose only proposition is that they provide a "third place" between work and home. It molds the way we dress, the way we eat, the skills we choose to acquire and the hobbies we undertake. It largely determines our social status. Not least, it places bounds on the way we present ourselves and the things we feel able to say out loud.

At this point, a garden-variety pop futurist would commit to the flat declarative: All of this is going to change. In the advance of automation, there will be very little that is meaningful left for anyone to do. The point will be reiterated, made again for the folks who were texting or otherwise tuned out the first time around: jobs are going away. You Better Get Ready.

The temptation, when presented with one of these would-be business oracles, is always to hiss with suppressed laughter at the shallowness of the argument and the simplicity of whatever "takeaway" they offer. But what if they're even halfway right? What if the thing that furnishes the economy with its basic structure, and day-to-day experience with its most fundamental organizing principle, is starting to erode before our eyes?

In their recent book *Inventing the Future*, Nick Srnicek and Alex Williams perceive in this set of circumstances an epochal opportunity for the left. Their argument, broadly, is that going forward, there simply won't be enough meaningful work to furnish a global labor force of five billion or more with employment capable of sustaining them—and that it is in any event perverse to defend jobs we know full well to be bullshit.[48] Instead of squandering energies in the sentimental defense of a proletarian way of life that no longer corresponds to any set of facts on the ground, they propose that there is a far more valuable effort progressive forces could dedicate themselves to at this moment in history: the struggle for a universal basic income, or UBI.

As the name suggests, most UBI plans—and the variants are many—propose that the state furnish all of its citizens with some kind of sustaining stipend, regardless of means tests or other qualifications. Most versions propose a grant at least equal to the local poverty line, in theory liberating recipients from the worst of the want and gnawing fear that might otherwise beset them in a time of mass disemployment.

The UBI is by no means strictly an argument from the utopian fringes of the left. Indeed, the terminology "basic income" itself is a market-friendly reframing of something that Fabian socialists used to think of as the "social dividend."[49] In the United States, no guaranteed annual income initiative has ever gone further than the Nixon Administration's 1969 experiments with the unfortunately named Family Assistance Plan (FAP).[50] More recently, the Dutch city of Utrecht and the Finnish national government have recently trialled similar measures under the market-liberal VVD party and Juha Sipilä's center-right coalition, respectively.[51] (A June 2016 Swiss UBI initiative failed, with 76.9 percent of voters opposed.)

With support across the conventional political spectrum, it may seem like some kind of UBI is far and away the most cogent response to widespread automation we have available, a cushion to buffer those who might otherwise plummet to Earth.

But the devil always nestles in the details of any such proposal. Held up to sustained inspection, the UBI can often seem like little more than a neoliberal giveaway. Its proponents on the market right clearly anticipate it as a pretext to do away with existing benefits, siphoning whatever transfers are involved in it back into the economy as fees for a wide variety of educational, healthcare and family services that are now furnished via social provision. And whichever direction it comes from, arguing for the accelerated disappearance of work is a very high-stakes gamble to make, in a world where the welfare state and its safety net are distant and receding memories and the horizontal and mutualist infrastructures that might replace them have not had time to develop.

One could, therefore, be forgiven for concluding that in practical terms, the achievement of a universal basic income will result not in anything like total leisure and unlimited self-actualization, but in the further entrenchment of desperation and precarity. When far more powerful forces are already waiting to exploit its emergence and divert its flows for their own ends, it seems unnecessarily cavalier of people who think of themselves as being on the left to "demand" a generic UBI. To the degree that we buy the Srnicek and Williams line, what we need to insist on is the implementation of income guarantees in a context that protects our ability to spend that windfall as we see fit.

Other, less central aspects of the visions we're presented of a world without work might trouble us as well. In his book *The Zero Marginal Cost Society*, Jeremy Rifkin fetishizes fully automated logistics, without considering how often logistics workers specifically have constituted the most radical faction of industrial labor. Without for a moment romanticizing the circumstances that gave rise to their militancy, we might want to remember how frequently in the past it's been workers toiling in the most oppressive industries who have offered themselves as the insurgent brake on unfettered capital accumulation. On our way to a world of total automation, we may often have time to contemplate what a society winds up looking like when its most mutinous voices have fallen silent.

It can be briefly amusing to stand alongside the accelerationists as they proclaim, "Workers of every nation unite! You have nothing to lose but your jobs!" But the euphoria soon fades, swept away by the swiftly sobering recognition that there is terribly little chance for a soft landing in any of this, for any one of us.

Though we may debate the degree to which choice and conscious authorship are involved in it, it seems important to note that automation is a directional process whose initial stages we've already entered. In this respect David Graeber's empty, signifier-shuffling "bullshit jobs" are a signal from the future. They're not so much a return as an anticipation of the repressed: the surfacing in the present, and pricing into contemporary ways of doing and being, of the recognition that there simply won't be enough meaningful work for anyone to do following the eclipse of human judgment.

The UBI, as a rearguard action aimed at ensuring the continuity of business as usual, seems to be predicated on the survival of at least some higher-order executive jobs. But what its advocates neglect to consider is how total the process of supplantation will be. If we allow anything like this to happen, it will be a wave that sweeps any notion of consequential work away, for the wealth managers and creative directors and project managers as much as the truck drivers and pipefitters. What we will discover, I think, is that we urgently need to reinvent (particularly, but not just) a left politics whose every fundamental term has been transformed: a politics of far-reaching solidarity, capable of sustaining and lending nobility to all the members of a near-universal unnecessariat.

But we will also discover something else. We needed work, though not in any hackneyed dignity-of-labor sense. We certainly didn't need to rouse ourselves to Stakhanovite exertions on behalf of uncaring employers; we didn't benefit from being forced to simulate team-spiritedness, amidst all the profoundly dispiriting banality of our fluorescent-lit cubicles; and it goes without saying we didn't need to suffer the insults of cretinous customers, working out their neuroses and class frustrations across the counter. All too often work cost us our health, our dreams, our lives. But it also offered us a context in which we might organize our skills and talents, it gave us some measure of common cause with others who labored under similar conditions, across all bounds of space and time, and if nothing else it filled the hours of our days on Earth. Though these goods came at far too high a price, I don't know that we are wise to consider living entirely without them, or are practically prepared to do so.

Even under the very best of foreseeable circumstances, circumstances in which we are successfully able to organize the infrastructures of solidarity we will need to call upon for our sustenance once work has gone away, I don't know that we're psychically equipped to withstand total freedom from obligation.[52] As feeling beings, we become habituated to any emotion long and persistently experienced, and eventually desensitized to its appearance. Some degree of variation, effort and friction—in other words, some measure of its absence—is necessary to the experience of pleasure.[53] In a world without work, as Keynes suggested almost a century ago, we dispense with most all of the friction and effort bound up with the struggle to survive, and therefore finally and implacably arrive at the question of what life is for. At a time when the alienation and anomie attendant upon the withdrawal of work is literally killing (some of) us[54], perhaps it's worth considering what the answers might cost us.

Some researchers insist that in the aftermath of total automation, we will learn to value people not for the advantage we're able to generate through work, but for who we are inherently, as unique and irreplaceable individuals. I leave that thought here without further comment.

In the end, it's difficult to stand back far enough to weigh the meaning of the changes rippling across this thing we call the economy, something so total in our lives that its outer bounds are virtually impossible to perceive. What we can see is that for all the sorriest, most predictable and all-too-human of reasons, human discretion is progressively becoming decentered within it.

As algorithms develop the ability to plan optimal courses of action through mind-bendingly complex multivariate decision spaces, and blockchain-based distributed autonomous organizations the ability to capture and organize wealth, it seems as though human intention is sure to follow. Such decenterings may not be particularly upsetting to anyone who's ever sat with a set of questions we inherit from feminist, post-structuralist and ecological thought: questions about the death of "Man," the agency of nonhuman actors, the consequences of our decisions for the other life we share a planet with, and the extreme unwisdom of trying to articulate some kind of binary distinction about the boundary between humanity and its others in the first place.

I believe questions like these come from the best that's in us, and I cannot imagine how impoverished we would be if nobody had ever thought to press them. But it remains difficult for me, at least, to conceive what an economy might be for, if not the generation and apportionment of wealth as humans experience it.

Machine learning

The algorithmic production of knowledge

We've already discussed the massive volumes of data that stand to be collected by a true internet of things, the torrential trains of ones and zeroes coursing through and between all the world's networked devices. We've seen how digital fabrication devices can turn data into material artifacts of the most extraordinary delicacy and precision, how the desire to make shared data incorruptible furnishes the blockchain with its very purpose and reason for being. But we haven't yet paused to reflect on just what data *is*.

Let's start with the thought that whatever set of events life presents us with, we need to situate ourselves in the world, evaluate our circumstances and the possibilities they afford us for purposive action, and then decide among the options we're presented with—and this is true whether we're deciding who to befriend on the first day of kindergarten, choosing the right seeds to plant on the shadier side of our community-garden plot, or wrestling a quarter-billion-dollar fighter jet through a high-G dogfight with a similarly equipped enemy. A simple way of defining data, then, might be *facts about the world, and the people, places, things and phenomena that together comprise it*, that we collect in order that they may be acted upon.

But before we can act upon any such collection of facts, we have to make sense of it. A commonplace of information science holds that data, information, knowledge and wisdom form a coherent continuum, and that we apply different procedures at every stage of that continuum to transform the facts we observe into insight and awareness. There are many versions of this model, but they all fundamentally assert that we *measure* the world to produce data, *organize* that data to produce meaningful, actionable information, *synthesize* that information with our prior experience of the world to produce knowledge, and then—in some unspecified and probably indescribable way—arrive at a state in which we are able to apply the things we know with the ineffable quality of balanced discernment we think of as wisdom.

The various versions of this model all generally assume that data itself is neutral and objective. Whenever we say "data," however, what we're really referring to is that subset of the world's infinite aspects that have been captured by some instrument or process of measurement. (In fact, the French word for "sensor," *capteur*, directly reflects this insight, and some of the more thoughtful observers of information-processing technology have argued that in English the word "capta" would be a more accurate way of describing that which is retained.)[1] For our purposes, what is vital to remember is that there's no such thing as "raw data." Whatever data we measure and retain with our sensors, as with our bodily senses, is invariably a selection from the far broader array available to us; perception itself is always already a process of editing and curation.

As we saw in our discussion of the blockchain, the conventional way of deriving actionable information from large bodies of data was to apply structure to it, by storing it in the linked cells of a relational database. For example, such a database might record each of Amazon's user accounts sequentially, with cells containing the account holder's first name, last name, delivery address, the various credit cards they have on file, and so on. Retrieving information in this case is a simple matter of submitting a structured query to the database, and even this straightforward process is generally buried beneath the still-simpler front-end interface of a consumer-facing website: for example, we make such a query every time we click on a link that reads "View Your Orders" or "Manage Payment Options."

But managing flows of so-called big data—a buzzword that simply denotes the extremely high volume, velocity and variety of contemporary data production—stresses such conventional techniques to the breaking point. Storage capacity sufficient to cope with the onslaught simply may not be available. Populating a database accurately requires a significant investment of resource and effort, which may not be forthcoming. And in any event, most of the world's data—and virtually all of it that's germane to systems that operate in physical space and real time—does not happen to reside in the neat tables or crisply cellular structure of any database, and never will. So the new way of handling such situations is to look for emergent patterns in previously *unstructured* data, like a large body of text, a series of images, or indeed a real-time video feed. In fact, this is what "big data" is all about. There's something uncanny, almost Deleuzian about this process of interrogation: as they are iteratively resolved in ever-higher fidelity, the patterns themselves begin to suggest the questions that might be asked of them.[2]

The way such streams and flows are induced to render up whatever patterns are latent within them is by passing them through an algorithm—or more likely, several of them.

With its faintly exotic etymology and unfortunate near-homophony with a completely unrelated concept in mathematics, "algorithm" is one of those words that does so much to shroud discussions of information technology in an unnecessary aura of complexity. There needn't be any mystery on this count, though: all the word means is a finite, structured, sequential and highly explicit set of instructions, a procedure for doing *this* to *that*. A well-specified recipe is an algorithm, as is the process of alphabetizing a list of names.

As you may by now suspect, algorithms are everywhere beneath the surface of contemporary life.[3] They govern what songs or films a streaming service will recommend, the price at which a given commodity will be offered to market, where a restaurant will seat its customers, which potential partners will appear in a dating app, and (if you're unwise enough to use a browser without an ad blocker installed) what ads are served to you. In contemporary society, a very great deal of material power reposes in the party that authors an algorithm. They determine your credit-worthiness, your insurability and the priority with which you will receive medical care in a mass-casualty emergency. (This last example generally involves assessing a patient's condition against a set of procedures specified on a laminated card, and it's an excellent reminder that not all algorithms are necessarily executed by software.)

Algorithms also manage processes that are still, for the most part, at the edge of everyday experience, but drawing ever closer: they instruct a bipedal robot how to pick up a package without losing its balance, a drone how fast each of its rotors must spin to maintain level pitch, or an autonomous car how to recognize obstacles in the roadway.

Because of the colossal volume of data that passes through them, changes to any of the more widely relied-upon algorithms can have consequences that ripple through the entire society. Every time Google tweaks its search algorithm, or Facebook the one it uses to govern story placement, certain business propositions suddenly become viable, and others immediately cease to be; more profoundly yet, certain perspectives on reality are reinforced, and others undermined. These particular tweaks, we should be clear, are made manually, invariably in response to some perceived vulnerability or weakness—in Google's case, that content farms and other low-quality sites were rising too high in their search results by gaming its algorithm, in Facebook's the accusation that their trending news feature was biased against right-wing sources. But not all such algorithmic refinement is manual.

What links all of these situations is their dynamism. Because the circumstances of the world evolve so rapidly, an algorithm that is expected to face up to the challenges of everyday life can only suffer from being static and set in stone. Compelled to make its way in a fundamentally unpredictable and even turbulent operating environment, like any of us an algorithm will ideally be equipped with the ability to learn from its experiences, generalize from what it's encountered, and develop adaptive strategies in response. Over time, it will learn to recognize what distinguishes a good performance from an unacceptable one, and how to improve the odds of success next time out. It will refine its ability to detect what is salient in any given situation, and act on that insight. This process is called "machine learning."

What distinguishes this from "deep" learning, as some would have us call the process through which a machine develops insight? And why does it seem to have become so prominent in recent years?

In the beginning was the program. Classically, using computers to solve problems in the real world meant writing programs, and that meant expressing those problems in terms that could be parsed and executed by machine. Research into artificial intelligence proceeded along these lines for decades, culminating in the so-called expert systems of the 1980s, which attempted to abstract the accumulated expertise of a human diagnostician or trial lawyer into a decision tree built on a series of explicit if-then rules.[4] These systems did work, for some crude approximation of "work," but they were clumsy and brittle, failing completely when encountering situations their programmers hadn't envisioned.

And there was a still-deeper problem with this high-level approach to artificial intelligence. Many of the things we'd like algorithmic systems to do for us—whether recognizing handwriting or natural speech, identifying people and other discrete objects in the visual field, or succeeding at the continuous exercise of identification we think of as the sense of vision itself—confound explicit articulation, and therefore expression in the form of executable code. These are things our brains do trivially and without conscious thought. But precisely for this reason, because we cannot explicitly reconstruct how we arrive at the decisions involved, we're generally unable to encode them as instructions computational systems would be able to make use of.

In other words, we might be able to imagine the set of principles that allow us to isolate the things we perceive in the visual field, and gloss them as "cat" or "coffee mug" or "Ricky," but we'd have a very hard time making those principles concrete enough to articulate and convey to a machinic system not overfond of ambiguity. What's more, we have an astonishing ability to keep track of the stable identity of things through relatively profound changes in state—we still recognize the cat in bright sunlight, Ricky after he's grown a beard, even the mug after it's been shattered on the floor—and this is still more difficult to account for. We might achieve these tasks with no discernible effort at all, but if machinic systems are ever to have the slightest hope of mastering them, they would have to be provided with some way of acquiring knowledge that does not involve explicit instruction.

Enter the neural network, a way of organizing individual processing units into meshes that mimic the way neurons are interconnected in the human central nervous system. In its basic contours, this idea had been floating around computer science for decades; the first conceptual glimmerings had come in a 1943 paper, and the first "perceptron," or artificial neuron, was built in hardware at Cornell in 1957.[5] Though they may not have borne fruit until much later, neural networks were by no means an intellectual backwater—if anything, they were the staple of artificial intelligence research throughout the 1980s, and were actually deployed at scale in commercial applications like check reading by the late 1990s. But riven by arcane doctrinal disputes, and undermined by the stark limitations of the available hardware, the field languished. It wasn't until the early years of this century, and the belated refinement of these techniques, that computer science finally began to produce systems robustly capable of learning from experience.

The contemporary neural network is built on a layered model of perception. At its most fundamental level are processing elements called *input neurons*, which work just as the brain's neurons do, firing in response to a specific stimulus. In machine-vision applications, for example, these are tasked with detecting features like edges and corners, and are therefore responsible for the crudest binary figure-ground calculation: is there something in the image, or not?

If the answer is "yes," these primitives will be passed on to a higher layer of neurons responsible for integrating them into coherent features. As neurons in each successive layer fire, a picture of the world is filled in, at first with low conceptual resolution ("this is a line," "this line is an edge"), then with increasing specificity ("this is a shadow," "this is a person standing in shadow"). And then an accumulation of finer and finer detail until the criteria for top-level recognition are triggered, and an *output neuron* associated with the appropriate label fires: this is Ricky standing in shadow. The algorithm has learned to recognize the subject of the present image by attending to statistical regularities among the thousands or millions of such images it was trained on. And so it will be for each of the higher-level objects a neural network can be trained to recognize: they must be built from the bottom up, in a cascade of neural firings.

What gives the neural network its flexibility, and allows for it to be trained, is that the connection between any two neurons has a strength, a numerical weighting; this value can be modulated at any time by whoever happens to be training the algorithm. The process of training involves manipulating these weights to reinforce the specific neural pathways responsible for a successful recognition, while suppressing the activation of those that result in incorrect interpretations of an image. Over thousands of iterations, as the weightings between layers are refined, a neural network will learn how to recognize complex features from data that is not merely unstructured, but very often noisy and wildly chaotic, in the manner of the world we occupy and recognize as our own.

Stripped of its mystification, then, machine learning is the process by way of which algorithms are taught to recognize patterns in the world, through the automated analysis of very large data sets. When neural networks are stacked in multiple layers, each stocked with neurons responsible for discerning a particular kind of pattern, they are capable of modeling high-level abstractions. (This stacking accounts for the "deep" in deep learning, in at least one of the circulating definitions.) It is this that ultimately gives the systems running these algorithms the ability to perform complicated tasks without being explicitly instructed in how to do so, and it is is how they now stand to acquire the capabilities we have previously thought of as the exclusive province of the human.

The training of an algorithm can happen in one of two different ways. In the more conventional *supervised learning*, an algorithm is offered both training examples and their corresponding labels. The task to be performed might be binary—given this series of transactions, some of which are known to be fraudulent, is this particular one valid, yes or no?—or categorical—given one of a series of images to be identified, which category does the depicted object belong to?—but both types of tasks will be trained by manually reinforcing the pathways that lead to a correct answer.

For example, a thousand files containing training images of three classic American muscle cars of the 1960s might be presented to an algorithm for analysis, along with the respective labels *1968_Camaro*, *1968_Mustang* and *1968_Charger*, and it will be asked to place each image in the correct category. At first, when presented with a fresh image, it will do no better than chance. But as its weightings are tweaked, the algorithm will learn to identify those features which are definitive of each one of the possible options before it: a distinctive grill or fender or hood scoop. Eventually, given an accumulation of such details, it will arrive at a judgment as to which category it thinks the car in the image belongs to. (Some degree of anthropomorphism is difficult to avoid in describing how this process works; of course, the algorithm doesn't "think" anything at all, but has assigned a weighted score to the image, representing the probability that the car in the image is the one its calculations suggest.)

We might say, then, that the first goal of machine learning is to teach an algorithm how to generalize. A sound algorithm is one that is able to derive a useful *classifier* for something it hasn't yet encountered from the things it has been shown. Perhaps after reviewing its thousand images, for example, our algorithm concludes that a taillight configuration of six vertical rectangles is very highly correlated with the label *1968_Mustang*. When applied to a new data set, this classifier can be graded by the metrics of *accuracy* (were all of the images tagged as Mustangs identified correctly?), *precision* (were all of the Mustangs known to be in the set correctly identified as such?), and *recall* (of the known Mustangs, how many were successfully identified?). Precision is an index of an algorithm's discriminative quality, while recall is correlated with its ability to return a complete set of results.

Note that this particular classifier is a highly reliable discriminator, in that both Camaros and Chargers have round taillights. Nevertheless, it will still fail to capture some, and perhaps many, of the Mustangs known to be present in the training set—those not pictured from an angle at which the taillights are visible, for example. In other words, if used on its own, this classifier will produce high *accuracy* (zero false positives), but low *recall* (many false negatives). As we'll see, given that false positives and false negatives are not equally costly in the real world, this state of affairs may in fact sometimes be desirable; the important precondition to any valid use of learning algorithms will always be to ask careful questions about which metric actually matters most in a given situation.

But the relative weakness of taillight configuration as a classifier in this example also speaks to the difficulty of identifying which features of a data set might lead to a higher degree of confidence in identification. In order to permit ready discrimination between alternatives—whether those alternatives are objects that might conceivably be present in an image, phonemes in an audio stream, or characters in a body of text— such a feature must be unambiguous, distinctive in some way and independent of any other variable. The effort involved in extracting appropriate candidates from a data set is called "feature engineering," it is still generally done manually, and it remains among the most time-consuming and expensive aspects of training an algorithm.

The problems we associate with bad machine learning are those that arise when an inappropriate feature is used in classification, or the process of abstraction otherwise goes wrong. Broadly speaking, there are two ways in which this can happen: *overfitting* and *bias*. Overfitting means that an algorithm has "memorized" training data rather than learning to generalize from it, which most often happens when the training set sharply diverges from what it experiences in the real world. Perhaps all of the Camaros our algorithm was shown in the training phase happened to be red, and as a consequence it has mistakenly settled on this feature as a definitive classifier, rather than an independent variable. It will therefore have problems with accurate identification when presented with a black Camaro.

Or it could suffer from the opposite problem, bias. In the context of machine learning, bias means that even after extensive training, an algorithm has failed to acquire anything essential at all about the set of target objects it's being asked to identify. An algorithm displaying high bias is basically taking random stabs in the dark, however much confidence it may seem to be mustering in its labeling, and will without hesitation identify outright static as a house, a whale or a chair. (We should be careful to distinguish this sense of the word from its more usual, pejorative sense, in which the implicit prejudices of the party responsible for training an algorithm are reflected in its output—though that happens too, as on the notorious occasion on which a Google Images algorithm identified a picture of black people as "gorillas," apparently because the only training images labeled "people" it had ever been provided had light skin.)[6]

However they might undermine an algorithm's practical utility, or embarrass the software developers involved, errors of bias and overfitting can be corrected. They will eventually yield to patient retraining, involving recalibration of algorithm's internal weightings. At the outside, a human teacher can directly furnish the learning system with heuristic cues, so-called "privileged information"; just as we might expect, these insights sharply accelerate and improve the algorithm's ability to recognize artifacts.

None of this will help, however, if a training set is simply too small or homogeneous to permit generalization to the contents of the real world. An algorithm raised up on such a set will only ever perceive what it has been taught to perceive, whatever should happen to be placed in front of it. It was largely this tendency, coupled to a positive feedback loop, that produced the wildly hallucinogenic images of Google's briefly popular Deep Dream software. The original Deep Dream filter was trained exclusively on the Stanford Dogs Dataset, a body of imagery produced for a competition in which machine-vision algorithms were tasked with distinguishing among 120 different canine breeds.[7] Little wonder, then, that it would see dogs in everything it was shown, especially when same image was passed through the algorithm again and again, sharply amplifying its quality of dogness.

The uncanny ability such an algorithm has to zero in on the all-but-inarticulable essence of something is illustrated by a neural network Yahoo is currently training to automatically characterize images as "not safe for work." When set loose to generate images of its own, it renders a fleshy, Gigeresque landscape that registers as entirely unwholesome, yet never quite resolves into anything specifically identifiable as obscene; whatever writhing, disembodied genitalia you may perceive in the images are artifacts of your own perception.

Done carefully and conscientiously, with whatever hallucinogenic potential it may hold carefully suppressed, supervised machine learning produces impressive results. It has certainly been embraced at scale by commercial enterprises like PayPal and NBC Universal, who use the technique in training algorithms to identify potentially fraudulent payments, or predict which low-demand media properties can most profitably be moved to cheaper offline storage.

But these contexts are fairly static. They evolve only slowly, and so both an algorithm and its teachers enjoy the luxury of time. Faced with unacceptable results, trainers can tune the algorithm, run material to be classified through it, and tweak it again in response to the output, until they arrive at an outcome they're happy with. The challenge ramp ascends sharply, though, when systems are faced with a dynamic multivariate decision space, like directing a car safely through urban traffic. The software controlling a moving vehicle must integrate in real time a highly unstable environment, engine conditions, changes in weather, and the inherently unpredictable behavior of animals, pedestrians, bicyclists, other drivers and random objects it may encounter.[8] (Now the significance of those reports you may have encountered of Google pre-driving nominally autonomous vehicles through the backstreets of its Peninsular domain becomes clearer: its engineers are training their guidance algorithm in what to expect from its first environment.)

For autonomous vehicles, drones, robots and other systems intended to reckon with the real world in this way, then, the grail is *unsupervised deep learning*. As the name implies, the algorithms involved are neither prompted nor guided, but are simply set loose on vast fields of data. Order simply emerges.

The equivalent of classification for unsupervised learning is *clustering*, in which an algorithm starts to develop a sense for what is significant in its environment via a process of accretion. A concrete example will help us understand how this works.

At the end of the 1990s, two engineers named Tim Westegren and Will Glaser developed a rudimentary music-recommendation engine called the Music Genome Project that worked by rebuilding genre from the bottom up. (The engineers eventually founded the Pandora streaming service, and folded their recommendation engine into it.) Music Genome compared the acoustic signatures and other performance characteristics of the pieces of music it was offered, and from them built up associative maps, clustering together all the songs that had similar qualities; after many iterations, these clusters developed a strong resemblance to the musical categories we're familiar with. Nobody had to tell the algorithm what a slow jam was, what qualities defined minimal techno, or how to distinguish Norwegian black metal from Swedish death metal: it made these determinations itself, inductively. The program may not have had any names for these categories, but given any specific piece of music, it was capable of assigning that composition to a cluster any human aficionado would recognize as being appropriate, instantaneously and with a very high degree of accuracy.

This is just how unsupervised learning would work when applied to our example. Rather than being assigned to a known category (i.e. *1968_Charger*) by an instructor, an unsupervised algorithm will group together an emergent cluster of all of the images sharing a particular constellation of features: this particular headlamp configuration, this distinctive paint scheme, this wheelbase. Three robust and well-defined clusters should emerge from the thousand images, possibly orbited by a few edge cases and outliers. In this case, the algorithm will probably not be able to identify the images as belonging to anything beyond *Cluster_1*, *Cluster_2* and *Cluster_3*, but provided with the labels for each would immediately be able to identify any newly presented images of cars. (We should also consider the possibility that it is working in synchrony with a text-recognition module capable of reading trunk-lid or fender badges, in which case it may very well be able to arrive at such determinations unaided.)

And this is the hinge at which machine learning meets big data. The more data it has available to train on, the better an algorithm is able to identify features and useful classifiers, and the more robustly defined the clusters it is likely to discern. The ultimate aim here is unsupervised feature learning, in which an algorithm builds up a sense of what is salient in the world without anyone ever having told it what to look for. Such a system isn't merely developing a picture of the world from first principles, but doing just that from moment to moment. It's as if it were specifically designed to attack the old philosophical question of persistence—just what is it that binds the baby I was to the person I am to the corpse I'll one day be? Does this coffee mug or this chair retain coherent identity across contexts?

Such learning must be "unsupervised" because, again, these questions are no longer abstractions. The algorithms being trained in this way are intended to operate reliably in the real world, as the machinic faculty of discrimination at the heart of autonomous systems charged to operate in the vast unpredictability of the everyday—robots, vehicles, weapons platforms. The consequences of failure here can all too easily be fatal.

In mid-October 2015, the automobile manufacturer Tesla released a new version of the software running their Model S and Model X series cars.[9] Called 7.0, it was an example of the sudden upgrades in capability we are coming to expect from the software-driven objects all around us. This wasn't simply an incremental improvement, though: version 7.0 brought with it a much-anticipated feature that Tesla chose to call Autopilot. This made use of each car's existing suite of onboard cameras and sensors—a forward-looking, long-distance radar system to see through bad weather, cameras equipped with image-recognition software, and a battery of ultrasonic proximity sensors—to achieve a limited degree of autonomous operation.

As far as Tesla was concerned, this capacity was meant to augment, rather than supplant, human guidance. That it *was* limited, however, wasn't always clear from the company's official pronouncements. "The car can do almost anything," enthused CEO Elon Musk, talking up Autopilot at an unveiling event. "We're able to do lane keeping on freeways, automatic cruise control, active emergency braking … It'll self-park. Going a step further, you'll be able to summon the car, if you're on private property." Anyone enticed by this reeling-off of capabilities—or his earlier brag that a driver could take a Model S from San

Francisco to Seattle "without touching the controls at all"—could perhaps be forgiven for missing the hesitant "almost" with which he hedged the claim.[10]

Musk further touted his product's almost uncanny ability to learn from experience, referring to each Model S owner as an "expert trainer" who could tutor Autopilot simply by driving with the mode engaged. Whatever measurements were captured in this way would then propagate across the Tesla network, furnishing the set of learning algorithms at Autopilot's core with an astonishing training set: one million miles' worth of high-resolution driving data added to the collective repository in this way, weighing up to 10 gigabytes per mile, each and every day.[11] Like no real-world product that came before, the entire fleet of Tesla vehicles running version 7.0 would build on whatever knowledge they derived from their encounter with the world, constantly adapting, constantly sharing, constantly improving.

None of that saved Joshua Brown, who was killed in May 2016 when Autopilot steered his 2015 Model S, at full speed, straight into the side of a tractor-trailer turning across his lane.[12]

Brown was history's first known fatality in a crash involving an autonomous vehicle. But he was also a longtime Tesla enthusiast, well known in the owner community; Musk had actually tweeted a video Brown made celebrating Autopilot to his 4.4 million followers, a little over a year prior to the accident.[13] By the standards of adroit public relations as well as those of common decency, the company was compelled to respond with some kind of statement.

Tesla chose to hang a generic title on its blog post commenting on the crash. It was called "A Tragic Loss," as though the victim deserved not a single syllable more than the absolute minimum gesture prescribed by courtesy; perhaps their attorneys had advised them that anything more specific would be injudicious.[14] The copy in the body of the statement was similarly *pro forma*, explaining that the "customer who died in this crash had a loving family and we are beyond saddened by their loss," as though the presence of a loving, or any, family was the only factor that made Brown's death worth mourning.

A dutiful recitation followed of all of the occasions on which the Model S user interface and documentation informed a driver of the "need to maintain control and responsibility for [their] vehicle" while using Autopilot. Even in context, it reads like something intended as nervous self-reassurance. Tin-eared though this may have been, however, it wasn't yet the oddest aspect of a very odd piece of writing. A single sentence buried halfway through the post delivers this disquieting explanation for the cause of the crash: "Neither Autopilot nor the driver noticed the white side of the tractor trailer against a brightly lit sky, so the brake was not applied." Horrifyingly, Brown's Model S never slowed, never even thought to slow, because it didn't see anything it might have needed to slow for.

This apparent whiteout gives us some insight into the way a Tesla Model S equipped with Autopilot perceives the world. In failing to detect the outline of a white truck against a white sky, this ensemble of sensors and interpretive algorithms foundered at the most basic task of vision, resolving a figure from its background. That it did so is unsurprising, though, when we consider what Autopilot was actually designed to do: keep the car centered on well-maintained freeways with clear, high-contrast lane markings. In other words, the moment the first driver took to the roads in a car running Autopilot, a gulf opened up between what the function could actually do and its implicit premise—a premise underwritten by everything from Musk's public commentary to Tesla's choice of naming. Joshua Brown accepted that premise at face value, and it killed him.

In the wake of Brown's death, Tesla tried mightily to steer public opinion toward the conclusion that any lapse in vigilance was entirely his own. A followup post on the corporate blog, complaining about negative media coverage of the crash, reiterated the official position that Autopilot is nothing more than "a driver assistance system that maintains a vehicle's position in lane and adjusts the vehicle's speed to match surrounding traffic."[15] It didn't address why, that being the case, they hadn't chosen to call the feature Autolane.

It wasn't just the feature's name, of course, that left Brown with the idea that he was safe in relinquishing control of his car. Autopilot was introduced at a time of significant hype about autonomous vehicles, by no means all of it Musk's own, and if we understand the choice of name as being part of a commercial product-differentiation strategy, we also need to consider what Tesla thought it needed to be differentiated from. The notion that a car might safely operate itself under conditions of highway driving was in the air more broadly in the culture, and the release of Autopilot merely reinforced it.

Those most knowledgeable about the current state of the art in machine learning and autonomous guidance had argued that it was irresponsible of Tesla to release any such feature, whatever its name, until it was capable of delivering on everything it implied.[16] But the company's behavior was unsurprising given the pressures it was exposed to in the contemporary market economy. The idea that a manufacturer might hold off from shipping a feature until it can actually achieve all the things its prospective users have been led to believe it can feels like an artifact from a long-gone age of centralized production, when the entire decision nexus of an industry might feasibly be gathered at a single conference-room table. It has virtually no chance of prevailing in a world where productive capacity is so widely distributed. Some party will always be hungry to claim the first-mover advantage, to benefit from the perception of being first to market with autonomous capability, and will do assuredly do everything this side of the law to make promises that they've achieved it. It will take more than a disclaimer in the licensing agreement, or a few lines of boilerplate tucked away at the bottom of the press releases, to keep people from believing them.

The gulf between what we believe about automated systems are capable of and what they can actually do is only one of the frictions that confronts us as such systems like Tesla's Autopilot become ever more prominent in shaping the circumstances of everyday life. Not one of these systems is simple in itself, and they interact in complicated ways. They subtly alter the ways we see and engage with the world, and in particular they pose

troubling implications for our ability to apprehend the arrangements of power we contend with. But developing some sense
of what they do is critical to understanding the deal we strike
whenever we surrender control of a situation to the judgment
of algorithms.

The tacit bargain that automation offers us is that in exchange
for some perceived enhancement of performance, we relinquish
discretion, and at least some degree of control over a situation.
Sometimes this act of stepping away is trivial—virtually no one
other than the individual dispossessed of a job directly suffers
when robotized sleds replace human workers in the warehouse—
and sometimes it feels more like a vital surrender of judgment, as
in the development of that class of systems the United Nations
refers to as "lethal autonomous robotics."[17] This suggests a
common-sense way of reckoning with the impact of automated
systems, the axes of what we might call a matrix of concern:
the more people affected by a particular act of automation, the
more vulnerable those people are, and the harder it would be to
reverse its effects, the more cautious we should be in enacting
it. Our task as a society would then be to determine just where
in this envelope any given proposed displacement lies. By these
lights, we ought to have a great deal of concern when someone
is proposing to bring learning algorithms to bear directly to bear
on decisions of great public consequence, on a population that is
already at risk, with immediate and life-changing consequences.

As we've seen, data analytics is a fourfold process that involves
collecting large volumes of facts about the world; *sifting* them
algorithmically, to reveal whatever patterns are latent within
them; *inspecting* those patterns to determine optimal points for
intervention; and finally, *acting* on that knowledge to reshape
the trajectory of the system being studied, so that its future
evolution more closely conforms with desire.

This is a powerful and highly generalizable set of capabilities,
and in principle it can be applied to the management of any
complex system, from the steering and guidance of a car to the
shaping of public policy. When applied to the maintenance of

public order, this capability is called *predictive policing*. The idea is that, equipped with nothing more than a sufficiently rich set of data on past incidents, public safety departments can predict crime hotspots, and even individual criminals, with a high degree of accuracy, far enough ahead of time that they are able to circumvent any actual offense. (Proponents of this approach invariably cite the "precrime" unit of Steven Spielberg's 2002 *Minority Report,* evidently mistaking the film's depiction of dystopian oppression for an aspirational goal.)[18] There are a few different approaches and strategies bound up in the practice of predictive policing, but what they all have in common is that they propose to sit in Olympian detachment, far removed from the play of events, and reach down into all the murk of our affairs to wrest the single salient truth from a whirling storm of confusion.

The simplest tools mobilized in predictive policing efforts, and in a way the most general, are dedicated to geolocating and otherwise parsing the things people say on social media, in the hopes of drawing actionable inferences from them. This is the province of "location-based social intelligence" applications like Snaptrends and SpatialKey, which promise to "identify, isolate and assess" threats, whether direct or indirect. A Snaptrends brochure for prospective customers in the law enforcement sector makes the proposition explicit: "From angry Facebook posts to suggestive Instagram uploads, today's would-be criminals often leave A STRING OF CLUES across social media," and a public-safety agency made aware of those CLUES can deploy its resources in time to preempt the commission of crime.[19]

Such tools use sentiment analysis, a facet of the emerging pseudoscience of "intent recognition," to extract actionable intelligence from utterances.[20] But it's astonishing that anyone takes sentiment analysis seriously in any but the most trivial applications, let alone what is all too often the life-or-death context of a police stop. The algorithms involved are notoriously crude and simple-minded, stumbling when confronted with sarcasm and other common modes of expression. They have trouble with word order, double negatives, ambiguous qualifiers and inverted sentence structures.[21] In short, they simply cannot be relied upon to distinguish even the most obvious snark from a genuine CLUE.

More insidiously, context necessarily colors the interpretation of otherwise-innocuous utterances, especially utterances swept up by the kind of braindead, single-keyword searches Snaptrends showcases in its promotional literature. When I use the word "heroin" in a social-media post, I could be responding when asked to name my favorite Velvet Underground song, or discussing allegations that the CIA's Air America was involved in drug trafficking in Laos in the late 1960s, or misspelling the gendered term for the protagonist of a work of fiction, but what I am almost certainly not doing is openly offering the Schedule I drug known by that name for sale.

And yet this starkly unlikely scenario is what is being inferred in an act of collection of this sort. It will register against my identity, tagging me as well as anyone unwise enough to communicate with me as people with a known interest in illicit drugs, as we are snared in automated round-ups of "activity clusters" and "relationship networks." Should our activity climb past some threshold of intensity that is never specified by either Snaptrends or its client agencies, we may become the subject of intensified monitoring, or even physical surveillance. (Those worried about the clear potential for mission creep and overreach will surely breathe a sigh of relief at the reassurances of Racine, Wisconsin police public affairs officer Jessie Metoyer, who promised a reporter that, at least in the hands of her department, Snaptrends "would strictly be used for criminal investigation purposes.")[22]

Seemingly miffed by the implication that their product might entrain thoroughly illegal searches and seizures, Snaptrends falls back on a blame-the-victim strategy, arguing that if social media users don't want to wind up in the crosshairs of official attention, they might want to apply a greater degree of prudence in the things they choose to post. (A Snaptrends representative patronizingly explained that there can be "no expectation [of privacy] with open settings.")[23]

Even beyond the distasteful premise of this argument, it's unfair to expect this degree of sophistication from users in a milieu where privacy settings are often deliberately obscured—and for that matter, in which millions of Facebook users don't even understand that they're using the internet.[24] As absurdly, offensively shallow as all of this may be, it is what the automation of administrative awareness actually means. The only quality that distinguishes it from low comedy is the distant nagging understanding that life chances, and lives, hang in the balance wherever such tools are taken at face value by the undertrained, the uncaring or the outright gullible.

The next stage of "intelligent policing" is so-called redboxing, in which predictive algorithms preferentially dispatch police units to neighborhoods or specific locales considered to be at particularly high risk of crime. An analytic package called PredPol, which has been licensed by more than sixty American police departments, including those of Los Angeles and Atlanta, is among the redboxing market leaders—in fact, the company's logo is a stylized red box. PredPol furnishes patrol units with a list of the ten to twenty locations in their assigned area of operation where it believes crime is most likely to occur over the course of their shift.[25]

Different departments have their different ways of making use of this intelligence. The Modesto, California, PD parks their Mobile Overt Surveillance System vehicle, otherwise known as the Armadillo, in redboxed hotspots, as a heavily armored, all-seeing standing deterrent.[26] The LAPD takes an approach rather more suited to our mediated age, and tweets the location of identified redboxes so the civic-minded can keep a watchful eye on them. Still other departments simply "flood the zone" with patrol officers.

PredPol's site sports a variety of claims for the product's efficacy, all well larded with statistics and all worded with the most exquisite lawyerly precision. The company appears happy to leave a casual reader with the impression that use of its algorithm significantly reduces crime without ever actually coming out and making that claim, perhaps because it cannot.

But common sense suggests what will happen whenever a supervisory presence is brought to bear more heavily on one place than another: a higher percentage of whatever crimes that are being committed in that neighborhood will be detected, even if the baseline level of criminality in other places is identical, or still higher. That the obvious logical flaws in predictive approaches like this surrender to a few moments' consideration suggests a few basic possibilities, both disturbing: either their promoters don't know, or they don't care.

As Charlotte-Mecklenburg, North Carolina police chief Rodney Monroe points out, though, "We're not just looking for crime. We're looking for people."[27] And that is precisely the aim of what is without doubt the most notorious of current-generation predictive policing initiatives, the Chicago Police Department's so-called Heat List.[28]

This is an algorithmically compiled index of the 1,400 Chicagoans the city's police department considers most likely to commit, or suffer, homicide at some unspecified point in the future. It is not a matter of idle interest: having identified these individuals, CPD teams actually go out and visit them at their homes and street corners and places of work. Again, so far as the Police Department is aware, the named individuals have not yet committed any known crime of interest—and yet there they are, knocking on the door and asking to be let in for a brief chat. (I had promised myself that I wouldn't use the clichéd description "Orwellian" for any of this, but the official name for these visits, "Custom Notifications," really does seem to demand it.)[29] Whether this can be squared with the Fourth Amendment to the United States Constitution, which nominally protects citizens against unreasonable search and seizure, and the Fifth and Fourteenth, which guarantee them the right to the due process of law, is not yet a settled question. Concerns have also been expressed that the program amounts to a reintroduction of racial profiling through the back door—in other words that the Heat List is indeed, and in so many words, a *Minority Report*.[30]

But there's no way any of us can know for sure whether or not this is the case. Beyond generalities, its operators refuse to discuss the most basic questions about this tool, like how you get on the list, how you get off it, who has access, how long it persists and how its use is regulated.[31] The most they're willing to admit is that prior arrests and conviction records are heavily weighted in its algorithm, with the by-now usual implication that those with nothing to hide have nothing to fear. You don't have to believe each and every last person on the list is a model citizen in order to be wildly disturbed by this—and it's still more disturbing to contemplate this capability in the hands, specifically, of the Chicago PD, a force with a documented penchant for rogue operations,[32] a record of having literally maintained black sites,[33] and a thoroughgoing culture of impunity.[34] (A similar program was piloted in London in 2014, the fruit of a collaboration between consultancy Accenture and the Metropolitan Police; it remains to be seen whether the Met's interpretation is any less problematic.)[35]

You might ask what the problem is with programs like Snaptrends, PredPol or Chicago's Heat List, if they keep innocent people safe and free from harm? What's so offensive about algorithmically mediated interdiction, if it keeps young black men especially from being drawn (further) into the clutches of a prison-industrial complex all but certain to grind them to dust?

One way of answering might be to point out that PredPol and similar redboxing tools don't so much criminalize behavior as they criminalize the simple fact of physical presence. Suspicion is shed upon you not for anything you've done, or even for anything you *might* do, but simply because you happen to occupy an area of interest. (As one skeptical criminal-justice scholar characterized the insinuation it presents to a patrol officer, "I go in this box, and everybody's Michael Brown.")[36]

In response, PredPol's chief of research and development Jeffrey Brantingham is quick to reply that "this is about predicting where and when a crime is most likely to occur, not who will commit it."[37] But this is sophistry. Brantingham's is a distinction without a difference—as he certainly would have known, given that the geosocial model prevailing in the field, "travel-to-crime," which asserts that most offenses are committed within a relatively short distance of a criminal's home or base, was developed by his parents, Patricia and Paul, in the 1980s.[38]

Another way of considering the question might call attention to the salience of that which is *not* being measured by these systems. In economics as in physics there is a property called "path dependence," which is the tendency of a dynamic system to evolve in ways that are determined by decisions made in its past. That system might have taken any number of different developmental paths at its outset, but once embarked on a particular course, the choice of trajectories it will enjoy as time unfolds is strongly constrained by the choices that came before. There is a very real danger of path dependence in the use of predictive analytics, based as they are on the notion that meaningful inferences about the future can be drawn from a consideration of the prior distribution of events.

Predictive policing may seem to be concerned with the future, in other words, but the future in question is one oddly entangled with the past. A neighborhood in which a statistically significant spike in felony assault has taken place may find itself the focus of intensive patrolling moving forward, leading to new citations for felony assault being issued at a rate far above the citywide average, and therefore new cycles of police vigilance. A teenager who was once tagged in a Facebook picture alongside friends throwing gang signs may be swept up a social network analysis, find her whereabouts, activities and patterns of association tracked, and eventually be cited for some trivial offense that anyone else (or even she herself, prior to the descent of this watchfulness) might have gotten away with.

She will, of course, thereafter have a criminal record; given that predictive algorithms are known to weight prior offenses heavily as predictors of future run-ins with the law, she will show up sooner and higher on all such rankings, even as other people—equally or perhaps far more inclined to criminal behavior—slip through the weave and evade detection. And this is even before considering the impact of those many varieties of crime that are corrosive of a community's trust, insulting to its hopes and injurious to its fortunes, yet aren't measured by any kind of algorithm at all.

We have a word for all of this, and it's *bias*.

None of the operations of these tools are in any way free from human discretion, however much those responsible for engineering them might want us to believe otherwise. Heat List developer Miles Wernick, by training and experience a specialist in medical imaging, defends his creation against charges of racial, or any other, bias by claiming that the algorithm is intended "to evaluate the risk of violence in an unbiased, quantitative way." A representative of the organization sponsoring Wernick's work, the National Institute of Justice, expands on his point: the individuals named on the Heat List "are persons who the model has determined are those most likely to be involved in a shooting or homicide, with probabilities that are hundreds of times that of an ordinary citizen."[39]

To be sure. But we constantly need to remind ourselves that somebody designed that model—if not Wernick himself, then some other specific, identifiable actor, operating inside history. Somebody selected its sources, devised its features and weightings, or at the very least validated that some attribute happened upon by an automated feature-extraction process was indeed a likely signifier of criminal intent. At every step of the way, human judgments were folded into the ostensibly neutral operation of the algorithm.

Proponents argue that these tools transcend the fallible knowledge, the profoundly situated experience and the variable training of the individual public-safety officer, and supplant it with a cool and dispassionate collective intelligence derived from a million points of data. But what is that intelligence other than a distillation of the way we've chosen to order our societies in the past?

The choices we make in designing an algorithm have profound consequences for the things that are sorted by it. Even the choice of weighting applied to a single variable can lead to different effects in the application of an algorithmic tool.

Let's say that as a municipal administrator concerned with the maintenance of good order and the protection of the citizenry, you want to flag and neutralize as many potential murderers as possible, before they're able to do any harm. Your review of the data offers you only a few selectors to work with, but you eventually determine that of the seven individuals charged with homicide in your district in the past six months—*charged with*, mind you, not *convicted of*, because a separate agency holds that set of data, and you don't have access to it—100 percent of them are males from single-parent households, between the ages of eighteen and thirty, who lack anything beyond a high-school education. Each of them naturally has other qualities, life experiences and attributes, but this is the only set of features they all share. And so this becomes the cluster of features around which you develop your predictive algorithm. You have chosen to optimize for *recall*.

In the six months that follow, every time someone who matches these criteria comes into your field of awareness, in the course of a traffic stop or an unrelated investigation, his file is flagged for intensive follow-up. This means not seven, not eight or nine potential murderers have been diverted into your intervention program, but hundreds of them, each of whom precisely conforms to the contours of your model. And you can get in front of the press and the public, and tell them with a clear conscience that your model is *clean*. It never once mentions race, or anything like it. It is as limpidly neutral as can be.

Is it, though? Is there any way in which your set of sorting criteria might strongly correlate with other features of the target set—features that no ethical designer could ever legitimately consider, like race or income? Not that you would intentionally choose your selection criteria as a proxy for those features, of course, but it will be very hard for you to argue that you are entirely free from the mire of the past.

And just as important, are those factors in any way meaningfully predictive of a propensity to commit homicide? There is in principle no way of measuring the frequency of events that have failed to happen. But let's, for the sake of argument, assume that your algorithm didn't miss a single one of the residents of your district who would have gone on to pull the trigger on someone in that six-month period. Either what you developed is just preternaturally accurate or, what is far more likely, some false positives have been folded up into its assessment of likely criminality. In this case, that anodyne technical term—*false positive*—means that entirely innocent people have been saddled with the identity "criminal" and swept up into your dragnet, with everything that implies for their life chances. And in the United States, anyway, this is clearly illegal: it blatantly violates the Constitutional guarantees that all citizens in principle enjoy equally.

So in the United States, if the law is to be observed, recall *can't* be the criterion that is emphasized in the design of a predictive policing algorithm. It has to be accuracy. A successful system, by these lights, would necessarily tolerate some false negatives to ensure that it doesn't entangle any false positives. Making the terms of this bargain explicit: some actual bad actors will escape your net of computational awareness—and presumably go on to cause harms that theoretically could have been pre-vented—because the alternative is Constitutionally and ethically intolerable. Other societies could, of course, arrive at just the opposite determination: that sweeping the occasional innocent into the clutches of an algorithmic gill net is the regrettable, but eminently acceptable, cost of full assurance. Thankfully, that's not the society we happen to live in at the moment. You, as the party responsible for the design of a predictive algorithm, can choose to do otherwise.

We are told that the Heat List works—that 70 percent of the people shot in Chicago during the first six months of 2016 were already on it, and 80 percent of those arrested in connection with these incidents.[40] But that definition of "working" is dif-ficult to square with the reality that the number of homicides committed with a firearm have continue to rise in the city since the List's introduction and the advent of Custom Notifications. Chicago police superintendent Eddie Johnson explains this as a shortfall in execution, rather than conception: "We are targeting the correct individuals, we just need our judicial partners and our state legislators to hold these people accountable."[41]

And more pressing still is the question of what using a tool like this does to us. If a tool like the Heat List "works," what was the cost of that efficacy?[42]

The promise of preventing some future harm seems to justify just about any action taken in the present. It's hard to argue with this when the future harms imagined involve a level of everyday violence no one should ever be asked to become used to. But the very first thing we learn when we evaluate systems like PredPol and the Heat List is that the consequences of adopting them cannot in any way be said to break over us equally. The geographer Ben Anderson makes this uncomfortably plain in his account of the way these systems work: "Certain lives may have to be abandoned, damaged or destroyed in order to protect, save or care for life" that is considered to be more valuable.[43]

This is an explosive thing to admit, especially at a time when the Black Lives Matter movement is bringing sustained attention to bear on issues of structural injustice, reflexive overpolicing of communities of color, state violence, and impunity for state actors implicated in that violence. We can be sure that in no society will the terms of this bargain ever be spoken aloud by the parties proposing it, and certainly not in so many words. But we shouldn't fool ourselves as to what's actually happening when we embrace tools that claim to magick away centuries of discrimination.

And this speaks more deeply still to the question of automation, and all the contexts in which it might be welcomed for its supposed rationality, objectivity and neutrality. The evidence presented to us by the current generation of algorithmic tools suggests that this is a fool's errand, that there can and will be no "escape from politics" into the comfort of governance by math. What we will be left with is a picture of ourselves, a diagram of all the ways in which we've chosen to allocate power, and an unforgiving map of the consequences. Whether we will ever summon the courage to confront those consequences with integrity is something that no algorithm can decide.

What happens when pattern-recognition systems disclose uncomfortable truths to us, or at least uncomfortable facts?

We hardly lack familiarity with the conscious introduction of uncomfortable facts into public debate. Self-delighted pop contrarians like Malcolm Gladwell and the *Freakonomics* team of Steven D. Levitt and Stephen J. Dubner have built careers on observing seemingly counterintuitive correlations that turn out to have a reasonable amount of explanatory force—for example, claims that the observed downturn in violent crime in the United States following 1991 can be traced to the more liberal access to abortion that American women had enjoyed starting twenty years earlier.[44] Their arguments tend to take the form "everything you think you know is wrong," and despite what might appear to be a slap-in-the-face quality, they're easily assimilated by the mainstream culture. If anything, the factoids dispensed by observers like these often become part of the conventional wisdom with astonishing rapidity.

But the reason why these narratives get adopted so quickly has a great deal to do with their inherent conservatism, the ways in which they can be wielded to support prejudices with existing potency in the culture. What if an algorithmic trawl through the available data surfaces a significantly more abrasive pattern of facts, something that's harder to square with the way we'd prefer to present ourselves and our institutions? For example, what if a multidimensional analysis conducted for a big-city police department revealed, with absolute statistical certainty, that hiring mildly overweight white male veterans of the US armed forces between the ages of twenty-five and forty-five, who purchase domestic beer in cans and consume mixed-martial arts media, is overwhelmingly correlated with use-of-force incidents and subsequent liability claims? Is this the kind of interruption of conventional wisdom that would easily be tolerated?

We've seen that a coffee mug or a curb can be identified by machine-vision systems with relative ease. But most of the objects and other features an algorithmic system will be tasked with characterizing have identities and meanings somewhat more charged than that—and this, of course, is where things start to get complicated. You can teach an algorithm to recognize a table readily enough, based on its characteristics and the ways in which it relates to the world's other contents. It might be able to identify, with successively finer degrees of precision, a *vehicle*, a *car*, a *police car*, a *New York City police car*. That's straightforward enough. But how do you teach it to recognize *poverty?*

Or *do* you teach it to recognize any such abstraction in the first place? We assume that if an algorithmic system is to have effective agency in public affairs, it must respond to the same categories we do. What is more likely, however, is that an unsupervised learning system will have no *a priori* notions of "person" or "community" at all, let alone "taxpayer" or "citizen" or "grievance." Where we might think of ourselves as working class, or Scots Irish, or Sikh, or a San Diegan, or a Republican, none of those categories mean anything to a learning algorithm, except possibly as tags for closely correlated syndromes of human behavior.

A learning algorithm will derive the categories that are salient to it, building them from the bottom up. Here the rhetorical function of data in the sense we're accustomed to—as something marshaled in support of an argument—is inverted, as the patterns and syndromes of fact disclosed to us instead begin to *suggest* arguments that might be made about the state of the world.[45]

And as a result, such systems may, just like a child, innocently come up with fairly pointed and uncomfortable questions. Why *does* this group of people not receive as many resources as those others, when it clearly limits their ability to act in the world? Why *are* service calls in this district responded to so much more quickly than those originating in this other neighborhood? So long as such questions do not appear to originate from some tacit bias within the algorithm itself, I believe (to paraphrase Brian Eno) that they ought to be honored as a hidden intention wherever they arise[46]—a gift from the collective unconscious, and a rare hint that the most effective way of solving the problem at hand might involve frontally engaging a set of circumstances we ordinarily prefer to ignore.

Sometimes this will involve asking pointed questions about the nature and intended purpose of the sensemaking tools we are offered. The premise of algorithmic technologies is not merely that they detect patterns, after all, but that they help us *recognize* them, and this in turn implies that there is something semantically meaningful to us in that which is identified. Why is this object of interest? What does our interest in it imply?

In learning to question what motivates the design of our sensemaking tools, we might want to ask, for example, what desire is being spoken to when machine-vision engineers devise an algorithm that sorts people passing through the gaze of a camera by gender. The justifications underlying the development of such an algorithm range from ends most of us would be likely to endorse—the automated characterization of images circulated online by child pornographers, for example, to aid in the protection of the children involved[47]—to others we might be far less comfortable with, many of which are founded in the fact that women and men have differential value as audiences for advertising.[48] We should be attentive to the reasons why a specific party proposes to deploy a specific technology in a specific context, and sometimes the answers to such questions will indeed tell us everything we need to know.

But there's an additional factor complicating our evaluation of algorithms belonging to this particular class, and it's independent of any justification that may be offered for their use. At the current state of development, when an algorithm proposes to "determine gender," it does so by retrieving measurements of facial structure from an image—jawbone length, distance between the eyes, and so on—and comparing these values to the ones associated with the label *male* or *female* in whatever set of images it was trained on.[49]

Biology may not be destiny, in other words, or gender itself anything but a performance,[50] but you wouldn't know any of that from reading the descriptions of systems like these, in which advanced methods like genetic algorithms and support vector machines are marshaled to render a simple binary decision.[51] Whatever the justification behind deploying a system based on such methods, all questions of identity, fluidity, multiplicity or an individual's right to construct the way they are perceived by the world are here foreclosed, while a certain degree of misgendering is automated.

Not every algorithm is going to face complexities of this exact type, of course, but here bias (an incomplete or inadequate view of the world held by the algorithm's designers) and legibility (the sifting of a set of facts so as to render the patterns within it available for inspection) combine to produce an effect I think of as *overtransparency*. This is a surfacing of some state of affairs, whether based in fact or "fact," that causes a significant degree of social friction or harm, and it is bound to be a routine property of our broader embrace of algorithmic orderings. Preventing the emergence of situations like this, keeping automated systems from drifting back toward the inscription of received social categories, will require constant vigilance, some degree of technical sophistication and the mobilization of opinion—and all of these things require the exertion of energy. What I worry is that those with the most to lose from overtransparency may have the least energy available with which to counter it.

The burdens of overtransparency, perhaps unsurprisingly, will weigh particularly hard on the poor and the powerless. But some portion of that burden will fall on every one of us, whatever our status or situation. For example, when walking down a city street, we still tend to nurture the unconscious assumption that we are somehow insulated in our privacy by the others surrounding us. But the advent of powerful facial-recognition algorithms, and particularly the escape of those algorithms from their original context, threatens our ability to remain anonymous in this way—and by extension, our ability to assemble in public, demonstrate collective grievances and assert popular power.

This is the lesson of the recent Russian application FindFace, which lets users upload a picture of someone unknown to them, and compare it to those shared to the Russian-language social network Vkontakte by its roughly 200 million users. FindFace's primary innovation isn't so much its raw pattern-matching ability—so far, the matches it comes up are accurate only around 70 percent of the time—but its speed; developer Alexander Kabakov brags that "[w]ith this algorithm, you can search through a billion photographs in less than a second."[52]

It didn't take users much longer than a second to figure out what they wanted to do with it. By the time FindFace had been in the wild for a month, it had already been used by a photographer to identify hundreds of random strangers riding the St. Petersburg metro,[53] and by an organized cabal of misogynist trolls to out and otherwise harass women working in the sex industry.[54] What may have seemed like an amusing party trick when described in the abstract begins to look a lot more serious when packaged as an app and made available to a broad public. The stakes get higher still when that capability is grasped by the state: Kabakov and his partner are currently concluding an agreement with the Moscow city administration to furnish the municipality's 150,000 CCTV cameras with their face-recognition algorithm.

This story epitomizes so many of the more troubling aspects of our encounter with algorithmic tools, all at once. It demonstrates the modularity of technology, how easily an algorithm developed in one context can be ported to another. It demonstrates how a developer's commercial interest so often overwhelms any concern they may have preserved for ethical behavior, or the fortunes of anyone affected by the tools they bring into being. It surfaces and makes plain the violence that has always been implicit in the power to see and the power to sort. Most specifically, it demonstrates how assumptions that have framed urban experience since human beings first gathered in cities are being undermined by newly emergent technical capability.

There are, of course, other ways in which the advent of overtransparency threatens freedom of assembly. So-called "group event detection" algorithms applied to the real-time analysis of video allow police forces to determine when a group of two or more has formed.[55] Simulations of crowd behavior are used to better understand how social disturbances arise, pinpointing the "catalyzed space-time clusters of rebellion" unrest ripples out from, and identifying how those clusters can be disrupted.[56] Still other algorithms determine how many troops will be needed to suppress outbreaks of disorder, built right into municipal management systems in so many words, as a dropdown menu option available to administrators.[57] As applied to the city, the language of algorithms is that of "anticipatory surveillance," "scalable anomaly detection"[58] and preemptive control. The kind of conclusions that drop out of this body of work ("to quell the riot, you have to arrest 40 percent of the rioters") chill the blood, especially when coupled with the ability to identify specific individuals of interest as they move within the surging crowd.

But equally important is that virtually none of the algorithmic tools used in crowd control were originally developed for this set of applications. A learning algorithm that has outstripped the baseline of human cognitive performance may be of little enough concern in the lab, or even as part of a trade-show demo, so long as those things are self-contained and inaccessible. The moment it escapes from that context, though—whether its source code is uploaded to the GitHub repository, published in an academic journal, patented and made available for licensure, or simply reverse-engineered by another party—it is in the wild, and can be folded into any number of other systems, advancing ambitions arbitrarily remote from any it was developed to serve. And so it is that code leaps from one platform to another, like a plasmid swapped between organisms in the shallow primordial seas.

Kabakov may have intended FindFace as a diversion, or possibly as a pretext to flirt with women he wouldn't have dared to approach otherwise. The authors of the group-detection software were probably sincere about deploying it in the context of group homes and eldercare. But these technologies have transparently obvious political implications for people who live in places where the freedom of assembly is not guaranteed.

And you could not hand an authoritarian government a more perfect tool for the application of draconian hygiene than something capable of alerting the secret police that a knot of potential dissidents has formed, and identifying them by name. (Sometimes, indeed, little repurposing is required, especially when market actors work in close concert with the state. When the *MIT Technology Review* reports that Chinese search giant Baidu is able to use map searches to "determine, up to three hours in advance, when and where a dangerously large number of people might congregate," it's not at all hard to imagine who their prime customer might be.)[59]

Security expert Bruce Schneier is eminently correct to remind us that "many of these technologies are nowhere near as reliable as claimed."[60] But again, just as with Tesla's Autopilot, the meaningful question isn't whether these technologies work as advertised. It's whether someone *believes* that they do, and acts on that belief. In the end, the greatest threat of overtransparency may be that it erodes the effectiveness of something that has historically furnished an effective brake on power: the permanent possibility that an enraged populace might take to the streets in pursuit of justice.[61] In this light, these algorithms should be seen for what they really are: a series of technical counters to liberty, and steps toward the eclipse of freedoms we have enjoyed since the dawn of the modern public.

Among the most disconcerting aspects of the world we are building is that we will never know the reasons underlying a great many of the things that happen to us in the course of our lives. Already a literal and uninflected description of daily life sounds like nothing so much as the conspiracy theory of a paranoid schizophrenic: we're surrounded by invisible but powerful forces, monitoring us from devices scattered throughout our homes, even placed on our bodies, and those forces are busily compiling detailed dossiers on every last one of us. They pass the contents of these dossiers onto shadowy, unaccountable intermediaries, who use everything they learn to determine the structure of the opportunities extended to us—or, what may be worse, not extended. We'll be offered jobs, or not; loans, or not; loves, or not; cures, or not. And the worst of it is that until the day we die, we'll never know which action or inaction of our own led to any of these outcomes.

This account is enough to stir up visions of Kafka, Borges and Philip K. Dick huddled up in some damp and miserable afterlife, plotting their hundredfold revenge on humanity for some long-forgotten transgression. You wouldn't necessarily want to repeat it word-for-word to a cop, or an intake counselor, or anyone else you needed to convince of your stability and levelheadedness. But there it is, laid out in schematic: the terms under which we now live out our lives.

As the examples of PredPol and the Heat List demonstrate, our ability to inspect the way in which algorithmic power is exerted in the world is already complicated by the impenetrability of the systems involved. They're proprietary business secrets, or the details of their construction aren't being shared with us because some shadowy bureau has determined that their disclosure "would endanger the life or physical safety of law enforcement personnel or any other person." Or it's simply that their guts are lying open before us—every line of code commented with the greatest conscientiousness, the name of every register plain as day—but the whole utterly taxes our ability to comprehend.

As legal scholar Frank Pasquale points out, algorithmic systems are the proverbial "black boxes," in that they produce material effects in the world without necessarily revealing anything about how they did so.[62] This profound murk hampers our ability to evaluate whether or not we feel that the algorithms operating on us are acting in ways consonant with our values.

Whether wielded by a market actor or an institution of state, then, the reasoning behind the judgments rendered by such black boxes is often unavailable for inspection—and this is most likely intentional. Among Pasquale's fundamental points that the structure of what we do and do not know about the way these algorithms work is a site of the most intense interest. Quite simply, some parties derive advantage from the fact that we don't understand the tools used to rank and order us. And this results in a pronounced and troubling asymmetry in the world, when the actors in a position to determine our lives know far more about us than we know, or will ever be able to find out, about them.

The circumstances that are determined in this way aren't simply which songs a streaming service will choose to play you, which restaurant you'll be steered toward upon arrival in an unfamiliar city, or which driver Uber will send to pick you up at the tail-end of a Friday night on the town. They're far more consequential decisions than that—life-altering, even. We've already seen how an HR manager equipped with a workplace-analytics suite can use it to decide questions as laden with import as who to hire and who to let go, how the exercise of the law and the operations of the criminal justice system are equally shaped by the use of algorithmic assessment tools. Similar processes guide the apportionment of financial resources, enhancing or undermining our ability to function as independent actors in the economy.

Of the four major ways in which households in the developed world are sustained economically—via formal employment, the extension of credit, capital gains (at the high end) and government transfers (at the low)—algorithms already condition access to three, and will certainly determine the choice of products you are offered should you be fortunate enough to require the services of a wealth manager. Those algorithms are developed by parties who answer to no one other than their clients or employers, and the tools they produce are almost never assessed on any criterion other than the minimal one that they are broadly seen to work. We should understand this as what it is: an unprecedented intervention by a small set of private and unaccountable actors in the structure of opportunity, and the distribution of life chances.

Among the financial circumstances that are determined in this way, the one with the most pervasive reach is credit score. Via an entirely unsurprising process of mission creep, a narrow and algorithmically determined creditworthiness has become an index of reputational worth that affects your fundamental ability to participate in a fully formalized economy.[63] Just as the Social Security Number was pressed into service as a *de facto* national identity number, so too has credit score been deployed as a selection criterion in contexts it was never intended for and never designed to function in. An individual's credit score affects their employability—a 2013 report prepared by the Demos public-policy research organization concluded that nearly half of all employers used the index to determine hiring decisions for some or all positions[64]—their access to housing, even their access to that most vital of contemporary utilities, a mobile-phone service plan. (If you doubt this last, try signing up for a mobile plan in a country where you lack a credit history.) And all of this, of course, becomes still more important in a time when the state has broadly retreated from the provision of benefits.

Once someone is past the age of majority, moreover, their lack of a credit history is not a neutral fact. It's a charged lacuna, something that can be interpreted as a positive suggestion that one's financial activities are informal, offshore or otherwise illicit—or simply, and perhaps more damningly, that they just aren't reliable in the ways our society constructs reliability. (I think of the "Credit Poles" in Gary Shteyngart's mordantly dystopian *Super Sad True Love Story*, lampposts topped with LED signboards that display pedestrians' credit ratings in real time, and blink a damning red when one's score falls below the threshold.)

The extension of credit operates obscurely, in ways that seem designed to confound oversight and to route around regulations on the way in which creditworthiness is calculated. Consider an algorithm currently being used to assess creditworthiness, based on "subtle patterns of behavior that correlate with repayment or default"[65]—in this case, patterns of mobile-phone usage. This algorithm has been developed by a startup named Branch.co, that seeks to extend financial services to the same market of "the unbanked" we encountered in the context of cryptocurrency technologies. Branch uses both data—the content of text messages and emails—and metadata—the frequency and duration of calls—to build a character model of its subscribers, even weighing whether or not you've bothered to furnish the contacts in your address book with last names. The price of noncompliance with their model of good character is punitive: the interest rate such low-scoring borrowers are assessed literally doubles.

Branch, like many institutions in similar situations, presumably keeps the precise composition of its risk assessment algorithm secret for two main reasons. The first is simply that they derive value from its being a proprietary trade secret, or believe that they do. They think that it gives them a competitive advantage, and they don't want rivals nullifying that advantage by copying it. That part is straightforward enough. But the second reason is that, like all such metrics, these stats can be juked: Branch's algorithm is subject to Goodhart's Law, the principle that "when a measure becomes a target, it ceases to be useful as a measure."[66] In other words, they believe that if it became more widely known just how their algorithm arrived at its determinations, it would be easier for unreliable people to act in ways that would fool it into classifying them as trustworthy.

On the surface, then, this is the same reason that Google holds the precise composition of its search algorithm closely: to prevent it from being gamed by interested parties. But altering a web page so that it might rise higher in a ranking of search results is relatively uncomplicated. By contrast, performing good citizenship in the way Branch's algorithm would require is exhausting; considering the number of separate factors it weighs, and the semi- or even subconscious level at which some of them operate, it may not even be possible. Who, after all, is capable of maintaining conscious control over all the signals we broadcast through our behavior, at the level of data and metadata both?

Here a judgment is being made about what it is that makes a specific human being reliable, in a very narrow context, and has encoded that judgment in a numeric value. That score thereafter serves as a global representation of that person's character. Having developed such a representation, Branch, like any other party in its position, can either license it to other companies as a stand-alone index of reliability, or provide it through an API so it can be folded into some other machinic weighting. And so the judgement once made spreads across the network, and shows up in any number of remote contexts, very much including ones it may never have been intended for.

To recap: *we don't know if the information on which a determination of creditworthiness was founded is correct.* The parties that develop such scores almost never take responsibility for founding prejudicial decisions on bad data—at best, perhaps, they delete that data, rarely with so much as an apology tendered. By the time they do make this correction, though, it may be too late; the information has already cascaded onto other commercial partners, data brokers or other third-party service providers, either in itself or as bundled into an aggregate score.

As well, *we don't know if the algorithm complies with the relevant law.* In the United States, for example, the Federal Trade Commission's inventory of Equal Credit Opportunity Rights explicitly "prohibits credit discrimination on the basis of race, color, religion, national origin, sex, marital status, age, or because you get public assistance," and this is intended to protect certain classes of people who have historically been denied access to financing.[67] Without access to an algorithm, there is no way of knowing whether it observes those provisions—or, perhaps more worryingly, whether the behaviors it weighs transparently serve as proxies for factors that lenders are specifically forbidden by law to consider in their provision of credit.

And finally, without access to its composition, *we can't reconstruct whether the conclusions an algorithm arrives at bear even the slightest relationship to someone's actual propensity to repay a loan.* Like any other sorting algorithm, the ones used in the determination of creditworthiness always direct our attention to a subset of the information that is available. That information may have less bearing on someone's trustworthiness than other facts which might well be more salient, but which by their nature are less accessible to the lender. The mathematician and alternative-banking activist Cathy O'Neil has documented, for example, that lenders systematically refuse credit to borrowers on the basis of "signals more correlated to being uneducated and/or poor than to the willingness or ability to pay back loans," and these signals can be as arbitrary as the fact that they exclusively used capital letters in filling out their loan application.[68]

There might very well be other information that casts a specific individual's reliability in a much better light, but simply isn't available to the lender in numerical form, or available at all. Perhaps behavioral models will improve, as lenders sweep up ever-larger bodies of correlated fact; one German provider claims to use 8,000 data points in determining borrower reliability.[69] But perhaps these models won't actually get any more accurate—and the point is that, in the absence of any right to inspect them, there will be no way any of us will ever know for sure. As long as the systems are "working"—that is, they are producing net benefit and a positive return on investment—any concern for mistaken results, whether it involves the production of false positives or false negatives, can be waved away as a quibble. As things stand now, there is little to no incentive for anyone to fix the situation, and this is especially distressing when that same credit score conditions access to so many of the other goods produced by our society.

For many years now, ever since it first became clear that control over so many of our life chances had passed into the hands of parties equipped with tools like these, concerns about the obscurity of their functioning have prompted calls for "algorithmic accountability." This effort has notably picked up momentum in recent months, culminating in the framing of measures like the European Union's new General Data Protection Regulation, scheduled to take effect in April 2018.[70]

The law has two major provisions. The first is intended to protect vulnerable people from the consequences of automated decisions, and it articulates a series of categories still more comprehensive than the one enunciated by the US Federal

Trade Commission: "racial or ethnic origin, political opinions, religion or philosophical beliefs, trade union membership… data concerning health or data concerning sex life or criminal convictions and offenses."

The desire to protect the vulnerable is, of course, entirely laudable. We've already seen, though, what the problem is with articulating lists of protected categories like this, which is that certain kinds of innocuous data can be used as proxies for factors that developers are forbidden to use in crafting an algorithm. If the law prevents you from using household income as a determination factor in choosing whether to offer someone a loan, you can just use their postal code, which will after all tend to be strongly correlated with income; if health status and medical history are off limits in making a decision about insuring someone, use their browser history, and mine it for its predictive value.[71] If a regulation bans the use of specific items of sensitive data, it leaves open the possibility that proxy values can be found that produce precisely the same discriminatory result. Conversely, as we cannot even in principle specify ahead of time what kinds of correlations might emerge from the analysis of a sufficiently large data set, the only way to prevent all such correlations from being used with discriminatory intent is to ban data capture in the first place—and that's obviously off the table in any technologically advanced society. As Oxford researchers Bryce Goodman and Seth Flaxman point out, then, the EU regulation is either too narrowly written to be effective, or so broadly interpretable as to be unenforceable.

This suggests that it isn't so much the obscurity of any specific algorithm that presents would-be regulators with their greatest challenge, but the larger obscurity of the way in which sorting algorithms work. And this impression is reinforced by the law's second major provision, which aims directly at the question of algorithmic opacity. Its Articles 12 and 13 create "the right to an explanation," requiring that anyone affected by the execution of some algorithmic system be offered the means to understand exactly how it arrived at its judgment, in a "concise, intelligible and easily accessible form, using clear and plain language."

Again, laudable—and again problematic, on two grounds. The implicit logic operating here is that once we are furnished with an explanation, we will be able to act on it in some way. But this places the burden of responsibility on the person the law refers to as the "data subject," who is required to seek out an explanation, and then exercise prudence in their choices once it's been provided to them. The right enunciated here is thoroughly consonant with the neoliberal practice of governmentality, which tends to individualize hazards and recast them as issues of personal responsibility or moral failure, rather than structural and systemic issues. It's a conception of good governance that conflates transparency with accountability: if the information is available, you're expected to act upon it, and if you don't, it's nobody else's fault but your own. This clearly relies entirely too much on the initiative, the bravery and the energy of the individual, and fails to account for those situations, and they will be many, in which that individual is not offered any meaningful choice of action.

Furthermore, this sort of accountability is ill-suited to the time scale in which algorithmic decisions take place—which is to say, in real time. Explanation and redress are by definition reactive and *ex post facto*. The ordinary operation of a sorting algorithm will generally create a new set of facts on the ground,[72] setting new chains of cause and effect in motion; these will reshape the world, in ways that are difficult if not impossible to reverse, long before anyone is able to secure an explanation.

It's evident that the authors of this well-intended regulation either haven't quite understood how algorithms achieve their effects, or have failed to come up with language that might meaningfully constrain how they operate. Their perplexity goes to a deep feature of the way in which predictive algorithmic systems work. Predictive analytics is all about discovering reliable correlations between two seemingly unrelated patterns of fact—for example, between a person's propensity to fill out a loan application in uppercase letters, and the likelihood that they will eventually default on that loan. But as Goodman and Flaxman point out, there's never any concern for causal reasoning involved in making this correlation, nor any attempt to work out how or why these two observations might be related to one another. Nobody's arguing that some-one's idiosyncratic spelling practices *caused* their shaky financial situation; in fact it's highly unlikely that there's any direct connection between the two to speak of. Both are epiphenomenal of some deeper syndrome of behavior. And while that syndrome might well be of interest to a psychologist or a social worker, it's completely immaterial to a prospective lender. From their perspective, it's enough simply to note that a correlation exists, and that it's sufficiently robust to permit the presence of the one to serve as a predictor of the other. So much for the right to an explanation.

And this begins to gesture at the ultimate complication with laws designed to produce algorithmic accountability. It's one thing to feel like you're in the grip of someone else's agenda, that you don't (and won't ever) know how selecting one or another among the options you're being presented with might serve the shadowy ends of another; still worse is the fear that there is no overriding logic at all to the decisions that shape our lives, that these systems behind them exercise their considerable power in an arbitrary and capricious manner. Perhaps worst of all, though, is the fear that there *is* a logic behind such decisions, but that it resides on a plane of complexity permanently inaccessible to the human mind. This is the realm of "opaque intelligence."[73] Who can say, in a layered, cascading, probabilistic model of behavior, what originally triggered a determination that someone is trustworthy, insurable or reliable?

This is not hypothetical. It is affecting the choices we are being presented with right now. Many of the systems we already use every day work in ways that are not fully understood by their designers. On Facebook, for example, "there is no way to know with any certainty why any specific [news item] is included or missing from" the ticker of Trending News stories.[74] The algorithm that makes that determination has already breached the threshold of incomprehensibility. As internet researcher Christian Sandvig told *The Intercept*, the reason that a particular story or controversy appears or does not appear in that list "may not be recoverable." The one that governs the appearance of Trending News is far from the only such algorithm out there, sorting, ordering and classifying as you read these words, and doing so in a way that no human being alive will ever be able to account for.

Calls for algorithmic accountability face the most severe impediments when the computational models in question might have evolved on their own, without the involvement of any human programmer. This is the principle behind the development of so-called genetic algorithms; the technique is not universally applicable, but can often result in stunningly effective designs.[75] And when it does, no human mind will ever be able to account for the decisions it has made. Who would be so unwise as to claim authorship of any such thing? And what does accountability even mean in this context?

And if the logic of any one algorithm is indecipherable, try to imagine how hard it would be to reconstruct the logic behind a given decision when multiple algorithms mesh with one another to produce an outcome, the entire interaction unsurveilled by any human eye. In our tightly coupled, hyperlinked economy, there are any number of circumstances where our fortunes are shaped by such complex multiway interactions. It might not be possible for anyone to determine afterward, even in principle, whether a decision resulted from any particular process of reasoning, or was simply produced by a poorly buffered algorithm interacting with other automated systems in unforeseen, non-linear ways.

The idea that we can somehow force these black boxes open, then, and demand that they render up their secrets in the name of accountability, simply isn't tenable. While Pasquale's call for a move "toward an intelligible society" is entirely welcome, any such thing would require a well-coordinated combination of technical, organizational and regulatory measures. It is not at all clear who would be responsible for articulating those measures, who would have the incentive to undertake them, or how they might be enforced.

The question of incentive naturally prompts some reflection as to just who it is that benefits most from the unfathomable obscurity at the heart of algorithmic systems. And indeed—as Pasquale points out at length in his book, and as we've seen from the examples of Google and Branch—there are certainly circumstances in which some party's interest is advanced by our inability to determine how they arrive at their judgments.

But there's a more distressing possibility, which is that no human party may derive any benefit from it at all. This may simply be the price of invoking systems that operate at higher orders of complexity than any our organic minds can encompass. The kind of opacity we've considered here may therefore simply be the pilot wave of a deeper transition rolling through our societies, as algorithmic decision processes take hold in most spheres of life. In the world we are building, we may well contend with patterns of advantage we cannot discern, allocations of resource that make no obvious sense, arranged in ways (and for reasons) we'll never understand, to advance ends we can only dimly perceive. Even our finely honed cynicism, tuned against centuries' experience of human venality, may not be the surest guide to this set of circumstances.

The black-box quality we see in so many algorithmic systems— the deep obscurity of the methods they use to decide whatever matters that are placed before them—aggravates our ability to make wise choices about them in one final way.

As we saw from the examples of Autopilot and Branch, Snaptrends and PredPol, what often matters most in weighing the degree to which we surrender control to an automated decision-making process isn't so much what a system can actually do, but what we believe it can do. In the absence of better information—guided mostly by the folk beliefs about the capabilities of autonomous systems that completely saturate popular culture, leavened significantly by commercial hype— our estimates of machinic competence can grow to the point that they become dangerous. As Tesla enthusiast Joshua Brown discovered, with fatal consequence, this confusion of desire, belief and actual capability operates at the individual level. But it also functions at the level of entire societies.

A case in point is, again, automated driving. A few years back, a friend with experience in the trucking industry pointed out some of the many complications that would surely beset any attempt at automating away the human driver. He noted that the challenge wasn't merely guiding a cargo vehicle from one point to another, which is comparatively simple, but somehow accounting for everything else that needs to happen in and around that vehicle in order to accomplish the real goal: moving *freight* from one point to another.

As he explained it, "autonomous trucking" really means automating a whole bundle of processes and procedures dedicated to cargo handling, including specialized protocols for the management of live loads or hazardous materials; it means automating the balancing of loads in a moving vehicle, and (at least until route-optimizing algorithms dispense with the necessity of doing so) the swapping of loads between them; and it almost certainly means at least some redesign of loading bays and docks around the world, to accommodate whatever ancillary automation is required by all of this. And reasonably enough, given the magnitude of the effort involved in all this, he concluded from this that automated trucking is some ways off yet.[76]

But all of that doesn't mean that every aspect of the challenge he sketched out won't be essayed, and attacked, and worn down by attrition, however complicated it might have seemed from the outset. Once the conceptually central element of the problem— vehicle control, guidance and navigation—is accomplished, every other subtask wrapped up in logistics suddenly seems like an eminently reasonable and achievable goal, *even if each of them is in itself far more complex than the task of moving the vehicle across a continent.*

Belief, in other words, exerts a peculiar kind of gravitation, pulling history toward it—especially when the belief concerns something as widely desired, for as many reasons, as autonomous trucking. When desire is that overdetermined, the problem sufficiently modular or reducible, and the (hardware and software) components that might be assembled in a solution already in existence in some context, however remote, the resolution of a challenge like this can come to seem very close at hand indeed. It would be absurd to think that that isn't already affecting investments, hiring, training and other allocations of resource, and that it isn't already reflected, however subtly, in the posture and disposition of all the institutions touched on by trucking.

What comes to be the object of belief, in short, resculpts the space of possibilities we're presented with. The conviction that autonomous operation isn't merely possible in principle, but actually imminently practicable, operates at multiple levels, and creates multiple kinds of consequences. I think it's by now reasonably well understood that the truly vexatious complications of automation are almost never technical but legal, regulatory, institutional, and those invariably take longer to settle out than any mere matter of invention and development.

In the meantime, just as was the case with Tesla's Autopilot, a chasm will open up between belief and realization, and we should understand that this is a "meantime" that might span anywhere from months to decades. And what we will contend with in the interim is an impoverished universe of possibilities.

Consider the set of arguments put forth by Florida state senator Jeff Brandes. In his successful 2014 attempt to eliminate subsidies for mass transit in his district, Brandes argued that it was futile to invest in mass transit when an age of autonomous vehicles was dawning upon us: "It's like they're designing the Pony Express in the world of the telegraph."77 Never mind that Pony Express riders historically delivered mail, packages and other things the telegraph could not have; the argument from technological inevitability is a vivid and compelling one, especially for Americans nurtured practically from birth on the belief in a gleaming technological future. If autonomous cars really are just a year or two away, why invest in modes of public transit that would surely be rendered obsolete before they even entered service?

This sentiment carried the day, and the light-rail line Brandes opposed was never built. But Pinellas County, where Brandes prevailed, is a place that desperately needs mass transit. As David Morris reports in *Fortune*, the city and its surrounding region "are consistently near the bottom in a number of transportation and livability indexes. They suffer high average commute times, astronomical pedestrian fatality rates, and massive per-capita spending on the private automobiles that, given today's inadequate public transit system, even the very poorest need to get by." And this will remain true for all the time between the present and any appearance of an automated mobility system capable of serving their needs.

Again, by being politically useful, the mere perception that automation is imminent has produced a new set of facts on the ground. Here the imaginary folds back against the actual, constraining the choices we have in the here and now, forcing us to redesign our lives around something that may never come into being. The lesson for all of us is clear: beliefs about the shape of the future can be invoked, leveraged, even weaponized, to drive change in the present. Even in advance of its realization, automation based on machine learning and the algorithmic analysis of data serves some interests and not others, advances some agendas and not others.

Artificial intelligence

The eclipse of human discretion

Taken together, the practical efforts we've discussed in this book—the massive undertakings of data collection and analysis, the representation of the world in models of ever-increasing resolution and sophistication, and the development of synthetic discretion—have a distinct directionality to them. As groups of people, each acting for their own reasons, bring these discrete capabilities together and fuse them in instrumental ensembles, we finally and suddenly arrive at the place where we must have known we were headed all along: the edge of the human. We have hauled up at the shores of a general artificial intelligence, competent to take up the world as it is, derive meaning from its play of events, and intervene in its evolution, purposively and independently.

For some, this has been a conscious project. At every step of the way, their efforts have been marked by wishful thinking, sloppy reasoning and needless reductionism. Distressingly often, the researchers involved have displayed a lack of curiosity for any form of intelligence beyond that they recognized in themselves, and a marked lack of appreciation for the actual depth and variety of human talent. The project to develop artificial intelligence has very often nurtured a special kind of stupidity in some of its most passionate supporters—a particular sort of arrogant ignorance that only afflicts those of high intellect, as if, when Dunning-Kruger syndrome appears in the very bright, it strikes with tenfold force.[1] But for all these home truths, it has also made very significant progress toward its goals.

There is some truth to what AI supporters argue: that over time, as research succeeds at mastering some aspects of the challenge of teaching a machine to think, those aspects are then no longer thought of as "true artificial intelligence," which is progressively redefined as something perpetually out of reach. For some of the more enthusiastic, it must feel like the prospect of recognition for their achievements is forever receding.

As one supposedly impossible goal after another yields to the advance of automation, falling one after another with the flat clack of dominoes, many of us cling to the subconscious assumption, or hope, that there are some creative tasks technical systems will simply never be able to perform. We tend to think of these in terms of some access to the ineffable that is putatively distinctly and uniquely human, whether that access takes the form of artistic inspiration or high spiritual refinement.

The essence of learning, though, whether human or machinic, is developing the ability to detect, recognize and eventually reproduce patterns. And what poses problems for this line of argument (or hope, whichever it may be) is that many if not all of the greatest works of art—the things we regard as occupying the very pinnacle of human aspiration and achievement—consist of little other than patterns. Richly elaborated and varied upon though they may be, there is nothing magic about them, and nothing in them that ought to prevent their characterization by sufficiently powerful processing engines. The humanist in me recoils at what seems like the brute-force reductionism of statements like this, but beyond some ghostly "inspiration," it's hard to distinguish what constitutes style other than habitual arrangements, whether those be palettes, chord progressions, or frequencies of word use and sentence structure. And these are just the sort of features that are ready-made for extraction via algorithm.

Everyone will have their own favorite examples of an art that seems as if it must transcend reduction. For me, it's the vocal phrasing of Nina Simone. When sitting in a quiet hour, listening to all the ache and steel of life in her voice, it's virtually impossible for me to accept—let alone appreciate, or find tolerable—the notion that everything I hear might be flattened to a series of instructions and executed by machine. I feel much the same way, in vastly different registers, about the cool curves of an Oscar Niemeyer structure, about Ruth Asawa's sculpture, the all-but-anonymous but nevertheless distinctive hand behind the posters of Atelier Populaire or the final words of James Joyce's "The Dead"—about every work or act of human craft I've ever encountered that sent a silent thrill of recognition, glee and *rightness* running through me.

As I say, these are my examples; you'll surely have your own, and I'm sure they do similar things to you. That we feel these shivery things in the presence of the works that move us feels like, must be, evidence of inspiration, if not of a soul plugged right into the infinite.

But we know by now that such structures can be detected, modeled, emulated and projected with relative ease. Something as seemingly intuitive as a Jackson Pollock canvas yields to an analysis of painterly density, force, and velocity. Similarly, entirely new Bach compositions can be generated, passages of music Bach himself never thought nor heard, simply from a rigorous parametric analysis of the BWV. Nor is it simply the icons of high culture that fall before such techniques. One of the redemptive beauties of the human condition is that just about any domain of endeavor can become an expressive medium in the right hands, and someone working in just about any of them can aspire to the condition of art. Every designer has their go-to moves, every storyteller their signature tropes, and every trial lawyer their preferred patterns of precedent and emphasis. Given only sufficient processing power, though, sufficiently well-trained feature-extraction algorithms, and access to a sufficiently large corpus of example works, abstracting these motifs is not much more than trivial.

A recent project called Next Rembrandt set out to do just this, and in at least the coarsest sense, it succeeded in its aims.[2] A team of engineers and data modelers sponsored by Microsoft and the Dutch bank ING plumbed the painter's corpus "to extract the features that make Rembrandt Rembrandt," deriving from them parameters governing every aspect of his work, from his choice of subject and lighting angle to the precise proportions of the "typical Rembrandt eye or nose or ear." Having crunched the data, they arrived at their "conclusive subject"— "a Caucasian male with facial hair, between the ages of thirty and forty, wearing black clothes with a white collar and a hat, facing to the right"—and then used this data set projectively, to create a portrait of someone who never existed, in the unique style of a master three and a half centuries in the ground.

You might quail, as I do, at the disrespectful, even obscene act of reanimation implicit in the project's tag line ("347 years after his death, the next Rembrandt painting is unveiled"). You will very likely cringe, as you should, at the absence of any possibility that the historical Rembrandt Harmenszoon van Rijn might consent to being used in this way. Your soul might die a little death at the bathos and utter banality of the lesson ING evidently derived from their sponsorship of this effort: "Next Rembrandt makes you think about where innovation can take us—what's next?" But to my eye, anyway, the generated painting does capture something of Rembrandt's soulfulness, that characteristic sense of seeming to have been captured on the cusp of a moment I associate with his work. If you shuffled this portrait into a stack with authentic Rembrandts, and asked me to come back in a year and pick out the one among them that had been produced *de novo* via the intercession of a generative algorithm, I'm not at all sure I'd be able to. And, of course, now that the algorithm has been developed, it can be used at will to generate any number of pastiches of equal precision, accuracy and detail, an entire unspeakable postmortal oeuvre—not, in other words, the next Rembrandt, but the one after that, and an endless succession of ones to follow.

This feels like a disturbing precedent. But curiously enough, the 340-odd authenticated Rembrandts known to exist present the would-be replicator with a relatively constrained parameter space. Consider by contrast the game of go. Its 19×19 board admits to some 2×10^{170} legal moves—as commentators seem contractually obligated to note, more configurations by many, many times than there are atoms in the universe. Perhaps this unfathomable void offers still greater scope for poetry, and a final preserve for the human?

Go is a positional game, a game of perfect information; there is no room in it for the operations of chance. Patterns of domination unfold across its board in unforgiving black and white, as one stone after another is placed on the grid of points, each one claiming territory and radiating influence to the points beyond. The set of ramifying possibilities represented by each successive move is a hypergraph far too deep to be swept by brute-force calculation techniques, like those which IBM's Deep Blue used to defeat grandmaster and longtime world chess champion Garry Kasparov in 1997, and so for many years it was thought that mastery in go would long remain the province of human intuition.

Up until very recently, this seemed like a safe bet. At the time chess fell to computational analysis, a mediocre human player could still hold off the most advanced go program available, even if that program had first been granted a significant handicap of four or five stones; even Deep Blue didn't have anything like the processing power necessary to sound the game's boundless depths. There is, of course, much more to go than simply its degree of permutational complexity. But this was the quality that made it irresistible to artificial intelligence researchers, some of the brightest of whom took it up on a professional level simply so they could get a better sense for its dynamics.

A few of the most dedicated wound up working together at a London-based subsidiary of Google called DeepMind, where they succeeded in developing a program named AlphaGo.[3] AlphaGo isn't just one thing, but a stack of multiple kinds of neural network and learning algorithm laminated together. Its two primary tools are a "policy network," trained to predict and select the moves that the most expert human players would make from any given position on the board, and a "value network," which plays each of the moves identified by the policy network forward to a depth of around thirty turns, and evaluates where Black and White stand in relation to one another at that juncture. These tools are supplemented by a reinforcement-learning module that allows AlphaGo to hive off slightly different versions of itself, set them against one another, and derive the underlying strategic lessons from a long succession of training games played between the two.

For all its capability, DeepBlue was a machine of relatively conventional architecture. In defeating Kasparov, it relied on a brute-force tree search, a technique in which massive amounts of processing power are dedicated to mapping out every conceivable move accessible from the current state of play. It is, no doubt, far easier to say this in retrospect, but there's something mechanical about this. It doesn't feel anything like intelligence, because it isn't anything like intelligence. Deep Blue was a special-purpose engine exquisitely optimized for—and therefore completely useless at anything other than—the rules of chess. By contrast, AlphaGo is a general learning machine, here being applied to the rules of go simply because that is the richest challenge its designers could conceive of, the highest bar they could set for it.

In March 2016, in a hotel ballroom in Seoul, DeepMind set its AlphaGo against Lee Sedol, a player of 9-*dan*—the highest rank. Lee has been playing go professionally since the age of twelve, and is regarded among cognoscenti as one of the game's all-time greatest players. His mastery is of a particularly counterintuitive sort: he is fond of gambits that would surely entrain disaster in the hands of any other player, including one called the "broken ladder" that is literally taught to beginners as the very definition of a situation to avoid. And from these vulnerable positions Lee all but invariably prevails. A book analyzing his games against Chinese "master of masters" Gu Li is simply titled *Relentless*.[4]

In Seoul Lee fell swiftly, losing to AlphaGo by four matches to one.

Here is DeepMind lead developer David Silver, recounting the advantages AlphaGo has over Lee, or any other human player: "Humans have weaknesses. They get tired when they play a very long match; they can play mistakes. They are not able to make the precise, tree-based computation that a computer can actually perform. And perhaps even more importantly, humans have a limitation in terms of the actual number of go games that they're able to process in a lifetime. A human can perhaps play a thousand games a year; AlphaGo can play through millions of games every single day."[5] Understand that here Silver is giving AlphaGo considerably short shrift. A great deal of what he describes—that it doesn't tire, that it can delve a deep tree, that it can review and learn from a very large number of prior games—is simply brute force. That may well have been how Deep Blue beat Kasparov. It is not how AlphaGo defeated Lee Sedol.

For many, I suspect, Next Rembrandt will feel like a more ominous development than AlphaGo. The profound sense of recognition we experience in the presence of a Rembrandt is somehow more accessible than anything that might appear in the austere and highly abstract territorial maneuvering of go. But there was something almost numinous about AlphaGo's play, an uncanny quality that caused at least one expert observer of its games against Lee to feel "physically unwell."[6]

It is true that human beings invented go, and elaborated its rules and traditions over some 2,500 years. So perhaps we should consider that the true achievement isn't the ability to play within the universe bounded by its ruleset, however exceptionally well, but imagining something that resonant, that satisfying and that beautiful in the first place. There is, no doubt, something to this—that we have nothing to fear from the rise of artificial intelligence until and unless it should begin to design games we find as captivating as go. But remember that the stack of neural networks and modules called AlphaGo was designed for the general acquisition of abstract knowledge—and that even as you read these words, it is still learning, still improving, still getting stronger.

Whether most of us quite realize it or not, we already live in a time in which technical systems have learned at least some skills that have always been understood as indices of the deepest degree of spiritual attainment. These questions have rarely been more present than they are in the case of a Yaskawa industrial robot, trained in 2015 to perform precision feats with a Japanese fighting sword as part of a promotional campaign called the Bushido Project.[7]

To accomplish this act of training, master swordsman and Guinness world record-holder Isao Machii was garbed in a full-body motion-capture suit, and recorded in high resolution as he performed the basic moves of his chosen art.[8] (The narration of the promotional video Yaskawa released is careful to refer to this art as *iaijutsu*, the technical craft of swordfighting, as opposed to *iaido*, the Way of the Sword; as we'll see, the distinction will become important.) This abstraction of lived, bodily human knowledge was transferred to the control unit of a Yaskawa Motoman MH24, a high-speed six-axis manipulator generally deployed in assembly, packaging and material-handling applications.

Rather astonishingly, Yaskawa chose to refer to this effort as the "Bushido Project." They would be perfectly aware that—as opposed to a more technical description of the swordfighting skills involved—the word *bushido* has the most provocative resonances. Japanese cultural activities with names ending in -*do* aren't positioned as mere pastimes, but as profound spiritual investigations into a single subject understood as life in microcosm.

Bushido, understood properly, is nothing less than the Way of the Warrior. Its virtues are those of duty, of reciprocal obligation, of self-control verging on abnegation of the self, and of being prepared at any and every moment to throw one's life away to protect that of one's master and house—all those qualities extolled at length in the *Hagakure*, the classic manual of samurai discipline. As supposedly entwined with the equally ineffable Japanese national spirit, *yamato-damashii*, bushido is a modern invention, with obvious appeal to the authoritarian state that successfully invoked it toward a variety of domestic and external ends between the 1920s and the end of the Second World War. However the concept may have been abused for political purposes, though, as constructed bushido is unquestionably something that resides in the human heart, or does not.

This matters when we describe a machine, however casually, as possessing this spirit.

At the time his feats of swordsmanship were captured by digital apparatus, Isao Machii had trained at the advanced level for some twenty-two years. Performed without ego or attachment, each stroke of his sword will be complete, perfect, whole and in harmony with the inmost nature of things. This necessarily raises some fairly profound questions when that same gesture is digitized in high resolution, and rendered as an instruction set that any articulated industrial machine with the necessary motive power and degrees of freedom can reproduce.

Once the necessary code is uploaded, any robot can perform the thousand cuts as well as Machii. Better, even: tirelessly, unweakeningly, ceaselessly, with uptime measured in strings of nines. It needn't be a Japanese robot, serve Japanese masters, nor in any way partake of *yamato* spirit. It will nevertheless be capable of drawing a sword through whatever material it encounters until the blade itself is worn away, or becomes useless through ablation.

Of more concern is the notion that this digitized instruction set is a package. It can travel over any network, reside in and activate any processing system set up to parse it. We may joke, uneasily, about the lack of foresight implicit in teaching a global mesh of adaptive machines the highly lethal skills of a master swordsman. But it also points toward a time when just about any human skill can be mined for its implicit rules

and redefined as an exercise in pattern recognition and reproduction, even those seemingly most dependent on soulful
improvisation.

One final thought. We're already past having to reckon with
what happens when machines replicate the signature moves of
human mastery, whether the strokes of Rembrandt's brush or
those of Machii's sword. What we now confront is the possibility of machines *transcending* our definitions of mastery, pushing
outward into an enormously expanded envelope of performance. And in many ways even this is already happening, as
algorithmic systems, set free to optimize within whatever set of
parameters they are given, do things in ways no human being
would ever think to.

Consider the curiously placeless quality of drone footage,
its unnerving smoothness and grace perhaps deriving from the
fact that often there is no specific human intention behind the
capture of a particular image or sequence of images. The target
is automatically perceived, acquired, reframed and captured, all
of it accomplished with a steadiness of hand so far beyond the
human norm that it is instantly recognizable.

Consider what go master Fan Hui said about the final turn
in AlphaGo's defeat of Lee Sedol: "It's not a human move. I've
never seen a human play this move. So beautiful."[9] The AI
player, unbound by the structural limitations, the conventions
of taste or the inherent prejudices of human play, explores fundamentally different pathways—and again, there's an aesthetic
component to the sheer otherness of its thought.

Consider the intriguing image that was not long ago circulated on Twitter by the entrepreneur Jo Liss: a picture of a
load-bearing bracket, before and after a computational process
of "topological optimization" has been applied to its design.[10]
The difference between before and after is stark. The pre-
optimized bracket looks unexceptional. It sports holes *here, here*
and *here* allowing it to be bolted to other components. Clearly
capable of performing to spec independent of orientation, it's
recognizably designed for standardization, ease of stocking
and use by unskilled labor. In short, it's the kind of thoroughly

generic, entirely fungible part you might find five hundred to a bin down at the neighborhood hardware store.

The "after" is Lovecraftian.

It is, no doubt, effective—almost by definition, more fit for its purpose than anything we'd come up with on our own. But it is decidedly, even aggressively strange. And it stands as a reminder that should autonomous systems develop their own logics of valuation and justification, they may not necessarily be so easy for human beings, or the infrastructures we've designed with our needs and limitations in mind, to mesh with, plug into or make sense of.

As it starts to condition the texture of everyday experience, this push past our own standards of beauty, resonance or meaning will do strange things to us, summoning up registers of feeling we'll find hard to describe with any accuracy. I have little doubt that we'll feel occasional surges of shocked delight at the newness, and yet essential correctness, of something forged by an intelligence of the deepest alterity—an image, a spatial composition, a passage of music, some artform or expressive medium we don't yet have the words for—and these may be among the precious few sources of joy and wonder in a rapidly ruining world.

I have equally little doubt that we'll more often find ourselves numbed, worn down by the constant onslaught of novelty when we have more pressing things to worry about. We'll feel pride that these intelligences have our DNA in them, however deeply buried in the mix it may be, and sorrow that they've so far outstripped the reach of our talents. It's surely banal to describe the coming decades as a time of great beauty and greater sadness, when all of human history might be described that way with just as much accuracy. And yet that feels like the most honest and useful way I have of characterizing the epoch I believe we've already entered, once it's had time to emerge in its fullness.

By virtually any meaningful standard, we would appear to be a long way from having to worry about any of this. Systems based on current-generation learning algorithms routinely stumble when presented with situations that are even slightly different than the ones their training has prepared them for, and fold completely before the kind of everyday ambiguities of interpretation that adults generally breeze through without noticing.

And this is true on many fronts. A test for machinic intelligence called the Winograd Schema, for example, asks candidate systems to resolve the problems of pronoun disambiguation that crop up constantly in everyday speech.[11] Sentences of this type ("I plugged my phone into the wall because it needed to be recharged") yield to common sense more or less immediately, but still tax the competence of the most advanced natural-language processing systems. Similarly, for all the swagger of their parent company, Uber's nominally autonomous vehicles seem unable to cope with even so simple an element of the urban environment as a bike lane, swerving in front of cyclists on multiple occasions during the few days they were permitted to operate in San Francisco.[12] In the light of results like this, fears that algorithmic systems might take over much of anything at all can easily seem wildly overblown.

As DeepMind taught us, however—with their AlphaGo significantly improving its play overnight, between the games of its series with Lee Sedol—algorithmic systems are able to learn *quickly*. The lesson of Tesla's Autopilot, where data from each individual car is continuously used to refine the performance of the entire fleet, is that algorithmic systems are increasingly able to learn *from one another*. And unlike we human beings, who find it increasingly difficult to take in new knowledge as we grow older,[13] any algorithm able to learn at all can keep doing so *indefinitely*, folding hundreds or thousands of human days of study into each 24-hour period, and doing so for as long as its trainers allow.

For all the flaws it's so easy to diagnose right now, the available evidence suggests that autonomous algorithmic systems will acquire an effectively human level of cognitive capability in the relatively near future, far more quickly than the more skeptical among us might imagine. More to the point, it is not at all clear what event or process (short of the complete collapse of complex civilization on Earth) might permanently prevent them from doing so.

I don't know what it will feel like to be human in that posthuman moment. I don't think any of us truly do. Any advent of an autonomous intelligence greater than our own can only be something like a divide-by-zero operation performed on all our ways of weighing the world, introducing a factor of infinity into a calculus that isn't capable of containing it. I understand full well why those who believe, however foolishly, that their advantage will be at a maximum under such circumstances, and their dominance made unassailable, are in such a hurry to get there. What I can't understand is why anyone else is.

Radical technologies

The design of everyday life

You are sitting at a café recommended to you by an algorithm, at a table that was cut on a CNC milling machine; you pay for your coffee with cryptocurrency, which you do by tapping your smartphone against the register; the voices of children playing an AR game filter in from the street. And while not a single aspect of this situation would have been possible even five years ago, none of it seems particularly remarkable to you. This is simply the shape of the normal in our time.

But it's worth noting that all of the qualities that make this situation what it is have been produced by technologies that are, as yet, relatively disarticulated from one another. And as they become better assimilated, they will tend to be integrated with other newly available technics, and fused into more complex propositions. This process of integration, in turn, will open up new and previously unsuspected possibilities for the behavior of things, and the texture of the everyday. The truly transformative circumstances will arise not from any one technology standing alone, but from multiple technical capabilities woven together in combination.

Discrete though they may seem, technologies like cryptocurrency, digital fabrication and augmented reality can be joined to one another because the systems involved all speak the same universal language of ones and zeroes. Condensed into modular chunks of code, their functionality—their ability to exert some specific material effect on the world—is more readily transferred from one product or service to another.

Access to that code can, of course, be tightly controlled by the party that developed it. Depending on the jurisdiction in which it was developed, the code responsible for producing a given effect may even be patented and licensed only to paying partners. But just as often, that code will be packaged along with any documentation necessary to its interpretation and use in a container known as a "library," and that library will be committed to an open-source repository like GitHub, where it can be downloaded for free by anyone who wants to make use of it.

This approach treats individual modules of code as the building blocks of a generative grammar. These elements can then be composed and assembled into higher-level propositions as and when needed, plugged into one another like so many Lego bricks. This is the logic behind well-documented APIs and cloud services, as it is of the modern web, and it is absolutely central to digital technology's ability to evolve new propositions with such startling rapidity.

Encapsulated in this way, strings of code that were designed to perform one useful function can now be repurposed and reappear in entirely new contexts. A given chunk of functionality may have been developed by a particular party, for a particular reason, by the lights of a particular culture. Once bundled in a library, though, it is free to travel and recombine, with very few limits on its application. This is how code that was developed to recognize when someone has fallen in an unattended nursing-home hallway winds up being used to monitor the behavior of a sidewalk crowd, or how code that determines a person's gender for the purpose of biometric access control is turned to the ends of targeted advertising. If a library to achieve a specified end exists, is widely used and is more or less robust, not many developers will take the time and trouble to reengineer it. The work is on the table, there for the taking, and available to serve any number of further purposes. Whatever values and priorities are inscribed in it will be incorporated by reference into everything it touches.

This is how formally discrete technologies can be brought together, and fused in powerfully hybrid propositions. But who is it, by and large, that's responsible for doing so?

No human institution, state or private, is yet of a scale that it can develop bespoke applications, devices and services for every last end it might conceivably want to pursue. There are, nevertheless, a small number of commercial enterprises whose size and concentrated technical competence now span much of the terrain of ordinary experience: Apple, Amazon, Google and Facebook, with Microsoft trailing a considerable distance behind. The American science fiction writer and commentator on technology Bruce Sterling calls these concerns "the Stacks," emphasizing the strategy of vertical integration by which each of them seeks to control the network, as well as the platforms, applications, physical devices and content that run on and are connected by it.[1]

Foremost among the Stacks, for the moment, anyway, is the company founded as Google, and later reorganized as a cluster of business units operating under the Alphabet umbrella. This single organization has had a hand in pioneering many of the technologies we've discussed, and what it hasn't developed it has simply been able to acquire. As a result, the company can in principle fuse together a suite of virtually hegemonic web products like GMail and the Chrome browser, the hundreds of millions of devices running the Android operating system, a high-resolution global mapping capability, the networked Nest thermostats and other home-automation systems, the Glass augmented reality visor, the Daydream VR headset, an autonomous-car initiative, the DeepMind artificial intelligence unit, the Sidewalk Labs smart-city effort, even the military robots produced by their Boston Dynamics division.

There is surely something troubling, if not outright dystopian, about this particular assembly of forces and capabilities. The thought that a single entity controls all of these products and services—and is able to tap and exploit the flow of information as it courses through and between them—is more than a little unsettling. Yet the truth is a good deal more complicated, and, in a small way, reassuring: Alphabet is not yet anything like all-knowing, and it may well never be. The Google Plus social-networking service, around which all the other web properties were reorganized, at no small expense and degree of user inconvenience, radically unperformed expectations; launched in 2011, it's wound up a quiet backwater in a world where Facebook and its properties dominate social media. It has been widely reported that the Nest team loathed founder Tony Fadell, and the division suffered from a string of embarrassing reversals during its time under the Google aegis;[2] to date, the parent organization has been unable to leverage the data presumably flowing upstream from its thermostats and networked cameras. Boston Dynamics was put up for sale in March 2016, in what has been characterized as a corporate retreat from the entire field of robotics (and what was notably, again, a failure to integrate organizational cultures following an acquisition).[3] The company's autonomous car initiative has suffered a long wave of defections among senior personnel, and keeps rolling back the date at which it plans to introduce its driverless technology;[4] it now estimates its vehicles will be fielded commercially no sooner than 2020. The Sidewalk Labs unit stumbled early on, when reportage by the *Guardian* brought to light troubling aspects of its proposals to American municipalities (including a plan to spend Federal mobility subsidies for low-income citizens on Uber rides).[5] And of course, as we've seen, the Glass product was outright rejected by a market of consumers manifestly unwilling to make Glassholes of themselves.[6]

So it's clearly foolhardy to underestimate the internal complexity of large, heterogeneous organizations, or the degree to which that complexity can confound even well-articulated intentions. It turns out that Alphabet, like any other enterprise of similar scale and complexity, is riven by internal rivalries, fractured commitments and contending priorities. And these all-too-human qualities leave the organization unable to wrest maximum advantage from everything it might, even from products and services it fully owns and controls. What is true of Alphabet in this respect is also true of Apple, Amazon and Facebook—as it would be of any entity of similar scale and ambition that might emerge to challenge their supremacy, whether private or public.

One school of thought might hold, then, that we are to a degree protected from the worst excesses of centralized control over emerging technology by the profound seamfulness and disharmony of any human organization. And in this case, as well, perhaps we are also protected by factors that are more specific to Alphabet's internal culture; in particular, it's not surprising that an organization avowedly and from bottom to top composed of people deeply attuned to science, technology and engineering might badly overestimate the general public's appetite for the things they themselves find so exciting.

But Alphabet may not actually furnish us with the best example of what a Stack looks like as it slouches toward hegemony. Consider, instead, what Amazon is doing as it links drones, robotics and the internet of things in a single, purposive, increasingly coherent proposition.

Each of the Stacks claims a piece of the puzzle that its peers would like to have, and this comprises its competitive advantage. Apple, of course, pioneered the strategy of ruthless, end-to-end vertical integration in its contemporary form. It ushered computation into the post-PC era through its iPhone and iPad devices, owns state-of-the-art mobile and desktop operating systems, sits cozily in the home through the Apple TV media player, and takes a 30 percent cut of everything sold through its App Store or downloaded from iTunes; it is now aimed squarely at wearables, point-of-sale payments, healthcare and semi-autonomous vehicles. Through Google, Alphabet dominates search, mapping and web browsing; in Android it controls the world's dominant mobile operating system; and, as we've seen, it has made strategic investments in a fantastic array of emerging technologies. Through its flagship social network, Facebook leverages the social lives of its 1.71 billion monthly active users—just short of one out of every four people on Earth—and through Instagram, no small share of their memories as well; through controversial projects like Free Basics[7] and its prototype fleet of solar-powered, autonomous Aquila drones, it is attempting to bring internet connectivity to "the last billion."[8]

And that leaves Amazon, the Seattle-based titan founded by Jeff Bezos in 1994. Having utterly dominated online commerce just about everywhere outside mainland China, it has pushed deep into cloud-computing infrastructure and automated logistics, and now sets its sights on the networked home.

Though Amazon's innovation comes at punishing psychic and physical cost to its workers, it has obsessively pursued technical efficiencies in the unglamorous backstage areas of warehousing, distribution and fulfillment. Most recently this has involved the launch of a program called Flex, in which same-day deliveries are outsourced to swarms of nonprofessional contract drivers scheduled by optimization algorithm.[9] It has also started to lease its own fleet of cargo aircraft, to reduce its dependence on carriers like FedEx.[10] It is even pursuing the idea that some degree of sorting might be pushed back up the supply chain to its wellsprings in the Pearl River Delta, with all the items destined to be delivered to a given neighborhood already allotted onto location-specific pallets on the other side of the Pacific.

A July 2016 Deutsche Bank research paper outlines how Amazon plans to consolidate its investments in logistical innovation, deploying a mesh of autonomous trucking, mobile warehousing and drone-based delivery assets, knit together by network-analysis and demand-anticipation algorithms. All of this takes place against the backdrop of America's decayed highway, bridge and road infrastructure, which I don't think is incidental, the state's withdrawal from public investment once again furnishing the impetus for the development of some wildly elaborate technical fix.

There is an armature here, or at least the beginnings of one, that reaches all the way from factories in coastal southern China directly into the myriad homes of the developed world. It does so in a way that neither Apple nor Facebook nor even Alphabet have yet managed to articulate, binding production and distribution to consumption and data capture directly, via propositions like the Echo and the Dash Button. Under Amazon's direct control, that elaborate distributed meshwork of trucks, planes, pallets and servers is effectively a single apparatus; every time you speak your needs to Echo that apparatus is activated to address them, and at the same time trained in how it might do so yet more efficiently next time around.

The Deutsche Bank analysts don't bother hedging their professional enthusiasm for this prospect: the scale and complexity of what Amazon stands to achieve here is so great that any emergent competitor would confront prohibitive difficulty in mounting a credible challenge to it, while a successful execution would so disrupt current ways of selling that "retail stores would cease to exist."[11] This is the apotheosis of what it means to be integrated as a Stack: Amazon owns the data centers, it owns the distribution and order fulfillment infrastructure, it owns the point of presence in your living room, it owns the data generated in the course of every user interaction and every physical delivery, and of course it takes a cut of any revenue generated by the consumption of content. Perhaps informed by the lessons learned in pioneering the provision of on-demand cloud infrastructure, all of this is sufficiently modular that even seemingly disruptive technologies like cryptocurrency or digital fabrication could be swapped in without missing a beat. And all of it, every moment of it, is predicated on the capture of data, the extraction of hitherto-unsuspected value from that data, and its use in creating ever-tighter loops of response to desire.

This is how a large number of separate digital technologies, developed at different times, in different places, by groups of people entirely unknown to one another, can be composed into a single functional ensemble of larger scale and import, and used to produce an experience of the everyday unlike any we've ever known.

Much of the technology yoked together in Amazon's effort seems to have originated internally, to the extent that aspects of the program were apparently overseen personally by Bezos himself.[12] Other than that this is an unusual degree of interest for a CEO to take in the details of implementation, in this respect the company is no different from the other Stacks: all of them spend billions of dollars annually generating, testing and refining new ideas, and trying to turn them into shipping products.

But the Stacks also innovate by acquisition, turning the entire planetary-scale entrepreneurial community into a vast distributed R&D lab. For example, Amazon apparently developed the foundations of its drone program in-house, but when it became evident that nobody on hand had the expertise in machine vision necessary to advance the program to its next stage, they simply hired an existing team of experts, and rebuilt the drone lab around them.[13] Similarly, they got a toehold in automation by buying the company that made the robots used in its warehouses, Kiva Systems.[14] While this practice is commonplace throughout the technology industry, it has been raised to an art in the age of the Stacks, especially as each of them expands beyond its original core competency. And a train of consequences follow from this that have a distinct bearing on what kinds of technologies are brought into existence.

Whether intended or otherwise, one of the primary effects of the Stacks' investment in young and emerging technical talent is to create a robust market for high-risk innovation with equally high "upside potential." At any given moment, there are thousands of startups busily exploring the edges of technological possibility, and shouldering all the risk involved in doing so. If their ideas come to nothing, so do they; they fade from the world without any further ado, and perhaps disperse their talent to other ventures. Should one of these fledgling concerns come up with a technique, a process or a useful bit of intellectual property, however, they will wind up being courted by one or more of the Stacks, with an eye toward eventual consummation in purchase. In fact the technology doesn't have to be anything flashy, so long as it shows insight or promise; the Stacks routinely acquire startups not so much because they need access to a particular technique, but because strategically denying their competitors design talent is a cost-effective way of preempting them.

The payouts involved in such acquisitions routinely reach into the tens of millions of dollars, and not infrequently hundreds of millions. Amazon bought video-delivery specialists Elemental Technologies for $296 million,[15] for example, and chipmaker Annapurna Labs for $370 million. Google acquired DeepMind for $500 million, networked-camera developer DropCam for about $55 million more than that, and Nest for just north of $2 *billion*. Just a year later, Facebook picked up Oculus VR for the same amount, and the messaging service WhatsApp for an eye-watering $19 billion.

Numbers like these are clearly a very strong incentive for talented developers to abandon the drudgery and anonymity of academic or corporate toil for chancier work in the startup sector, and so that is just what many of them now do. Surprisingly few of these entrepreneurially inclined developers actually intend to build and grow a sustainable business themselves, though. They are explicit about their intention to develop instead a "minimum viable product" as a technology or concept demonstrator, and more or less immediately thereafter flip their company to a deep-pocketed suitor.

One of the upshots of this is that there's a far larger, younger and more diverse cohort imagining and developing emerging technologies than ever before in history—and precisely because of means like GitHub, 3D printing and cheap Shenzhen production, virtually everyone among that cohort is able to generate prototypes of a sophistication that would have taxed the capabilities of the largest and wealthiest corporations of just a few years ago. As a whole, then, not many avenues for innovation will wind up going unexplored. If a given technical end is imaginable and even close to being physically achievable, it's a reasonable bet that somewhere on Earth, someone is at this very moment working feverishly to bring it to market. This situation is absolutely central to the vitality and perpetual inventiveness of contemporary technological development.

But there is, inevitably, a flipside to this vitality. The explosion in the number of people empowered to devise technology means there is virtually no idea so pointless, stupid or offensive that some startup somewhere will not invest resources in trying to develop it as a commercial product. And with such a tremendous multiplication of possibilities, any notion of a coherent ethics of technical development evaporates utterly.

What this means, in turn, is that there's nobody in a position to question the wisdom or propriety of a particular developmental direction. Monetize sleep, concoct a flavorless nutrient goo to replace food, engineer devices that transmit messages directly into the brain, develop robots for sex?[16] The refrain ought to be familiar by now: these are not hypotheticals. There are startups pursuing each of these goals, applying the methods and the mindset of contemporary software development to problem sets ever further afield. In each case, they are building a body of practice, perpetually refining their craft and technique, and pushing back the bounds of the possible. Perhaps at some point, they will run into the limits imposed by custom, regulation, psychology or undercapitalization. But all the while, they will be generating what the industry thinks of as "IP," intellectual property. And as we've seen, once that IP is released into the wild, there is no telling what kind of proposition it may wind up being conscripted into.

This, in schematic, is the dynamic that is in large part responsible for the oddly lurching and opportunistic quality of technological advancement in our time. There are no more Apollo programs, and relatively few strategic development plans as concrete, purposive and coherent as the one Bezos has invested in at Amazon. Most technical development is piecemeal, tactical and local, and only integrated into more comprehensive visions after the fact.

Each of the Stacks nevertheless has the same goal: to mediate and monetize everyday life to the maximum possible extent. Each of them starts from a slightly different historical situation, but is agnostic as to the specific nature of the means and tactics used in this pursuit as long as it makes reliable progress —preferably on a measurable, quarterly basis. Any path that suddenly appears before them will be explored, if it seems like it offers a potential for leapfrogging advancement. If this requires a manufacturer of computing hardware to master the design, construction and marketing of passenger vehicles, or an online book retailer to immerse itself in the arcana of robotics and drones, then so be it: there are to be no invidious limits of legacy or sector in their pursuit of hegemony.

This much was clear as long ago as 2007, when Apple dropped the "Computer" from their corporate name.[17] The progress of the Stacks is lubricated by the fact that, as one sector after another is decomposed and reformulated around the production, analysis and interactive provision of data, a new market territory falls squarely into their core area of expertise. Information is the substance of the new mobility, as it is of the new healthcare, the new urbanism, the new warfare and so on, and this affords the enterprise that has mastered information-work a near-infinite series of pivots. No longer a vendor of hardware, nor merely a service provider, the Stack has become an indispensable intermediary in all the relations that together constitute everyday experience.

It's not hard to perceive a certain deadening sameness that has begun to blanket the world under the sway of the Stacks, as the planet's extraordinary diversity of lifeways yield to the unlimited perfect reproduction of the modes of taste, self-expression and subjectivity these new hegemons are tuned to. All of them are headquartered on the west coast of the United States, three of them within a ten-mile radius of Stanford University. They share a set of assumptions about who their user is, how that person lives and what they want; they share a grounding in the Californian Ideology[18] and the casual technolibertarianism that has long reigned in the Bay Area; and latterly, they even tend to share a single overarching aesthetic.

It's hard to say what might distinguish a world in which Apple dominated, for example, from one in which Alphabet or Amazon reigned supreme. Perhaps the service and device eco-system would be open to a greater or lesser extent, and no doubt business prospects and entire lives would thrive or descend to nothing, depending on how capacious the interstitial spaces available in this world turned out to be. But at the level of routine existence: sameness, and a cluster of experiences approaching a Zenlike calm but for the degree to which they are branded.

Nothing forces anyone to buy from Amazon, of course, any more than anyone is forced to sign up for a profile on Facebook, search with Google, or use Apple computers, and there remain wide swathes of the planet where one can go weeks without overtly encountering any of their products or services. What's more, even in their core markets their dominance is of a relatively recent vintage, and it's unwise to ascribe to these particular enterprises a long-term tenacity and persistence they have yet to demonstrate. Yet it is already difficult, and becoming more difficult still, for anyone to equip themselves with modern technology without being subject to the totalizing influence of the Stacks.

There are precious few ways of availing oneself of networked information technology that do not invoke them at some level, whether as a provider of cloud services or other infrastructure, as a robust participant in standards bodies,[19] as a licensor of intellectual property, or as an investor with an ownership stake in some seemingly unrelated venture. And less concretely, they set agendas. The shared tastes, priorities and assumptions of a compact and relatively homogeneous body of people, most of whom work within a few miles of the Highway 85/101 interchange in Mountain View, sharply inflect the design of products made in Hyderabad, Seoul and New Taipei, in a way that can't simply be accounted for by network effects or convergent evolution.

For all the weirdness and vitality percolating up from the bottom of the technological food chain, a profoundly conservative tendency reigns at its apex. At present, the Stacks are able to reproduce and reinforce the conditions of their own survival through an array of canny strategic investments. Apple, for example, has organic capabilities that range from microprocessor design and fabrication to the provision of consumer financial services, securing it a position from which it will not easily be dislodged, and extending its ability to probe new markets at will.[20] But if theirs is the most complete portfolio among the Stacks, it is not by much.

It may be that this capacity to assemble, bind and merchandise new experiences is what gives emergent information technologies their port of entry into the everyday and the normal. Perhaps connected objects, the augmentation of perception, machinic discretion and all the other technics we've discussed will appear to us first and most prominently in the familiar form and guise of these masterbrands—levered into our lives through the apertures already available to them, folded in alongside existing services and propositions.

Or perhaps the existing Stacks will stumble and fade, and another set of actors will take their place—Samsung or Tencent, Tesla or Uber, branching out from their original competencies, developing a fully integrated product and service portfolio, and mediating the global everyday in a way they do not now. In particular, understand that it is by no means certain that technology will always be dominated by Western institutions, or guided by Western assumptions of what is desirable or achievable.

Indeed, there's some evidence that a shift away from Western values and priorities is already underway in global technical development. Consider the Chinese government's recently announced "social credit" scoring framework, which fuses smartphone, wearable and internet of things technologies with conventional social-networking services in a behavioral observation and control system of breathtaking scope and ambition.[21] In this sprawling scheme, just about every act taken by a Chinese citizen, whether online or off, impacts their "sincerity" score, and that score determines their access to social goods of all sorts. Think of it like credit score we're familiar with, but still more so: take out the recycling reliably, and maintain your privileges; play games too long or too frequently—or complain about the government on social media—and have your benefits cut.

Developed in close cooperation with Alibaba, an e-commerce platform far larger than Amazon by revenue,[22] and Baihe, China's dominant dating site, the social-credit scheme relies on a degree of overt corporate collusion with the state that would still be considered unusual in the West. And though Western authoritarians of various stripes may well dream fondly of the fine-grained social control such a system would enable, to date none have even dared to propose anything like what is now actually being built and deployed in China. So there's at least some reason to believe that whatever Stacks or Stacklike formations may emerge in the years to come, they may be guided by beliefs and principles unlike those broadly shared by the particular cohort that happens to dominate our moment.

But it is just as likely that the ascendance of any new set of large-scale technical actors would represent a distinction without a difference. There is already little enough that distinguishes a Samsung smartphone or virtual assistant from those produced by the North American Stacks; it's hard to imagine that any operating system or cloud infrastructure a non-Western actor might develop in the near to medium term would be a radical departure from the received norm. Precious little would change about the fundamental paradigm of devices, apps and web services, or the ecosystem of startups, incubators and venture capitalists on which innovation within that paradigm relies. The names, the logos and the shareholders might be replaced by new ones, but the colonization of everyday life by information technology, the measurement and monetization of ordinary experience, and the cementing of existing power relations would all proceed apace.

The Stacks have powerful ways of maintaining their position. They are well dug in, entrenched in the economy as in the minds of consumers[23]—able to call upon deep wells of customer loyalty, vast cash reserves and strategic investments in technologies that have yet to ripen. It's unlikely that they will disappear from our lives anytime soon. But it is invariably the worst sort of blunder to imagine the future as a straight-line extrapolation of the present, most especially when trying to weigh the impact of anything as destabilizing as the technics we've considered. If we want to understand how we might experience emerging informational technologies in the years to come, and get any meaningful handle on the ways in which they might come to inform our daily lives and choices and environments, we're going to have to take a leap beyond everything we know.

Perhaps we could find some clarity in the technique that many professional futurists and corporate foresight departments were trained to use, called "scenario planning". This method starts by recognizing that uncertainty always inheres in attempts to model the future. Instead of a single, unitary future, then, this technique offers multiple cases for an analyst to consider and weigh, side by side. This conceit helps us see that while our ability to act is invariably constrained by history, existing structures of power, and the operations of chance, we nevertheless have a degree of choice as to the kind of world we wish to bring into being.

As it was originally developed by Royal Dutch Shell's Long-Term Studies group,[24] scenario planning emphasized quantification, and the creation of detailed statistical models. The scenarios that follow aren't nearly as rigorous as all that. They are by no means a comprehensive survey of the possible futures available to us, nor is there anything particularly systematic about the way I've presented them. They are simply suggestive of the various choices we might plausibly make.

One final point about these scenarios: they are not periodizations. But for a few details, they could all coexist simultaneously, each one transpiring in a different place on Earth—they represent different trajectories societies can take, even when equipped with the same fundamental technics. The question they present us with isn't so much *What do our technologies let us do?* as it is *What do we choose to do with our technologies?* In considering them, we should always be asking: What decisions and commitments would we have to make now to tilt us toward the outcomes we want? And which ones would we be most likely to wind up in if we did nothing?

Green Plenty

In the first scenario, a commitment to the ethos of the commons infuses our relationship with emerging technology.

In Green Plenty the blockchain has matured as a technology, and autonomous corporations collaborate in comradely harmony with human beings across the entire landscape of everyday life. The state itself has been reorganized as a distributed autonomous organization in which every citizen is a shareholder, and it generally intrudes in people's lives only in the form of the gentlest of nudges. Sophisticated planning algorithms modulate the balance of demand and production in something very close to real time, through an extensive digital fabrication infrastructure maintained as a public utility; under their stewardship, a deeply circular and very nearly self-directed economy prevails. With most fabricated objects tagged with information about their material composition, alongside instructions for recycling, it's easy to disassemble products when they've reached the end of their useful life and sort their components for recapture or reuse; in fact, an automated recovery chain just as elaborate as the supply chain exists to do precisely that. It is clearer every day that the legitimating purpose of all economic activity is the production of universal bounty.

Here, a formal Universal Basic Income isn't necessary, because the goods of life are essentially free for the taking. The fruits of the Earth are distributed not merely equitably, but lavishly, as we always knew they could be. The grand framing narrative of commodity capitalism is finally shattered and left behind, the economics of want no longer relevant to a time when demand is estimated by wise algorithm, and fulfilled by automated production. The more audacious observers of technical advancement dare to speculate that the point is not far off at which molecular nanotechnology and the "effectively complete control over the structure of matter" it affords finally bring the age of material scarcity to its close.[25]

In places where Green Plenty has broken out, most large-scale interventions in the built environment are intended to democratize access to the last major resource truly subject to conditions of scarcity: the land itself. Placeless urban sprawl is overwritten by high-density megastructures woven of recovered garbage by fleets of swarming robots.[26] Equal parts habitat and ecosystem, they bear the signature aesthetic of computationally generated forms no human architect or engineer would ever spontaneously devise, and are threaded into the existing built fabric in peculiar and counterintuitive ways. But they afford everyone who wants to live in one of the planet's great urban cores safe and decent space in which to do so, and come to be loved for their own virtues.

Amidst all this, a delicate ecological homeostasis is maintained, underpinned by ubiquitous, high-resolution environmental sensing that allows for the fine-grained modulation of those activities that do unavoidably produce pollution. Work proceeds on the restoration of the biosphere, while a network of autonomous probes are cast outward to explore, and to mine the asteroids for their bounty. The circulation of matter and energy in Green Plenty bears the hallmarks of that steady state ecologists refer to as a "climax community": there is no growth in the classic economic sense, but everywhere there is life, beauty, adaptation and thriving creativity.

Green Plenty fosters the highest degree of experimentation at the edges of the human and of the self, the people liberated to explore new genders, relationship forms and family structures, or treat bodily augmentation as an expressive medium. Here whatever work people choose to undertake is understood as craft, and craft as something akin to play. With the compulsion to dominate leached out of it, even the competitive instinct takes on a lighter and more ludic quality.

This more or less a form of manifest Fully Automated Luxury Communism, a world of cornucopian excess for all. If this becomes possible anywhere, it will be hard to see how it can be prevented from happening everywhere. But while this scenario may stand in rebuke to the common complaint that it is easier to imagine the end of the world than the end of capitalism, it is troublingly founded on an *ex machina* retuning of human nature. It depends on something coming from outside to release us from the shaming psychic smallness of scarcity. What if no such thing ever happens?

The Widening Gyre

In this second scenario, we explore a pathway in which a thermodynamically sustainable alternative for proof-of-work is discovered, and blockchain-based cryptocurrency goes on to fulfill all the expectations its original champions held for it. This precipitates the withering of the state everywhere on Earth. With government's ability to sustain itself on tax revenue decisively undercut, it crumbles and fades—but does so before any kind of societal-scale coordinating process that might be able to replace it has had time to evolve.

There is no mainstream media anymore in the Widening Gyre, nor much of a shared culture to speak of. There is hardly any shared *reality* anymore—the fracturing of consensus is an epistemic challenge, as much as anything else, and it prevents institutions of any particular size from sustaining themselves, or new ones from forming in the first place. The stage is claimed by a set of smaller, more agile actors. Productive capacity is, for the most part, vested in networked workshops at neighborhood scale, organized as cooperatives and linked by networked processes of deliberation. Economic power is exercised by loose federations of such cooperatives, although coordination between them is complicated by the scatter of differing values and styles of governance, as well as the fact that they tender in competing local currencies.

Fabrication is cheap, widely available and just as widely used. The emphasis is on tactics of ad-hoc, improvisational or adaptive reuse, the built fabric reticulated by wildcat infrastructures in the style of the Indian *jugaad*[27] and its Brazilian near-equivalent *gambiarra*.[28] An unlimited profusion of local tastes prevails: the world wears a fractal fur of fabricated things, exuberantly colorful appliqués, plug-ins and bolt-ons that are cheerfully bereft of coordinating taste.

People have come to accept, as well, that they share that world with a phylum of autonomous, machinic agents of all types and descriptions, very few of which resemble conventional robots in any way. Once despised as a subaltern class, or feared for their literally inhuman strength and persistence, the members of this phylum have become too diverse to permit ready characterization; they are neither more nor less discordant than any other thing that populates the environment, and receive neither more nor less attention as a result.

The bill for the twentieth century has come due with a vengeance. The entire economy of the Widening Gyre sometimes seems geared to repairing the damage. Detailed augmentive overlays guide amateurs in the disassembly of the twentieth century's legacy structures and infrastructures; crews of them swarm over the land in gaily painted military-surplus exoskeletons, bringing down irreparable buildings, recovering precious materials for reuse, breaking up the expanses of cracked concrete so the land can be farmed. But there is no large-scale coordinated action to preserve the global environment, no way to prevent anyone from burning whatever quantity of coal they can get their hands on, and if humanity does manage to squeak by, it's clearly going to be a closer thing than anybody would prefer.

This is not the scenario of genteel collapse famously derided by the science-fiction author and critic Brian Aldiss as "the cozy catastrophe," in which a few privileged protagonists ride out the twilight of civilization in hand-me-down comfort.[29] Life in the Widening Gyre is hard for most people, most of the time— *physically* hard, grueling even. The cooperatives are subject to all the usual drawbacks of localism—fear of the outsider, and of the idea that originates elsewhere—and from the inside can easily feel conservative, even claustrophobic, to anyone who wanders out of step. There are more than occasional skirmishes on the boundaries between them, only barely held in check by desperate peace councils, and the insistent awareness that the survival of all is balanced on a razor's edge. Daily life has the tenor of a holding action. But it is not without its compensations. For those who are lucky enough to find a companionable fit, it is a life of fellowship, mutual aid and above all purpose, unmarked by any trace of boredom or ennui.

Stacks Plus

In Stacks Plus, most things are the way they are now, only more so. This is scenario that obtains in the Paris of our introduction, where the existing economic and political actors attempt to preserve dominion over a heating, drowning world by harnessing all the tools newly available to them, and more or less succeed in doing so.

Here the state and the market are nearly indistinguishable from one another—the former existing mostly as a guarantor of the latter, and executing all of its policies through an array of private-sector partners. Citizens are entitled to a Universal Basic Income; nobody starves, but most of the funds disbursed are swiftly recaptured as user fees assessed for services that used to be thought of as public goods. The institutions that might have been expected to function as a brake on this tendency—the academy, the arts, humanities and sciences, the elite media—are dominated at the highest level by people who are angel investors themselves, if not literally venture capitalists. There are very few effective public actors left outside the achieved neoliberal consensus, fewer still with any concrete memory of a different way of life, and just about nobody pays any sustained attention to them. Indeed, in many circles it's a moderate to severe breach of taste to even comment on the established order, and a decided faux pas to suggest that there might be other ways of ordering the world.

Digital fabrication has truly come into its own in Stacks Plus, driven by the urgent need to radically truncate sprawling transoceanic supply chains at a time when shipping is ever more exposed to risk and insurance costs are becoming untenable. There are, however, conditions on its use. Fabricators aren't restricted per se, or anything like it—in fact, each of the Stacks offers its own, highly refined model, and they are wildly popular. But these have been successfully locked down by the application of digital rights management. You print things at home at will, but they are branded things, and you produce them on a commercial, subscription basis; whichever one of the Stacks happens to have its brand slapped across the front of your unit takes a 30 percent cut.

In Stacks Plus, the development of blockchain technology faltered after the fundamental thermodynamic issues with proof-of-work proved to be insurmountable. Distributed ledgers are in broad use by those parties for whom the benefits outweigh the costs, but they never scaled universally; while they're absolutely critical to the exchange of value between large-scale institutions, they are no longer of particular interest to anyone outside of government or financial circles. The first flush of enthusiasm for cryptocurrency is remembered mostly for its flakiness and self-delusion, and is discussed, when it is discussed at all, with faint embarrassment, as though it were a once-trendy but now risible haircut or fashion choice.

For a slim shard of the world's favored, a bleak prosperity prevails. Life goes on for them pretty much the way it does now: peppered by increasingly catastrophic weather events, unpredictable outbreaks of savage violence, and a nagging, inchoate sense of loss, but otherwise very much business as usual. Unprecedentedly healthy, sparklingly bright, and diverse along every conceivable axis, the elite of Stacks Plus grind away ironically at jobs they know full well to be bullshit, in a gigantic, complicated ouroboros of pointlessness dedicated primarily to the manipulation of symbols. Their days are largely given over to the pleasures of friendship, conviviality and hard work; they arrange their brunches, vacations, hookups, gigs and pregnancies via app, and get around all but effortlessly, still delighted that the new autonomous Ubers relieve them even of the hassle of interacting with a driver. Almost everything is optimized for their comfort and convenience, based on data collection so detailed and comprehensive that most of the choices everyday life might otherwise present them with are anticipated and preempted. Virtually nobody complains—the credit plans, menu choices and travel upgrade options that are preselected for them always strike a perfect balance between affordability and the satisfaction of a desire they did not know they possessed until it was fulfilled.

Everyone else sweats it out. The Universal Basic Income may save people from having to hustle simply to put food on the table, and it just about covers the costs of housing and medical care. But it was instituted grudgingly, out of fear, and with an eye toward the subsidy of favored private partners, and it furnishes nothing beyond the most basic rudiments of a decent existence. For most, the gnawing anxieties of precarity have been replaced by something very nearly as unpleasant, and much more permanent: reconciliation to the fact that they have it as good as they ever will.

There are compensations, however. The Stacks don't care in the slightest if you're trans or poly or vegan or a weed smoker. In fact, they encourage the maximum possible degree of differentiation in self-expression, and are delighted to serve all markets equally. And while the Stacks and the state may arrogate to themselves the right to shape strategy and mediate the flow of experience, at the level of tactics ordinary people everywhere retain the power to contest, complicate, confound and resist—not merely those within shouting distance of the receding elite, but the shackdwellers and favelados as well. So while some are placated, succumbing to the powerfully seductive temptations of free-to-download virtual pleasureworlds and brightly gamified compliance regimes, others grasp everything they can. They become masters of hacking, subverting and exploiting, proving that the Stacks are not the only parties able to deploy technical expertise in the service of desire, nor the only ones able to forge technologies of diverse origin into instruments of purpose.

Some become particularly adept at cracking the digital rights management software that hobbles fabricators; the knowledge and tools required to do so circulate through a fully elaborated shadow economy, alongside unlicensed filament and all the illegal things people make with it. This is the vivid tableau presented in the video produced for M.I.A.'s 2013 song "Double Bubble Trouble." Here project kids wield 3D-printed assault weapons, use home-fabbed drones to establish their turf, give each other tribal tattoos that only become visible through augmentation, and fox surveillance by shrouding themselves in face-recognition-defeating niqab; the camera lingers on an Ultimaker 3D printer as prominently as it does on the clouds of vaped ganja. This is a fantasy of the street finding its own uses for technology, and if it's a very particular kind of wishful thinking, it at least gets the sense of cross-contamination right.

The sense that there is a fertile and creative hybridity fermenting at the bottom of the ladder may offer hope to at least some of those dispossessed by the arrangements that prevail in our own time, and it is what carves out room to breathe in the otherwise airless world of the Stacks Plus. But what if the possibility of popular resistance is detected and eliminated before it has had time to grow?

Perfect Harmony

This is what has come to pass in our fourth scenario. This is a landscape dominated, again, by a fused market/state—but this time one in which the neoliberal governmentality of the Stacks Plus has tilted sharply toward the authoritarian.

Affairs of all kinds are dominated by a universal, Chinese-style reputation scheme that rewards conformity, and penalizes deviation. The blockchain is at the heart of many things here, but not in any way its inventors intended. The central bank issues a digital currency, and all transactions take place in that currency. Every act of economic exchange is logged, monitored and mined for its significance. There are occasional and foolhardy attempts to do business off the books, but such anomalies are readily detected, and the parties responsible punished severely.

There are draconian controls not merely on what can be made with digital fabricators, but on fabrication technology itself. All fabricators must be registered, while constantly updated firmware prevents them from making certain classes of object at all. Nothing that might challenge the social and economic order in any way is ever allowed to breach the surface. The state retains full responsibility for the distribution of social goods, doling them out as rewards to parties in favor, and withholding them from suspect ethnicities and other fractious social formations.

Everyday life in Perfect Harmony is the voice-stress analysis of the call-center worker that allows for the training of the virtual agent that replaces her. It is the risk-assessment algorithm that predicted she would be laid off, and preemptively raised the APR on her loans, as well as the blockchain-mediated smartlock that turfs her out of her high-rise microflat the moment she comes up short on rent. It is the skeletal, 3D-printed drone that supervises her eviction, and the gait-recognition and station-keeping algorithms that keep it locked on her until she's safely offsite; the augmented reality interface that allows a security guard eight thousand miles away to watch her through that drone's eyes, and the fact that he'll do that work for fifty US cents an hour, grateful to have any job at all in the charnelhouse of his domestic economy. It's the high-resolution immersive VR that keeps the neighbors twitching in their flats next door, docilized, politically decorticated and completely uninterested in what's happening. It is the RFID tags ensuring that any moveable property belonging to her landlord remains on the premises. It is even the landlord itself—an autonomous parastatal enterprise without human shareholders, whose portfolio operates at such a narrow margin of profitability that her flat is already rented to a new tenant by the time she's a metro stop away. In this world all is aimed at the ruthless extraction of advantage precisely because everything is falling apart.

The economy itself has departed from human control. Under the guidance of opaque and haughty planning algorithms, the surface of the planet is traversed by vast processes whose scope, purpose and intention are incoherent to any human being. Have these new masters attempted a crash program of carbon sequestration, or something aimed at changing the planet's albedo so it reflects more of the sun's radiant heat back to space? Who can say? And in any event it's not wise to ask too many questions.

The citizens of Perfect Harmony know full well what they are: an unnecessariat warehoused and pacified, denied any place they might gather, stand and resist.

Even here, though, life goes on. It is impossible for any species as adaptable and tenacious as ours to live in unrelieved grimness. And so people break bread in Perfect Harmony, as they always have; drink and laugh together, as they always have. The big picture doesn't look promising, and everyone knows it, the blandishments of the market/state aside. But the random outbreaks of terror have for the most part been suppressed; some kind of corrective action is being taken on the environment, however obscure it may be; and if a brutal conformity reigns, it leaves just enough space for people to eke out the rudiments of a life they can call their own. Most choose to make of it whatever they can.

The final scenario has no name. Here we find failed civilization, on a planetary scale: societies panicking in the face of the first sharp shocks of climate violence collapse back into tribal allegiances and pseudoverities of blood and soil, and never meaningfully grasp any of the possibilities presented to them by new technology.

The landscape is scoured and blasted by desperate attempts to jumpstart the engines of the economy. The last forests wither beneath the effect of misguided geoengineering projects intended to right the climate, and finally succumb to slash-and-burn farming. The oceans are anoxic, reeking, dying. The food web unravels in every direction at once; the human population bottlenecks, hard. Small communities persist—scattered, hungry pockets held together by sheer will and a fierce, almost religious commitment to one another. But with all the easily accessible sources of energy burned away to thermal waste and pollution, their state of technical development rapidly plummets toward a floor it is likely to remain at for thousands of years to come.

The survivors' comprehension of the world that was is sharply limited by the fact that for the final few decades of its flowering, most human culture subsisted only in the cloud, and disappeared when the last server succumbed to the irreversible effects of time and entropy. Any cultural artifact that was not physically produced at scale, including the overwhelming majority of all the writing, music and visual expression created after 1995, is lost to human memory. Whatever remains of the rest is cherished as an heirloom and symbol of an all-but-inconceivably sweeter and more generous age.

Do these few sketches represent the only choices available to us, or even the entire spectrum of variation possible between them? Of course not. None of them takes particular note of the equally transformative potentials emerging from biotechnology and the life sciences—stem-cell therapies, for example, the CRISPR genome-editing process, or the various ways in which we are becoming-cyborg. Collectively, they no doubt underweight the influence of social and demographic trends that have nothing to do with technology *per se*. Each of them, in the manner of Shell's original scenarios, is merely a distillation of certain tendencies we can already perceive in our use of one particular class of technologies.

But such distillations have their uses. They help us see how discrete technologies fit together in certain characteristic syndromes, how they multiply rather than add to one another's effects, how they drive societal change even as they are shaped by it, and just how often the ones that thrive do so because they dovetail with the needs of existing ideologies. They teach us that we can only understand what technologies really do, and how they really work, when we are able to stand back and weigh their consequences for all the social and natural ecosystems into which they are knit. Perhaps most importantly, they make it plain that certain kinds of risks and harms can actually be discerned ahead of time—and this, in turn, means that they might be circumvented or avoided, if only we are able to apply sustained and concerted action to doing so.

As individuals and as societies, we desperately need to acquire a more sophisticated understanding of how technologies work in the world, and who benefits most from the way they accomplish that work. In part, this means applying the tools of institutional and discourse analysis to the technical innovation ecosystem, both to prise out latent patterns of interest and to demonstrate that certain statements and framings are the product of interest in the first place. But part of it is just learning to ask the right questions whenever we're presented with a new technological proposition.

If there's anything we ought to have gleaned from the scenarios, or from our consideration of the Stacks before that, it's that contemporary technologies never work as stand-alone, isolated, sovereign artifacts. Whatever effect they have on the way we live our lives comes about precisely because they have been embedded in larger-scale social, technical and physical systems. Whatever possibilities may in principle inhere in them are constrained by path dependency; channeled by custom, informal regulation and law; and amplified whenever they intersect with some existing current of human desire. Whether or not they ever do serve their original intended purposes, we can be sure they will overspill those purposes, and operate beyond them in ways that have permanently escaped any possibility of control by their inventors.

Conclusion

Of tetrapods and tactics—radical technologies and everyday life

On the strand at Niigata, facing the gently lapping waves of the Sea of Japan, stands a breakwater comprised of the cast-concrete objects known as tetrapods. Each one is shaped like a blunted caltrop a few meters across, and weighs just about two tons. They've been deposited here in their thousands, as they have been along some 55 percent of the overall coastline of Japan, to combat beach erosion; a massive interlocked chain of them parallels the beachfront, stretching away into the distance as far as the eye can see.

Because of their pronged shape, tetrapods can't help but self-organize into some semblance of order once they've been set down. Locking into place as the seabed settles beneath them, they form a dense yet porous barrier that dissipates the force of waves and crosscurrents, and—theoretically, anyway—keeps the sand of the beach from being washed out to sea. Over time the whole assemblage becomes part of the coastal ecosystem, forming a synthetic habitat for birds, crabs, seaweed and other wildlife. These brutal objects are, in their way, spontaneous infrastructure.

It's the shoreline at Niigata that comes to mind whenever I

encounter promises about all the wonderful things that some new technology is supposed to do for us, especially when it's supposed to do those things automatically. Beyond whatever aesthetic damage they do to the coastline, it is now thought that the tetrapods racked up all along the water's edge actually accelerate the erosion they were intended to forestall; they are mostly produced these days as a tacit state subsidy of the Japanese concrete industry.[1] At best a misguided allocation of energy and investment, they are in some ways worse than useless.

And so it seems to be with so many of the technologies that are offered to us on the premise that they will spontaneously produce the conditions of equity, justice or freedom. The tetrapods on the Niigata strand suggest to us that there are all kinds of circumstances that capture and overtake technical interventions, any number of factors that stand to subvert designerly intention. This is what the great British cyberneticist Stafford Beer meant when he argued that "the purpose of a system is what it does."[2] On this theory, it doesn't matter whether some technology was intended by its designer to enslave or to liberate, to preserve or to destroy. All that matters is what it is observed to do, and we ought to evaluate it on that basis alone. If the project of coastal engineering based on concrete tetrapods demonstrably channels subsidy to a few favored firms and constituencies, does so without preventing beach erosion, and is allowed to persist in doing so over long stretches of time, then we are bound to conclude that this is its sole actual purpose.

This is the razor we need to apply to augmented reality, or 3D printing, or distributed autonomous organizations: what is salient is not anything their visionary designers may have had in mind when imagining them, but what states of being they are actually seen to enact. And if given technologies cannot be evaluated at the level of their designers' intention, we need to be still more wary of the promises made to us by developers, promoters and others with a material interest in seeing them spread. The most misleading aspect of this body of rhetoric perennially resides in the gulf between technoutopian claims about what some emergent innovation "might" or "could" give rise to, on the one hand, and anything it has actually been seen to do on the other.[3] Very often the claimed benefits never do come to pass, while the easily foreseeable (and, in fact, explicitly foreseen) negative consequences invariably do crop up, and are left for others to deal with. This is why I repress a shudder whenever someone speaks of the emancipatory or liberatory "potential" of some technology under discussion. To have hope and to nurture it in others doesn't need to mean that we let go of rigor.

Equipped in this way, we see the claims so often made for new technologies in a different, harsher light. Adrian Bowyer explicitly devised his self-replicating digital fabricator to undermine the logic of material scarcity on which capitalist enterprise depends, and this argument has been picked up and extended in recent years by authors like Rifkin, Mason, Srnicek and Williams, in their reflections on the shape of an emergent post-capitalist order. From the shadowy Satoshi Nakamoto to Nick Szabo to Vitalik Buterin, the inventors of the blockchain overtly intended to erode statism and central administration. Virtually everywhere, decision algorithms are touted to us on the promise that they will permanently displace human subjectivity and bias. And yet in every instance we find that these ambitions are flouted, as the technologies that were supposed to enact them are captured and recuperated by existing concentrations of power. They will not spontaneously bring scarcity to an end, or capitalism, or oppression. Laminated into standing ways of doing, making and selling, the only thing they seem to be capable of spontaneously reproducing is more of the same.

In fact, the lesson of the tetrapods is that where technology is concerned, *nothing* happens automatically, nothing happens for free, and if you're not very, very careful, you might just wind up achieving an outcome at the widest variance with any you intended. If you're committed to a technology—as the Japanese government and concrete industry are to the tetrapod—then you are more or less compelled to find things for that technology to do, whether it works defensibly well in those roles or not. If, on the other hand, you're committed to achieving a particular social outcome, a particular distribution of power in the world, you'll only occasionally find that one or another technology serves your end. You're compelled to undertake the much harder work of organizing for that outcome directly.

If you want to end the depredations of scarcity, then, better by far that you work for the just distribution of the goods we already have than wait for some cornucopian machine to solve the problem for you. If you want to contest the power of the state, take concrete steps to claim decision-making power locally, rather than hoping that someone will release the code of an autonomous framework that instantly renders states obsolete. If you're interested in eliminating class and racial bias in the criminal justice system, work with one of the many civil society organizations established and chartered to do just that before handing the powers that be yet another tool and rationalization for their use of force. In every case the hard, unglamorous, thankless work of building institutions and organizing communities will demand enormous investments of time and effort, and is by no means guaranteed to end in success. But it is far less likely to be subverted by unforeseen dynamics at the point where an emergent and poorly understood technology meets the implacable friction of the everyday.

As it happens, I personally quite like tetrapods, as abstract aesthetic objects; I have a cluster of three miniatures sitting on the table in front of me as I write, each no wider across than a coffee mug is tall. But it's not the aesthetic pleasure these objects afford me that I tend to dwell in, when I recall what the tide sounded like as it broke against the concrete. I think instead of the public funds that went to deploy the tetrapods, investments that might have been placed more profitably elsewhere. I think of the despoiled coastal ecosystem, and the long, long stretches of Japanese coastline where it's impossible to lay eyes on scenery that hasn't been interfered with for reasons of industrial-scale cupidity. Mostly I think of the receding sands, slowly but steadily sifting out to sea. And I think: all these circumstances are the legacy of a conscious attempt to alter the conditions of life.

Whoever it was that made the original decision to invest in tetrapods, that party held the power to make change: the concentrated ability to redirect flows of attention and interest, information and investment, and ultimately matter and energy. This is the fundamental aim of all technology, as it is of all politics. Everything else is a sideshow, as the quotation from the "Theses on Feuerbach" inscribed on Karl Marx's grave marker reminds us. "The philosophers have only interpreted the world in various ways," it reads, in golden capitals crisply incised in the granite. "The point, however, is to change it."[4]

In our time, there may be no group of human beings that has taken this thought more sincerely to heart than those who work in the various fields of information technology. Changing the world is what they set out to do every day of their working lives, and their industry's impressive record of having actually done so over the last half-century makes this at least a superficially credible ambition. The theories of change people involved in this effort hold tend to be pretty straightforward. When faced with uncertainty, technologists are fond of invoking the visionary engineer Alan Kay, who argued that "the best way to predict the future is to invent it."[5]

Only the rarest inventions actually do change the world in this way, in themselves and simply by virtue of having been brought into being: the telegraph, penicillin, the atomic bomb, the birth-control pill. Innovations of this order are powerful enough to fold reality around them, forcing power itself to flow through new and different channels. The chain of causality in each of these cases is relatively easy to establish, and it is in them that the technodeterminist argument acquires its most convincing sheen of plausibility. You can certainly ask why a society, when granted the secrets of the atom, would immediately seek to weaponize that knowledge, just as you would be justified in asking why the effort to regulate fertility unfolded on the terrain of women's bodies rather than those of men; pre-existing social logics are never entirely absent from the equation. But it seems churlish to argue that these technical innovations did not more or less directly cause change to occur in the world. They did, and our ordinary language acknowledges the fact: mention "The Bomb" or "The Pill," and nobody needs to ask which one you meant.

Most inventions, however, exert no such transformative force on the world. Adrian Bowyer, after all, set out to invent the future in just the way Kay proposed, and yet we do not live in a world of infinitely self-reproducing fabricators, nor even remotely do we live amidst the freedom from want they were supposed to grant us. His RepRaps ran into a wall made of physics and economics, mortared together by the reliable human propensity toward laziness—who, after all, is going to grind out the parts of a new replicator when they can still be delivered from China more cheaply and more quickly?—and what we got instead was simply another class of product.

Similarly, Nick Szabo invented smart contracts to automate agreements between parties, and yet so far, thankfully, the world has yet to take him up on his offer. He failed to account for the tension between history, which unfolds in unpredictable ways, and the brutally reductive logic of a contract that unfailingly executes no matter what changes may have taken place in the time since it was signed. Such contracts will always be mismatched to human affairs, simply because they aren't flexible enough to provide for the negotiation that helps us adapt to unexpected contingencies.

We learn something new about the way things actually work from these examples: if the tetrapods taught us that the intention of a designed artifact can be suppressed, or even inverted, when it is captured by a larger social, technical or physical system, RepRap and the smart contract both teach us that such an artifact may be rejected outright if it presents too much friction at its interface with those systems.[6] Both RepRap and the smart contract failed because the networks of production and exchange they were intended to augment were already moored at multiple points to astonishingly tenacious, metastable systems: the broader culture and its legal and economic conventions, that statistically significant collection of drives and propensities we dub "human nature," and the physical universe itself. To a very great extent, it is this quality of drag that the political theorist Jane Bennett calls "the material recalcitrance of cultural objects"[7] which accounts for the conservatism that everywhere underlies the superficially exuberant play of technological innovation.

But pointing out that it is exceedingly difficult to achieve *conscious, intentional, purposive and directed* change in the world through the introduction of some novel technical means is not at all the same thing as saying that emergent technologies have no effect on the state of affairs we experience. Nor does it imply that such technically induced alterations to the state of the world as do appear are necessarily somehow uncongenial to existing institutions. Tetrapods, blockchains, fabricators, algorithms—none of them might produce precisely the outcomes their designers intended, least of all politically progressive ones, but there's no question that they all cause flows of matter, energy and information to shift in their presence, and some of those new flows will be highly desirable to incumbents.

Some superficially "disruptive" propositions, for example, like autonomous trucking or the pervasive instrumentation of the home and the human body, are likely to fare perfectly well because they present no challenge to the actors that presently hold economic power, or even allow those actors to pursue their existing ends in a more efficient way. Whatever direction the radicalism of such propositions may be expressed in, it's orthogonal to any that might threaten the process of capital accumulation. Of all those we've discussed, these are the technics whose wholesale adoption will unfold most rapidly.

The notion that many arrangements of long standing are being threatened by emergent technologies is not entirely a fiction, though, and equally there is little question that certain very wealthy and powerful individuals and institutions stand to lose a great deal of the grandeur they now enjoy. As the brand names and must-have apps of the moment rotate through our lives in ever-quicker succession, all those who work the enterprises involved—to say nothing of their investors, vendors and clients—no doubt experience this precession as a nerve-wracking, high-stakes drama of soaring triumph and ignominious defeat. (The consequences of such disruption are real for others, as well: consider the impact on the Finnish tax base, for example, when mobile-phone titan Nokia, not so long ago capitalized to the amount of $300 billion, lost 90 percent of its value in just over a decade.)[8]

But these skirmishes at the surface layer never fundamentally alter the deeper propositions presented to us by contemporary technics: that everyday life is something to be mediated by networked processes of measurement, analysis and control; that access to resources and life-defining opportunities can justly be apportioned by algorithm; and above all that human discretion is no longer adequate to the challenges of complexity presented to us by a world that seems to have absconded from our understanding. The shift in fortunes experienced by a single company, or even sector, never come anywhere close to derailing these core logics of our epoch, nor the posthuman capitalism they enable. The ecosystem that turns affect and experience into data, and data into revenue and the shape of life chances, is largely armored against the decisive, single-stroke disruption—and, if we are to believe the theoreticians of machine learning and adaptive intelligence, the ability to anticipate and preempt existential threats the apex participants of this ecosystem enjoy will only improve over time. There will be no masterstroke that all at once undoes their grip on our economies, the structure of our daily choices, or our imaginations.

Part of what keeps us from seeing this clearly is path dependency, or more simply momentum. We're not so much becoming-cyborg as we are already halfway distributed, with our work, our familial and social lives, our memories, our capacity to imagine and even our cognitive processes in a very real sense strewn across the mesh of data centers and server farms, transmission infrastructures and interface devices that constitutes the contemporary global network. We are fully committed to this scattered apparatus, many of us, and to some degree —that material recalcitrance again—we're compelled to go wherever it takes us.

Entrained in this way as we are, each new capability that is developed and offered to us begs the question of its origins. It presents us with certain forward lines of flight, but we rarely pause to ask whether any of those lines happens to proceed along a direction that we intended to travel in when we embarked. This year's laptop is lighter than last year's model, and next year's will be lighter still; this version of the app uses an image-search algorithm a thousand times faster than that in the last version; the new car firmware provides for semi-autonomous operation, and that is sufficient unto the day. These days, the software updates mostly unfold politely in the background, unspooling quietly in the overnight hours, while buying a new laptop or phone every year or two has become virtually compulsory if we want to keep using the applications and other software everyone else does. In either case, the hassle of choice has largely been engineered out of the process. But that act of engineering deprives us of an opportunity to consider whether we really wanted to carry our workplace and all its responsibilities around with us everywhere we went, subscribe to a service that lets anyone identify us from a picture, or surrender control of our vehicle to an algorithm that might operate on a moral calculus different from any we might be comfortable with.

Whenever we get swept up in the self-reinforcing momentum and seductive logic of some new technology, we forget to ask what else it might be doing, how else it might be working, and who ultimately benefits most from its appearance. Why time has been diced into the segments between notifications, why we feel so inadequate to the parade of images that reach us through our devices, just why it is that we feel so often feel hollow and spent. What might connect our choices and the processes that are stripping the planet, filthing the atmosphere, and impoverishing human and nonhuman lives beyond number. Whether and in what way our actions might be laying the groundwork for an oppression that is grimmer yet and still more total. And finally we forget to ask whether, in our aspiration to overcome the human, we are discarding a gift we already have at hand and barely know what to do with.

If we're disturbed by what we find when we do finally answer queries like these to our own satisfaction, if we dislike the picture of the world and our place in it that we're left with, we find ourselves confronted with a final set of questions: Can these radical technologies be renounced? Can they be resisted? And if not, can they at least be steered toward somewhat more congenial ends?

The possibility of renunciation is easily enough dispensed with. Short of a determined, Kaczynskian flight from the consensual world and all its entanglements, the algorithmic management of life chances in particular will still exert tremendous pressure on the shape of one's choices, even the structure of one's consciousness. And even then—whatever steps they may have taken to secrete the traces of their existence from the network's gaze, however blissfully unaware they may remain of its continuing interest in them—the dweller in a remote, off-the-grid cabin can be certain that data concerning them and their activities will continue to circulate indefinitely, turning up in response to queries and being operated on in unpredictable ways. That the network may know them primarily as a lacuna, that they may with a little luck evade its influence being brought to bear on their own body, does nothing to change the fact that its ambit is total.

Any gesture of refusal short of going off the grid entirely will be still less likely to result in the desired independence from the processes of intimate, persistent oversight and management now loose in the world. Just as whatever degree of freedom to act we enjoy is already sharply undercut by commercial pressures, and the choices made in aggregate by others, so too will our scope of action be constrained by the shape of the place that is left for us by the functioning of automated and algorithmic systems, the new shape of the natural, the ordinary and the obvious—for that is how hegemony works. If neoliberalism, like any hegemonic system, produced subjects with characteristic affects, desires, values, instincts and modes of expression, and those subjects came in time to constitute virtually the entirety of the social environment any of us experience, it's hard to see how matters could be any different in the wake of the posthuman turn. It is exceedingly hard to outright refuse something which has become part of you—and made you part of it—in the most literal way, right down to the molecular composition of your body and the content of your dreams.

The possibility of resistance offers somewhat more hope. Rare indeed is the oppression so total that there is no scope whatsoever for resistance to it. Though they emphasize different aspects of this experience—from cleverness and concealment to outright mulishness—thinkers as different from one another as Michel de Certeau, bell hooks, James C. Scott and Gayatri Spivak all agree that even amidst the most draconian circumstances, people find a way to make do and even flourish.[9] So perhaps we ought to be asking whether there remains a space for tactics in the drive toward total automation, the eclipse of human discretion and the transvaluation of all the values that gave rise to everyday life as we recognize it.

Historically, most such acts of rebellion took place in the register that James C. Scott calls *infrapolitics*. This is the stratum of gossip and bitter jokes, of shucking and jiving, of shirking, goldbricking and foot-dragging, of pilferage and work-to-rule strikes—of every stratagem that the poor and the powerless have ever deployed in the attempt to keep their masters from being able to appropriate the fruits of their labor, place bounds on their sense of self and define their reality entire. As we've seen, however, the ability to detect behavioral anomalies and departures from acceptable performance profiles algorithmically and remotely is already well advanced. Though they presently stumble at precisely the kind of coded speech that the marginalized have always used to establish and maintain spaces free from oversight—Verlan, Cockney rhyming slang, Polari, 3arabizi—it would be foolish to assume that sentiment analysis and intent recognition will not develop further in the years ahead. And of course totalizing systems like the Chinese social-credit scheme now under active development propose to weave a net capable of capturing, characterizing and punishing all such insurgent acts and utterances, whether public or private; whether or not, indeed, they are conscious at all.

And that leaves the possibility, however slim, of working to enact progressive social change within the technosocial frameworks that are now available to us. If we want to take Marx at his word and steer the world in the direction of justice, though—however we may define it—we need a better, more supple theory of technological change, more suited to a time in which our tools work as networks and distributed assemblages. That theory needs to help us understand how agency and power are distributed across the meshing nodes and links of our collective being, how to evaluate the effect on our lives of that which cannot be understood in isolation and cannot be determined in advance, and how to assemble discrete components in ensembles capable of prevailing over the recalcitrance of things and actually making change.

Acquiring this sophistication will help us avoid the blunders well-intentioned thinkers often make, in offering recipes for the transition out of capitalism that are based on technologies they simply don't understand very well. When Jeremy Rifkin argues, for example, that a "3D printing process embedded in an Internet of Things infrastructure means that virtually anyone in the world can [make] his or her own products for use or sharing, employing open-source software," we may very well share his hope for the defeat of scarcity and the emergence of a planetary commons. But in proposing 3D printing, the internet of things and open-source software as the engines of this transition, we know he cannot possibly have reckoned with the contestations, the complexities and the outright vulnerability to capture that vex every single term in this equation. We know that what undermines his vision is not its impossibility in absolute, physical terms, but how badly it underestimates the investments of effort and life energy required to sustain it against the recalcitrance of the world. And we wonder why this just-so story fails to convince. Instead, we need to furnish ourselves with a deeper account of the institutional processes by way of which technology is actually produced in our world, or the powerful entrenched interests that are dedicated to preventing any such thing as a post-scarcity commons from taking root. It is only by understanding these factors from the outset, and learning to anticipate their influence, that our designs might have any chance of being able to counter them.

And beyond theory lies practice. Can we make other politics with these technologies? Can we use them in ways that don't simply reproduce all-too-familiar arrangements of power? At the moment in which I write, for all the reasons I've laid forth here, I'm not particularly optimistic on this count; we appear to be laboring under a certain hegemony of the Stacks and, more precisely, of the approach to technology that they emblematize.

Their power to mediate experience is not yet total, but it's not terribly far short of that, either. It resides in the smartphone that is the last thing many of us look at before we sleep, and the first thing we turn to upon waking; in the apps with which we manage time and attention, negotiate the city, and pursue the ends of mobility, sociality and productivity; in the algorithms that parse our utterances, model the flow of our bodily and psychic states, and prepare strategies in response to them; and in the cloud that binds these things together, as indispensable as it is ubiquitous and hard to see clearly. Like any hegemony, that of the Stacks actively reproduces itself, sustaining and being sustained by a continuous and all but unquestioned framework of assumptions about what technology is for, how it is developed, and who makes it. And in doing so, it tends to deny the space in which alternatives might be nurtured, to the extent that those alternatives have all but literally become unthinkable. In our time, even the most seemingly transgressive visions of technology in everyday life invariably fall back to the familiar furniture of capital investment, surplus extraction and exploitation. We don't even speak of progress any longer, but rather of "innovation."

If what we find in the radical technologies we've discussed is the power to transform the very ground of our social being in a particularly inimical way, it difficult to imagine that any choice we can make as individuals or small clusters can do much to undermine the prerogatives of the institutions of scale that are interested in seeing this transformation made real, from Amazon to the Chinese state. And yet, daunting as it may be, that is the task that now lies before us, the charge that is ours to discover, inhabit and make our own.

For even in this airlessness, there is possibility. The assumptions on which the Stacks and their entire approach to technology rely are, after all, our own, and we retain the ability to reformulate them. Perhaps we could start the process of reframing what it is we expect from our tools by attending to those activists who are offering insight from within the technology community itself—the cyberfeminist research collaborative Deep Lab, for example, the participants in the annual Radical Networks conference, and all the many groups dedicated to critical engineering, critical making and critical algorithm studies. There is a current of technically capable and socially progressive inquiry corresponding to every section of this book, and space is being made by all of them. The fundamental insight they offer us is this: people with left politics of any stripe absolutely cannot allow their eyes to glaze over when the topic of conversation turns to technology, or in any way cede this terrain to its existing inhabitants, for to do so is to surrender the commanding heights of the contemporary situation. It's absolutely vital, now, for all of us who think of ourselves as in any way progressive or belonging to the left current to understand just what the emerging technics of everyday life propose, how they work, and what they are capable of. A time of radical technologies demands a generation of radical technologists, and these networks are the material means by way of which we can help each other become that.

And perhaps we could do a better job of pushing back again the rhetoric of transcendence we're offered. Every time we are presented with the aspiration toward the posthuman, we need to perceive the predictably tawdry and all-too-human drives underlying it, including the desire to profit from the exploitation of others and the sheer will to power and control. It doesn't take a trained psychologist to detect that these motives are present, and being clearer about them might give us at least momentary leverage over those pushing so hard for our own eclipse, who in doing so have consecrated their considerable gifts to the task of achieving the smallest, shallowest and most shaming of dreams.

Finally, as Raymond Williams long ago taught us, one of hegemony's features is that there remain within it always pockets of unassimilated material from social moments past, and the first weak signals of social forms just coming into being.[10] Even if just barely, then, like the ghostly patterns of data left behind on an imperfectly erased hard drive, our arrangements of the world bear traces of lifeways that were founded in solidarity and neighborly conviviality, and an everyday life that was more spacious and tolerant of imperfection. At the same time, if we sit patiently with them, we can sense in certain things around us the slightest premonitory tremble of lifeways yet to be—ways of being human unbound by the tangible and intangible shackles that so often constrained those who came before us. These are the seeds of possible futures, seeds that with effort and care might yet be grown into a wiser, more considered, more just and generous way of living together upon the Earth.

Acknowledgements

The very first person I need to thank here is Leo Hollis. The book you hold in your hands simply wouldn't exist were it not for his consistent belief in me, however unjustified it may have been. You know the scene in *Inception* where Joseph Gordon-Levitt and Tom Hardy, as intruders in the virtual world of another man's mind, are being besieged by the ghostly brigades of their subject's "militarized subconscious"? Gordon-Levitt's character is standing at the door of a warehouse, plinking away ineffectually at the encroaching horde with an assault rifle, when Hardy shoulders him aside. With the words, "You mustn't be afraid to dream a little bigger, darling," he hoists a massive South African grenade launcher, lobs a round onto the opposite rooftop, and blows things up *reeeeal good*. That was Leo to me ... except instead of a grenade launcher, he mostly relied upon double espressos from the Algerian Coffee Stores.

I'd also like to thank Mark Martin and his editorial team at Verso, for their good cheer, patience with my last-minute revisions, and indulgence of my more-than-occasional insistence on a particular way of wording things; designers Neil Donnelly and Ben Fehrman-Lee and typesetter Matt Gavan, for transforming those words into an aesthetically pleasing object; and publicists Jennifer Tighe and Wes House, for making sure people who might have an interest in that object know that it exists. Nothing is ever achieved alone, and to whatever degree that you've enjoyed this book, you have their labors to thank for it.

I am grateful to the insight, solidarity, support and energy furnished, in various ways, by Ash Amin, Jon Ardern, Timo Arnall, John Bingham-Hall, Ian Bogost, Shumi Bose, Jaya Klara Brekke, Ricky and Mika Burdett, Alberto Corsín Jiménez, Aimee Meredith Cox, Ayona Datta, Sally Davies, Benjie de la Peña, Nicholas de Monchaux, Nigel Dodd, Nick Durrant, Warren Ellis, Nuno Ferreira da Cruz, David Faris, Daisy Froud, Andrei Goncharov, Stephen Graham, Suzi Hall, Alaina Harkness, Usman Haque, Chris Heathcote, Catarina Heeckt, Robin Howie, Sha Hwang, Tom Igoe, Anab Jain, Shanthi Kalathil, Sophia Kakembo, Michelle Kasprzak, Mike Kuniavsky, Laura Kurgan, Annie Kwon, Derek Lindner, David Madden, Adrian McEwen, Justin McGuirk, Ana Méndez de Andés, Michal Migurski, Dietmar Offenhuber, Frank Pasquale, Bre Pettis, Lucia Pietroiusti, Alison Powell, Pamela Puchalski, Jack Linchuan Qiu, Philipp Rode, Saskia Sassen, Gaia Scagnetti, Fred Scharmen, Jack Schulze, Susan Wile Schwarz, Brett Scott, Richard Sennett, Steven Shaviro, Jonathan Silver, Stavros Stavrides, Cordy Swope, Rena Tom, Shan Vahidy, Tricia Wang, Gill Wildman, Amanda Marisa Williams, Sarah Williams, Jillian C. York, Adriana Valdez Young, and a few folks who need to remain nameless here but hopefully know who they are. Though their contributions were indispensable in helping me get my head around concepts I scarcely understood at the outset, the traditional disclaimer applies: any errors in comprehension, interpretation or characterization you may run across in these pages are entirely my own.

I'm indebted to the MetaFilter community for pointing me at sources, acquainting me with unfamiliar perspectives and forcing me to sharpen my argument. One thread in particular, on the "theology of consensus," was rich in comments that chimed with my own experience, confirming my intuition that I was headed in an interesting direction. I thank everyone who contributed to it. More specifically, I wish to express my gratitude to the user known to me only as kliuless: indefatigable if unknowing research assistant, without whose efforts my sections on cryptocurrency and the blockchain would have been so much shallower.

I'd also like to acknowledge the profound inspiration furnished to me by Godfrey Boyle and Peter Harper's 1976 compendium *Radical Technology*, and particularly the legendary illustrations contributed to that volume by Cliff Harper. If the righteous and resonant vision they offered—of advanced technology grasped by the people themselves, and repurposed for socially, politically, economically and ecologically progressive ends—cannot be sustained in our own time, my own work here has been an attempt to discover how and why this turned out to be the case, and what might still be done about it.

Finally, in the truest sense, this book was a coproduction with my love and life partner Nurri Kim. Beyond constantly challenging me intellectually, pointing me at useful resources, accommodating my needs for space and time in which to think and write, and demanding that I live up to the expectations I set for others, you offered me a frankly mortifying level of support and care in the endgame, when I hardly left the house for weeks at a stretch, and could barely be roused to maintain myself in any way beyond brewing the coffee. I can only hope to reciprocate that level of heartful care as you turn toward your own life's work.

Radical Technologies was written to the sounds of Orem Ambarchi, ANOHNI, AUN, Barn Owl, William Basinski, Rhys Chatham, Current 93, Deafheaven, Earth, Floor, Lento, Liturgy, Locrian, Machinefabriek, Nadja, Planning for Burial, Russian Circles, SubRosa, SUNN O))), Swans, True Widow, Mika Vainio, and Zeal & Ardor, with some assistance from Joan Baez.

Suiting by George Dyer of Threadneedleman Tailors, Walworth Road, London SE17.

Adam Greenfield uses and endorses Philz Coffee Jacob's Wonderbar Blend.

THIS BOOK IS TO BE PLAYED AT MAXIMUM VOLUME.

Notes

1 Smartphone

1. As of early 2016, smartphone penetration in major markets ranges from a low of 17 percent in India to 89 percent in South Korea: Jacob Poushter, "Smartphone Ownership and Internet Usage Continues to Climb in Emerging Economies," Pew Research Center, February 22, 2016, pewglobal.org.

2. This work resulted in two complementary academic papers: Mizuko Ito, Daisuke Okabe and Ken Anderson, "Portable Objects in Three Global Cities: The Personalization of Urban Places," in *The Reconstruction of Space and Time: Mobile Communication Practices*, Rich Ling and Scott W. Campbell, eds., Piscataway, NJ: Transaction Publishers, 2009; and Ken Anderson, Scott D. Mainwaring and Michele F. Chang, "Living for the Global City: Mobile Kits, Urban Interfaces and Ubicomp," in Michael Beigl et al., eds., *Proceedings of Ubicomp 2005*, Berlin: Springer Verlag, 2005.

3. While there had been some early thought that such interface gestures might be branded—that is, defined rigorously as sets of numeric parameters, then claimed as the intellectual property of a particular enterprise, such that no competitor could offer them as a means of interaction without first licensing them from the rights-holder—that ambition, thankfully, turned out to be legally untenable. As a result, these gestures now constitute a universal, industry-wide language of touch. John Ribeiro, "US patent office

rejects claims of Apple 'pinch to zoom' patent," *PCWorld*, July 29, 2013.

4. Ann Fenwick, "Evaluating China's Special Economic Zones," *Berkeley Journal of International Law* Volume 2, Issue 2, Fall 1984.

5. "According to a report by the Shanghai Academy of Social Sciences, each year about forty thousand fingers are either cut off or crushed in factories in the Pearl River Delta alone, mostly during assembly line operations for the export business": Jack Linchuan Qiu, *Working-Class Network Society*, Cambridge, MA: MIT Press, 2009, p. 104.

6. Michael Blanding and Heather White, "How China Is Screwing Over Its Poisoned Factory Workers," *Wired*, April 6, 2015.

7. Jenny Chan, "A Suicide Survivor: The Life of a Chinese Migrant Worker at Foxconn," Truthout, August 25, 2013. See also Joel Johnson, "1 Million Workers. 90 Million iPhones. 17 Suicides. Who's To Blame?," *Wired*, February 28, 2011.

8. Just how healthy? A teardown analysis of various iPhone 6 models in the fall of 2014 estimated that the most basic device's bill of materials ran to some $247, including roughly $4.50 in labor costs. With an unsubsidized retail price between $649 and $689, each unit sold yielded Apple an astounding profit margin of between 69 and 70 percent. Arik Hesseldahl, "Teardown shows Apple's iPhone 6 cost at least $200 to build," *Re/code*, September 23, 2014.

9. Michael Schuman, "Is China Stealing Jobs? It May Be Losing Them, Instead," *New York Times*, July 22, 2016.

10. Todd C. Frankel, "The Cobalt Pipeline," *Washington Post*, September 30, 2016; Friends of the Earth, "Mining for smartphones: The true cost of tin," November 26, 2012.

11. Depending on what precisely is being measured, it is either first, or a close second, to the tablet computer. Michael DeGusta, "Are Smart Phones Spreading Faster than Any Technology in Human History?," *MIT Technology Review*, May 9, 2012.

12. There are important exceptions. India's patriarchal culture has produced a staggering gender gap in mobile access: some 28 percent of Indian women have a personal device, compared to 43 percent of Indian men; Eric Bellman and Aditi Malhotra, "Why the Vast Majority of Women in India Will Never Own a Smartphone," *Wall Street Journal*, October 13, 2016.

13. Cary Stothart, Ainsley Mitchum and Courtney Yehnert, "The Attentional Cost of Receiving a Cell Phone Notification," *Journal of Experimental Psychology: Human Perception and Performance*, June 29, 2015.

14. Google, "Understanding Consumers' Local Search Behavior," May 2014, think.storage.googleapis.com/docs/how-advertisers-

can-extend-their-relevance-with-search_research-studies. pdf.

15. Winston Churchill, "House of Commons Rebuilding," *Hansard*, October 28, 1943, hansard.millbanksystems.com/commons/1943/oct/28/house-of-commons-rebuilding.

16. Will Worley, "Syrian Woman Explains Why Refugees Need Smartphones," *Independent*, May 12, 2016.

2 The internet of things

1. Mike Kuniavsky, *Smart Things: Ubiquitous Computing User Experience Design*, Burlington, MA: Elsevier, 2010.
2. See quantifiedself.com
3. Ahnjili Zhuparris, "Menstrual Cycles, 50 Cent and Right Swipes," QSEU15 Conference, September 24, 2015, vimeo.com/151149664.
4. Jeff Sparrow, "Soylent, Neoliberalism and the Politics of Life Hacking," *CounterPunch*, May 19, 2014. counterpunch.org/2014/05/19/solyent-neoliberalism-and-the-politics-of-life-hacking/
5. Beth Mole, "Want an Apple Watch? For some Aetna customers, it'll soon be covered," *Ars Technica*, September 27, 2016. arstechnica.com/science/2016/09/want-an-apple-watch-for-some-aetna-customers-itll-soon-be-covered/ Marion Dakers, "Health insurer bribes customers to exercise with an Apple Watch," *The Telegraph*, September 27, 2016. telegraph.co.uk/business/2016/09/26/health-insurer-bribes-customers-to-exercise-with-an-apple-watch/
6. Amazon.com, Inc., "Amazon Dash Button," undated, amazon.com/Dash-Buttons/b?ie=UTF8&node=10667898011.
7. Jeunese Payne et al., "Gendering the Machine: Preferred Virtual Assistant Gender and Realism in Self-service," in Ruth Aylett et al., eds., *Intelligent Virtual Agents: 13th International Conference*, Berlin, Heidelberg: Springer-Verlag, 2013, cl.cam.ac.uk/~rja14/shb14/jeunese.pdf.
8. Cameron Glover, "How Google's Virtual Assistant Tackles Gender Inequality," *Tech.co*, May 19, 2016.
9. Brian X. Chen, "Google Home vs. Amazon Echo. Let the Battle Begin," *New York Times*, May 18, 2016.
10. Mike Reis, "Secrets from the Host Stand: 10 Things a Restaurant Host Wishes They Could Tell You," *Serious Eats*, January 3, 2013.
11. United States Equal Employment Opportunity Commission, "Special Reports: Diversity in High Tech," May 18, 2016, eeoc.gov/eeoc/statistics/reports/hightech/; Gregory Ferenstein, "The

Politics of Silicon Valley," *Fast Company,* November 8, 2015.

12. Pew Research Center. "Shared, Collaborative and On Demand: The New Digital Economy," May 19, 2016, pewinternet. org/2016/05/19/the-new-digital-economy/.

13. An Amazon customer service representative characterized these as "to improve the results provided to you and improve our services": amazon.com/gp/help/customer/forums/ ref=cs_hc_g_tv?ie=UTF8&forumID=Fx1SKFFP8U1B6N5&cd Thread=Tx26V9TT6C3TD21

14. Ian Kar, "Amazon Echo, home alone with NPR on, got confused and hijacked a thermostat," *Quartz,* March 11, 2016.

15. Bradley Dilger, "The Ideology of Ease," *Journal of Electronic Publishing,* Volume 6, Issue 1, September 2000.

16. J. M. Porup, " 'Internet of Things' security is hilariously broken and getting worse," *Ars Technica,* January 23, 2016.

17. Ms. Smith, "Peeping into 73,000 Unsecured Security Cameras Thanks to Default Passwords," *Network World,* November 6, 2014.

18. Matthew Garrett, "I Stayed in a Hotel with Android Lightswitches and It Was Just as Bad as You'd Imagine," mjg59 blog, March 11, 2016, mjg59.dreamwidth.org/40505.html.

19. Aaron Tilley, "How Hackers Could Use a Nest Thermostat as an Entry Point Into Your Home," *Forbes,* March 6, 2015.

20. Tim Ring, "Hack Turns Cheap D-Link Webcam into a Network Backdoor," *SC Magazine,* January 12, 2016.

21. Bruce Schneier, "The Internet of Things Is Wildly Insecure—And Often Unpatchable," Schneier on Security, January 6, 2014.

22. Matthew Petroff, "Amazon Dash Button Teardown," May 24, 2015, mpetroff.net.

23. Sarah Perez, "Amazon Expands Dash Buttons to More Brands, Effectively Makes the Buttons Free," TechCrunch, September 2, 2015.

24. Graham Harman, "Heidegger on Objects and Things," in Bruno Latour and Peter Weibel, eds., *Making Things Public: Atmospheres of Democracy,* Cambridge, MA: MIT Press, 2005. See, however, Richard Rorty, "Heidegger and the Atomic Bomb," in the same volume.

25. Anna Minton, *Ground Control: Fear and Happiness in the Twenty-first Century City,* London: Penguin, 2009.

26. See discussion of FindFace in Section 7, Machine learning.

27. Jeremy Gillula and Dave Maass. "What You Can Learn from Oakland's Raw ALPR Data," Electronic Frontier Foundation, January 21, 2015. eff.org.

28. Eric P. Newcomer, "For More of Midtown, Traffic Relief May Be a Mouse Click Away," *New York Times,* June 5, 2012.

29. American Civil Liberties Union, "You Are Being Tracked: How

License Plate Readers Are Being Used to Record Americans' Movements," July 2013, aclu.org.

30. These are, of course, monitored for other reasons as well. Kashmir Hill, "E-ZPasses Get Read All Over New York (Not Just at Toll Booths)," Forbes, September 12, 2013.

31. Much of the argument that follows originally appeared in my 2013 pamphlet, *Against the Smart City*, New York and Helsinki: Do projects, 2013.

32. Siemens Corporation, "Sustainable Buildings—Networked Technologies: Smart Homes and Cities," Pictures of the Future, Fall 2008.

33. Laura Kurgan, "Forests of Data," EYEO Festival, Minneapolis, MN, June 28, 2011.

34. For example, in New York City, an anonymous survey of "hundreds of retired high-ranking [NYPD] officials" found that "tremendous pressure to reduce crime, year after year, prompted some supervisors and precinct commanders to distort crime statistics" they submitted to the centralized COMPSTAT system. David W. Chen, "Survey Raises Questions on Data-Driven Policy," *New York Times*, February 8, 2010.

35. David Simon, Kia Corthron, Ed Burns and Chris Collins, *The Wire*, Season 4, Episode 9: "Know Your Place," first aired November 12, 2006.

36. Asian Business Daily. "Subway CCTV Was Used to Sneakily Watch Citizens' Bare Skin," July 16, 2013, (in Korean) asiae.co.kr/news/view.htm?idxno=2013071614443771298.

37. Jim Fletcher, IBM Distinguished Engineer, and Guruduth Banavar, Vice President and Chief Technology Officer for Global Public Sector, personal communication, June 8, 2011.

38. Michal Migurski, "Visualizing Urban Data," in Toby Segaran and Jeff Hammerbacher, *Beautiful Data: The Stories Behind Elegant Data Solutions*, Sebastopol CA: O'Reilly Media, 2012. See also Michal Migurski, "Oakland Crime Maps X," tecznotes, March 3, 2008, mike.teczno.com.

39. See, as well, Sen's dissection of the inherent conflict between even mildly liberal values and Pareto optimality. Amartya Kumar Sen, "The impossibility of a Paretian liberal," *Journal of Political Economy* Volume 78 Number 1, Jan–Feb 1970.

40. Jay Forrester, *Urban Dynamics*, Cambridge, MA: The MIT Press, 1969; Joe Flood, *The Fires: How a Computer Formula Burned Down New York City—And Determined the Future Of American Cities*, New York: Riverhead Books, 2010.

41. See, e.g., Luís M.A. Bettencourt et al., "Growth, Innovation, Scaling, and the Pace of Life in Cities," *Proceedings of the National Academy of Sciences*, Volume 104, Number 17, April 24, 2007, pp. 7301–6.

42. Flood, ibid.
43. See Amazon's interview with *Fires* author Joe Flood: amazon.com/ Fires-Computer-Intentions-City---Determined/dp/1594485062/ ref=sr_1_1?s=books&ie=UTF8&qid=1376668689&sr=1-1.
44. Edwin Black, *IBM and the Holocaust: The Strategic Alliance between Nazi Germany and America's Most Powerful Corporation*, New York: Crown Books, 2001.
45. Raul Hilberg, *The Destruction of the European Jews*, New Haven: Yale University Press, 2003.
46. Jasmina Tešanović, "Seven Ways of IoWT," IoWT blog, April 27, 2016, internetofwomenthings.tumblr.com/post/143491446241/ seven-ways-of-iowt.

3 Augmented reality

1. County10 News. "Teen Playing New Pokémon Game on Phone Discovers Body in Wind River," July 8, 2016; José Pagliery, "Pokemon Go leads teen to dead body," CNNMoney, July 9, 2016.
2. Melissa Chan, "Pokémon Go Players Anger 9/11 Memorial Visitors: 'It's a Hallowed Place'," *Time*, July 12, 2016.
3. Mike Wehner, "The Mysterious Pokémon Go Gym at the Border of North Korea and South Korea Has Disappeared," *Daily Dot*, July 13, 2016.
4. Brian Feldman, "Yes, You Can Catch Pokémon at Auschwitz," *New York Magazine*, July 11, 2016.
5. Steven J. Henderson and Steven K. Feiner, "Augmented Reality for Maintenance and Repair (ARMAR)," Columbia University Department of Computer Science Report AFRL-RH-WP-TR-2007-0112, August 2007, http://graphics.cs.columbia. edu/projects/armar/pubs/henderson_feiner_AFRL_ RH-WP-TR-2007-0112.pdf.
6. Tanagram Partners. "The Future of Firefighting - A HMD-AR UI Concept for First Responders," August 18, 2011, YouTube.com.
7. Thomas Grüter, Martina Grüter and Claus-Christian Carbon, "Neural and Genetic Foundations of Face Recognition and Prosopagnosia," *Journal of Neuropsychology*, Volume 2, Issue 1, March 2008: 79–97.
8. For early work toward this end, see Thad Starner et al., "Augmented Reality Through Wearable Computing," MIT Media Lab, 1997, cc.gatech.edu/~thad/p/journal/augmented-reality-through-wearable-computing.pdf. The overlay of a blinking outline or contour used as an identification cue has long been a staple of science-fictional information displays, showing up in pop culture as far back as the late 1960s. The earliest appearance I can locate

is *2001: A Space Odyssey* (1968), in which the navigational displays of both the Orion III spaceplane and the exploration vessel *Discovery* relied heavily on the trope—this, presumably, because in the fictional universe of the film they were produced by the same contractor, IBM. See also the *Nostromo*'s orbital contours in *Alien* (1979), Pete Shelley's music video for "Homosapien" (1981), and the traverse corridors projected through the sky of *Blade Runner*'s Los Angeles (1982).

9. Gunter Demnig, *Stolpersteine: Here Lived 1933–1945, An Art Project for Europe*, 2009, stolpersteine.eu/en/.

10. Steven Cherry, "Steve Mann's Better Version of Reality," *IEEE Spectrum*, March 8, 2013.

11. Richard Holloway, "Registration Errors in Augmented Reality," Ph.D. dissertation. UNC Chapel Hill Department of Computer Science Technical Report TR95-016, August 1995.

12. Eugenia M. Kolasinski, "Simulator Sickness in Virtual Environments," US Army Research Institute for the Behavioral and Social Sciences Technical Report 1027, May 1995. dtic.mil/cgi-bin/GetTRDoc?AD=ADA295861.

13. Steve Mann, " 'Reflectionism' and 'Diffusionism': New Tactics for Deconstructing the Video Surveillance Superhighway," *Leonardo*, Volume 31, Number 2, April 1998: pp. 93–102.

14. Lisa Guernsey, "At Airport Gate, A Cyborg Unplugged," *New York Times*, March 14, 2002.

15. John Perry Barlow, "Leaving the Physical World," Conference on HyperNetworking, 1998, w2.eff.org/Misc/Publications/John_Perry_Barlow/HTML/leaving_the_physical_world.html.

16. Governors Highway Safety Association. "Spotlight on Highway Safety: Pedestrian Fatalities by State," 2010, ghsa.org/html/publications/pdf/spotlights/spotlight_ped.pdf. Similarly, a recent University of Utah study found that the act of immersion in a conversation, rather than any physical aspect of use, is the primary distraction while driving and talking on the phone. That hands-free headset may not keep you out of a crash after all. Strayer, David and Frank A. Drews, "Cell-Phone-Induced Driver Distraction," *Current Directions in Psychological Science*, Volume, 16 Number 3, June 2007.

17. Lyn Lofland, *The Public Realm: Understanding the City's Quintessential Social Territory*, Piscataway, NJ: Transaction, 1998; Jane E. Brody, "Distracted Walkers Pose Threat To Self and Others," *New York Times*, December 7, 2015.

18. Adrian Chen, "If You Wear Google's New Glasses, You Are An Asshole," *Gawker*, March 13, 2013.

19. The differentiation involved might be very fine-grained indeed: users may find themselves interacting with informational objects that exist only for them, and only for that single moment.

20. Wagner James Au, "VR Will Make Life Better—Or Just Be an Opiate of the Masses," *Wired*, February 25, 2016.
21. Philip K. Dick, "How to Build a Universe That Doesn't Fall Apart Two Days Later," in Sutin, Lawrence, ed., *The Shifting Realities of Philip K. Dick: Selected Literary and Philosophical Writings*, New York: Vintage, 1996.
22. The first widespread publicity for Glass coincided with Google's release of a video on Wednesday, February 20, 2013; the 5 Point announced its ban less than two weeks later, on the fifth of March. Unsurprisingly, concerns centered more on the device's data-collection capability than anything else: according to 5 Point owner Dave Meinert, his customers "don't want to be secretly filmed or videotaped and immediately put on the Internet." This is, of course, an entirely reasonable expectation, not merely in the liminal space of a dive bar but anywhere in the city. Casey Newton, "Seattle dive bar becomes first to ban Google Glass," CNET, March 8, 2013.
23. Dan Wasserman, "Google Glass Rolls Out Diane von Furstenberg frames," *Mashable*, June 23, 2014.

4 Digital fabrication

1. John Von Neumann, *Theory of Self-Reproducing Automata*, Urbana: University of Illinois Press, 1966, cba.mit.edu/events/03.11.ASE/docs/VonNeumann.pdf.
2. You may be familiar with cellular automata from John Conway's 1970 Game of Life, certainly the best-known instance of the class. See Bitstorm.org, "John Conway's Game of Life," undated, bitstorm.org.
3. Adrian Bowyer, "Wealth Without Money: The Background to the Bath Replicating Rapid Prototyper Project," February 2, 2004, reprap.org/wiki/Wealth_Without_Money; RepRap Project, "Cost Reduction," December 30, 2014, reprap.org/wiki/Cost_Reduction. Partial precedent for Bowyer's design exists in the form of the Bridgeport mill—not autonomously self-reproducing, but capable of making all its own parts when guided by a skilled operator, c. 1930.
4. Elliot Williams, "Getting It Right By Getting It Wrong: RepRap and the Evolution of 3D Printing," *Hackaday*, March 2, 2016. See also Tim Maughan, "The Changing Face of Shenzhen, the World's Gadget Factory," *Motherboard*, August 19, 2015.
5. MakerBot Industries, LLC, "MakerBot Reaches Milestone: 100,000 3D Printers Sold Worldwide," April 4, 2016.
6. Jeremy Rifkin, *The Zero Marginal Cost Society: The Internet*

of *Things, the Collaborative Commons, and the Eclipse of Capitalism*, Basingstoke, UK: Palgrave Macmillan, 2014; Paul Mason, *Postcapitalism: A Guide to Our Future*, London: Allen Lane, 2015; Nick Srnicek and Alex Williams, *Inventing the Future: Postcapitalism and a World Without Work*, London: Verso, 2015.

7. For a pungent critique, see mcm_cmc, "Fully Automated Luxury Communism: A Utopian Critique," Libcom.org, June 14, 2015.

8. Jane Jacobs, *The Death and Life of Great American Cities*, New York: Random House, 1961.

9. United Nations, "Universal Declaration of Human Rights," December 10, 1948, un.org/en/universal-declaration-human-rights/.

10. The slightly less-polished Othermill is still cheaper. Other Machine Co., "Othermill," 2016, othermachine.co/othermill/.

11. James Hobson, "3D Printing Houses From Concrete," *Hackaday*, April 15, 2016; National Aeronautics and Space Administration. "3D Printing: Food In Space," May 23, 2013; Sean V. Murphy and Anthony Atala, "3D Bioprinting of Tissues and Organs," *Nature Biotechnology* 32, 2014, pp. 773–85.

12. A global registry of Fablabs is maintained by the volunteers at fablabs.io/.

13. Neil Gershenfeld, *Fab: The Coming Revolution on Your Desktop, from Personal Computers to Personal Fabrication*, New York: Basic Books, 2005.

14. William McDonough and Michael Braungart, *Cradle to Cradle: Remaking the Way We Make Things*, New York: North Point Press, 2002. See also David Holmgren, *Permaculture: Principles and Pathways Beyond Sustainability*, East Meon: Permanent Publications, 2002.

15. MatterHackers, "How to Succeed When Printing in PLA," April 29, 2016, matterhackers.com.

16. Protoprint Solutions Pvt. Ltd., "The World's First Fair Trade Filament for 3D Printing," 2016. protoprint.in/.

17. Megan Kreiger et al., "Distributed Recycling of Post-Consumer Plastic Waste in Rural Areas," *Proceedings of the Materials Research Society*, Volume 1492, 2013, pp. 91–6., dx.doi.org; Cecilia Paradi-Guilford and Scott Henry, "Can We Shift Waste to Value Through 3D Printing in Tanzania?," World Bank Information and Communications for Development blog, September 23, 2015, blogs.worldbank.org; on SWaCH, see Solid Waste Collection and Handling Seva Sahakari Sanstha Maryadit, "What Is SWACH?," 2013, swachcoop.com; on ethical filament, see Ethical Filament, ethicalfilament.org/.

18. Hannah Rose Mendoza, "Got Milk? Then You've Got 3D Printer Filament at a 99.7 percent Discount," 3DPrint.com, July 3, 2014.

19. An effort called Precious Plastic even aims to open-source the

plans for all of the machines necessary to recycle plastic. Dave Hakkens, "Precious Plastic," 2013, preciousplastic.com/plan/.

20. Fablab Barcelona, "Furniture Hacking," November 2015, fablabbcn.org/workshop/2015/05/05/furniture_hack.html.

21. Nicholas De Monchaux, *Spacesuit: Fashioning Apollo,* Cambridge, MA: The MIT Press, 2011.

22. I am assuming that the costs of powering digital fabricators are no more onerous than those associated with any other appliance of similar scale. Indeed, given the increasing facility with which photovoltaics, Stirling engines, and wind-turbine components can be printed, there is a reasonable argument to be made that any properly equipped workshop can henceforth be self-powering.

23. See oshwa.org/definition/.

24. Alicia Gibb, "On Creative Commons and Open Source," Open Source Hardware Association, May 21, 2014, oshwa.org; See also the discussion of the nuances here: Lenore Edman, "Open Discussion: Best Practice for Mislabeled Open Source Projects?," Evil Mad Scientist Laboratories, June 18, 2014, evilmadscientist. com.

25. See 507movements.com.

26. OpenDesk, opendesk.cc.

27. Open Source Ecology. "Global Village Construction Set," February 4, 2015, opensourceecology.org/wiki/Global_Village_ Construction_Set; See also Autodesk, Inc., "Instructables," 2016, instructables.com and Definition of Free Cultural Works, February 17, 2015, freedomdefined.org/Definition.

28. Pieter Van Lancker, "The Influence of IP on the 3D Printing Evolution," *Creax,* August 12, 2015.

29. Zachary Smith, "MakerBot vs. Open Source—A Founder's Perspective," Hoektronics.com, September 21, 2012; See also MakerBot cofounder Bre Pettis's response, "Fixing Misinformation with Information," September 20, 2012, makerbot.com/blog/ 2012/09/20/fixing-misinformation-with-information.

30. Michele Boldrin and David K. Levine, *Against Intellectual Monopoly,* Cambridge, UK: Cambridge University Press, 2008.

31. John Hornick and Dan Roland. "Many 3D Patents Are Expiring Soon," *3D Printing Industry,* December 29, 2013, 3dprintingindustry.com.

32. Josef Průša, "Open Hardware Meaning," September 20, 2012, josefprusa.cz/open-hardware-meaning/.

33. Johan Söderberg, *Hacking Capitalism: The Free and Open Source Software Movement,* Abingdon: Routledge, 2012.

34. Manon Walquan, "Un clitoris imprimé en 3D, une première en France," Makery, July 26, 2016, makery.info/2016/07/26/ un-clitoris-imprime-en-3d-une-premiere-en-france/; Carrefour Numérique, "Les réalisations du FabLab: Clitoris," July 27, 2016,

carrefour-numerique.cite-sciences.fr/fablab/wiki/doku.php?id=
projets percent3Aclitoris#photos
See also ufunk.net/en/tech/imprimer-un-clitoris-en-3d/.

35. Jacob Silverman, "A Gun, A Printer, An Ideology," *New Yorker*, May 7, 2013; See also Defense Distributed, defdist.org.

36. Liat Clark, "Australian Police: Exploding 3D Printed Gun Will Kill You And Your Victim," *Wired*, May 24, 2013.

37. Robert Beckhusen, "3-D Printer Company Seizes Machine From Desktop Gunsmith," *Wired*, October 1, 2012.

38. Ghost Gunner, ghostgunner.net.

39. Ateneus de Fabricació. "Materialitzem idees cocreem el nostre entorn," undated, ateneusdefabricacio.barcelona.cat/.

40. Pau Rodrîguez, "Un centre internacional de producció digital es converteix en Banc d'Aliments improvisat," *El Diario*, August 20, 2013.

41. Richard Sennett, *The Craftsman*. London: Penguin, 2008. p. 82 et seq.

5 Cryptocurrency

1. It's important to note that blockchain operations aren't really distributed in the sense generally meant by "distributed computation," in which different chunks of a large problem are farmed out to a network of independent processors, and later annealed. The Bitcoin blockchain, by contrast, is replicated identically across all of the network's nodes. The trade-off is that all of these copies are verifiably identical with one another, at the cost of other advantages of true distributed processing, chiefly speed.

2. As is customary among Bitcoin enthusiasts, in what follows I'll simply refer to this party—whatever their actual number, gender or nationality—as a presumptively Japanese, presumptively male individual named Satoshi.

3. Satoshi Nakamoto, "Bitcoin: A Peer-to-Peer Electronic Cash System," October 31, 2008, Bitcoin.org/bitcoin.pdf.

4. *Very* carefully. Joshua Davis notes, in an article for the *New Yorker*, that the highly regarded security consultant Dan Kaminsky made strenuous efforts to attack the Bitcoin codebase, and found his gambits anticipated and countered at every turn. Joshua Davis, "The Crypto-Currency," *New Yorker*, October 10, 2011.

5. Note, for example, that the putsch establishing the fundamentalist Christian Republic of Gilead, in Margaret Atwood's *The Handmaid's Tale,* was accomplished by locking all users flagged as women out of the continental digital transaction network.

Margaret Atwood, *The Handmaid's Tale*, Toronto: McClelland & Stewart, 1985.

6. WikiLeaks. "Banking Blockade," June 28, 2011, wikileaks.org/ Banking-Blockade.html.
7. Hashcash, hashcash.org.
8. David Chaum, "Blind Signatures for Untraceable Payments," *Advances in Cryptology Proceedings of Crypto 82*, 1983, pp. 199–203.
9. See Dolartoday, dolartoday.com/indicadores/.
10. In practice, this is not a trivial undertaking. By February 2016, the full Bitcoin blockchain had grown to the point that it weighed in at some 60GB; it took almost a full day for me to download, at typical residential data-transmission speeds, and occupied more or less the entire memory my laptop had available.
11. Bitcoin Project. "Some things you need to know," undated, bitcoin. org/en/you-need-to-know.
12. My account here is deeply indebted to Chris Pacia's tutorial, which despite the rather patronizing title is the only one of many Bitcoin explainers I've come across that explores this stage of the process in such detail, chrispacia.wordpress.com/2013/09/02/ bitcoin-mining-explained-like-youre-five-part-1-incentives/.
13. Among the Bitcoin community, the collapse of the Mt Gox exchange is legendary. See Yessi Bello Perez, "Mt Gox: History of a Failed Bitcoin Exchange," CoinDesk, August 4, 2015.
14. Jose Pagliery, "The Tipping Point of Bitcoin Micropayments," *CoinDesk*, November 15, 2014.
15. Gulliver, "Booking flights with Bitcoin: Taking off," *Economist*, February 26, 2015.
16. http://usebitcoins.info/.
17. Pete Rizzo, "Is Bitcoin's Merchant Appeal Fading?," *CoinDesk*, March 13, 2015.
18. I actually consider this more an indictment of Visa than of Bitcoin, by the way. Visa has been around, in one form or another, since 1958; if besting a completely unknown competitor by a mere factor of 3,000 is all that it has to show for its half-century head start, that doesn't strike me as saying a great deal.
19. Zack Whittaker, "Hackers can remotely steal fingerprints from Android phones," *ZDNet*, August 5, 2015.
20. Fergal Reid and Martin Harrigan, "Bitcoin Is Not Anonymous," An Analysis of Anonymity in the Bitcoin System (blog), September 30, 2011, anonymity-in-bitcoin.blogspot.co.uk/2011/07/bitcoin- is-not-anonymous.html.
21. Bitcoin Project. "Protect your privacy," undated, bitcoin.org/en/ protect-your-privacy.
22. An additional complication has to do with the distinction between ASICs and general-purpose computing engines. Unlike the

processors in smartphones, tablets, laptops or desktop machines, by definition, an ASIC-based mining rig is optimized for one and only one task: mining Bitcoin. When its utility in this role is at an end, it is useless for anything else. Such devices have among the shortest utilization cycles of any commercial information-processing hardware, at significant environmental cost.

23. See en.bitcoin.it/wiki/Weaknesses#Attacker_has_a_lot_of_computing_power.

24. Charles H. Bennett, "The Thermodynamics of Computation—A Review," *International Journal of Theoretical Physics*, volume 21, number 12, 1982, pp. 905–40.

25. In this sense, it's weirdly resonant with a tidbit drawn from the history of twentieth-century urbanism: Le Corbusier's promise that the sprawling layout of his Ville Radieuse would stimulate a production-based economy, by requiring that as much fuel as possible be burned in getting around it, wearing down tires and parts, etc.

26. Mark Gimein, "Virtual Bitcoin Mining Is a Real-World Environmental Disaster," *Bloomberg*, April 12, 2013.

27. Tim Swanson, *The Anatomy of a Money-like Informational Commodity: A Study of Bitcoin*, self-published, 2014.

6 Blockchain beyond Bitcoin

1. A relatively intimate account can be found in Morgen Peck, "The Uncanny Mind That Built Ethereum," *Backchannel*, June 13, 2016.

2. On June 5, 2016, 5,096 nodes worldwide, to Bitcoin's 5,790, while their respective market capitalizations stood at $1.1 and $6.9 billion. Data from ethernodes.org, bitnodes.21.co and coinmarketcap.com/currencies/bitcoin/.

3. Gilles Deleuze and Félix Guattari, *What Is Philosophy?*, London: Verso, 1994.

4. Nathaniel Popper, "Ethereum, a Virtual Currency, Enables Transactions That Rival Bitcoin's," *New York Times*, March 27, 2016.

5. Nick Szabo, "Smart Contracts," 1994, szabo.best.vwh.net/smart.contracts.html.

6. Ronald Bailey, "Live from Extro-5," *Reason*, June 20, 2001. At the same conference, Szabo also apparently presented "an ambitious project in which all property is embedded with information about who owns it"; see the discussion of smart property that follows.

7. See the comments of Vili Lehdonvirta and Robleh Ali, Government Office for Science. "Distributed Ledger Technology: Beyond

blockchain," 2016, p. 41, gov.uk/government/uploads/system/uploads/attachment_data/file/492972/gs-16-1-distributed-ledger-technology.pdf.

8. Michael Del Castillo, "Prenup Built in Ethereum Smart Contract Rethinks Marriage Obligations," *CoinDesk*, June 1, 2016.

9. Chrystia Freeland, "When Labor Is Flexible, And Paid Less," *International Herald-Tribune*, June 28, 2013.

10. Stafford Beer, "What Is Cybernetics?", *Kybernetes*, Volume 31, Issue 2, 2002.

11. Kickstarter exacts a 5 percent commission on successfully funded projects, kickstarter.com/help/faq/kickstarter+basics.

12. Graham Rapier, "Yellen Reportedly Urges Central Banks to Study Blockchain, Bitcoin," *American Banker*, June 6, 2016; see also Nathaniel Popper, "Central Banks Consider Bitcoin's Technology, if Not Bitcoin," *New York Times*, October 11, 2016.

13. Pete Rizzo, "Bank of Canada Demos Blockchain-Based Digital Dollar," *CoinDesk*, June 16, 2016.

14. See, e.g., a proposal for London's budget to be executed via blockchain. Arlyn Culwick, "MayorsChain: a blockchain-based public expenditure management system," July 4, 2015, mayorschain.com/wp-content/uploads/2015/07/Whitepaper_Mayorschain-0.01-4 July2015.pdf.

15. Simon Taylor, "Blockchain: Understanding the potential," Barclays Bank, 2015, barclayscorporate.com/content/dam/corppublic/corporate/Documents/insight/blockchain_understanding_the_potential.pdf.

16. Jarrett Streebin, "The Cost of Bad Addresses," Easypost blog, July 15, 2015; Rainu Kaushal et al., "Effects of Computerized Physician Order Entry and Clinical Decision Support Systems on Medication Safety: A Systematic Review," *Archives of Internal Medicine*. June 23, 2003; see also Gordon Schiff et al., "Computerised Physician Order Entry-Related Medication Errors: Analysis of Reported Errors and Vulnerability Testing of Current Systems," *BMJ Quality & Safety*, April 2015; Raymond Bonner, " 'No-Fly List' Riddled with Errors, Impossible to Get Off Of," *Informed Comment*, December 16, 2015.

17. Michael McFarland, "The Human Cost of Computer Errors," Markkula Center for Applied Ethics blog, June 1, 2012, scu.edu/ethics/focus-areas/internet-ethics/resources/the-human-cost-of-computer-errors; Wayne W Eckerson, "Data Quality and the Bottom Line," The Data Warehousing Institute, 2002.

18. Antony Lewis, "Confused by Blockchain? Separating Revolution from Evolution," *CoinDesk*, May 17, 2016; see also Chris Skinner, "Will the Blockchain Replace SWIFT?," *American Banker*, March 8, 2016.

19. Simon Taylor, "Chapter 1: Vision," in Government Office for

Science, "Distributed Ledger Technology: Beyond blockchain," 2016, pp. 20–30, gov.uk/government/uploads/system/uploads/attachment_data/file/492972/gs-16-1-distributed-ledger-technology.pdf.

20. Vitalik Buterin, "Bitcoin Multisig Wallet: The Future of Bitcoin," *Bitcoin Magazine*, March 13, 2014.

21. Slock.it UG, "DAO," undated, slock.it/dao.html.

22. At least, they intend to do so. The developers of the Eris DAO platform appear to regard this process as a mere formality, and therefore "incorporation and other legal matters will be dealt with at a later date": Dennis McKinnon, Casey Kuhlman, Preston Byrne, "Eris—The Dawn of Distribute Autonomous Organizations and the Future of Governance," hplusmagazine.com, June 17, 2014.

23. Aaron Wright and Primavera di Filippi. "Decentralized Blockchain Technology and The Rise Of Lex Cryptographia," March 10, 2015, papers.ssrn.com/sol3/papers.cfm?abstract_id=2580664.

24. Ethereum Project, "How to Build a Democracy on the Blockchain: Distributed Autonomous Organization," undated, ethereum.org/dao.

25. Stephan Tual, "On DAO Contractors and Curators," Slock.it blog, April 10, 2016, blog.slock.it/on-contractors-and-curators-2fb9238b2553#.3jnmvy1jm.

26. Elinor Ostrom, *Governing the Commons: The Evolution of Institutions for Collective Action*, Cambridge UK: Cambridge University Press, 1990.

27. Michael Cox, Gwen Arnold and Sergio Villamayor Tomás, "A review of design principles for community-based natural resource management," *Ecology and Society*, Volume 15, Number 4: 38, 2010; see also Ostrom's own work *The Challenge of Common-Pool Resources*.

28. Stavros Stavrides, *Common Space*, Zed Books, London, 2016.

29. Though, in fairness, Ethereum's DAO tutorial later points out steps that can be taken to limit an Owner's power, enacting these measures requires that Owner's consent.

30. Michael Del Castillo, "The DAO: Or How A Leaderless Ethereum Project Raised $50 Million," *CoinDesk*, May 12, 2016.

31. Tom Simonite, "The 'Autonomous Corporation' Called The DAO Is Not a Good Way To Spend $130 Million," *MIT Technology Review*, May 17, 2016; Jon Evans, "All The Cool Kids Are Doing Ethereum Now," *TechCrunch*, May 22, 2016; Emin Gün Sirer, "Caution: The DAO Can Turn Into A Naturally Arising Ponzi," *Hacking, Distributed*, June 13, 2016; Kyle Torpey, Tweet, May 11, 2016. twitter.com/kyletorpey/status/730535910949916672

32. Dino Mark, Vlad Zamfir and Emin Gün Sirer. "A Call for a Temporary Moratorium on The DAO," *Hacking, Distributed*, May 27, 2016.

33. Izabella Kaminska, "Legal Exploits and Arbitrage, DAO Edition," *Financial Times* Alphaville blog, June 21, 2016; indeed, it was a cleverly leveraged recursive call that drained The DAO of Ether in the events of June 2016, seemingly strong justification for Satoshi's original decision to strip the Bitcoin blockchain of complex looping functions.
34. Andrew Quentson, "Full Interview Transcript with Alleged DAO 'Attacker'," *Crypto Coins News*, June 18, 2016.
35. Anonymous. "An Open Letter to The DAO and the Ethereum Community," June 18, 2016, steemit.com/ethereum/@chris4210/an-open-letter-to-the-dao-and-the-ethereum-community.
36. Emin Gün Sirer, "Thoughts on The DAO Hack," *Hacking, Distributed*, June 17, 2016.
37. Mike Hearn, "The Future of Money (and Everything Else)," Turing Festival 2013, August 23, 2013.
38. Anne Amnesia, "Unnecessariat," *More Crows Than Eagles*, May 10, 2016, morecrows.wordpress.com/2016/05/10/unnecessariat/.

7 Automation

1. John Maynard Keynes, "Economic Possibilities for our Grandchildren," *Nation and Athenaeum*, Vol. 48, Issues 2–3, October 11 and 18, 1930.
2. *Economic Report of the President, February 2016.* Washington DC: Government Printing Office, 2016.
3. Tim O'Reilly, "Managing the Bots That Are Managing the Business," *MIT Sloan Management Review*, May 31, 2016; Charlotte McEleny, "McCann Japan hires first artificially intelligent creative director," *The Drum*, March 29, 2016.
4 Jason Mick, "Foxconn Billionaire Hints at Robotic Apple Factory, Criticizes Dead Employees," *DailyTech*, June 30, 2014.
5. An advertisement for Columbia/Okura palletizing robots touts, even ahead of their "surprising affordability," the fact that they "eliminate costly stacking-related injuries."
6. International Labor Organization. "Global Wage Report, 2014/2015," December 5, 2014, ilo.org/global/about-the-ilo/newsroom/news/WCMS_324645/lang--en/index.htm.
7. Grégoire Chamayou, *Drone Theory*, London: Penguin, 2015; P. W. Singer, *Wired for War: The Robotics Revolution and Conflict in the Twenty-First Century*, New York: Penguin Press, 2009.
8. United States Department of Health and Human Services, Centers for Disease Control and Prevention, "Motor Vehicle Crash Deaths," July 6, 2016, cdc.gov.
9. United States Department of Transportation, National Highway

Traffic Safety Administration. "Critical Reasons for Crashes Investigated in the National Motor Vehicle Crash Causation Survey," February 2015, crashstats.nhtsa.dot.gov/Api/Public/ViewPublication/812115; see also Bryant Walker Smith's comprehensive review of causation statistics, cyberlaw.stanford.edu/blog/2013/12/human-error-cause-vehicle-crashes.

10. United States Department of Transportation, National Highway Traffic Safety Administration. "Economic and Societal Impact of Motor Vehicle Crashes, 2010 (Revised)," May 2015, crashstats. nhtsa.dot.gov/Api/Public/ViewPublication/812013.

11. Lt. Col. Dave Grossman, *On Killing: The Psychological Cost of Learning to Kill In War and Society*, London: Little, Brown, 1995.

12. The reality of the US remote assassination program is comprehensively detailed in the *Intercept*, "The Drone Papers," October 15, 2015, theintercept.com.

13. Daniel Gonzales and Sarah Harting, "Designing Unmanned Systems With Greater Autonomy," Santa Monica: RAND Corporation, 2014. For a poignant, if chilling, depiction of an autonomous combat system nearing the threshold of self-awareness, see Peter Watts, "Malak," rifters.com, 2010.

14. American Civil Liberties Union, "War Comes Home: The Excessive Militarization of American Policing," June 2014, aclu.org; see also Daniel H. Else, "The '1033 Program,' Department of Defense Support to Law Enforcement," Congressional Research Service, August 28, 2014, fas.org/sgp/crs/natsec/R43701.pdf.

15. Alex Williams and Nick Srnicek, "#ACCELERATE MANIFESTO for an Accelerationist Politics," *Critical Legal Thinking*, May 14, 2013; Novara Media, "Fully Automated Luxury Communism," podcast, June 2015, novaramedia.com/2015/06/fully-automated-luxury-communism/.

16. Shulamith Firestone, *The Dialectic of Sex*, New York: Bantam Books, 1971.

17. Valerie Solanas, *SCUM Manifesto*, New York: Olympia Press, 1968.

18. Quoctrung Bui, "Map: The Most Common* Job In Every State," National Public Radio, February 5, 2015, npr.org.

19. Elon Musk, "Master Plan, Part Deux," July 20, 2016, tesla.com.

20. See the site of Amazon's fully owned robotics subsidiary at amazonrobotics.com, and the video of one of its warehouses in operation at youtube.com/watch?v=quWFjS3Ci7A.

21. Pew Research Center, "Digital Life in 2025: AI, Robotics and the Future of Jobs," August 6, 2014, pewinternet.org.

22. In fairness, while nobody invokes the Bui map directly, several of Pew's respondents did point out that truck driver is the number-one occupation for men in the United States, and that alongside taxi drivers, current holders of the job would be among the first

to be entirely displaced by automation. The Gartner research firm takes a still harder line, predicting that one in three workers will be displaced by robotics or artificial intelligence by 2025. See Patrick Thibodeau, "One in three jobs will be taken by software or robots by 2025," *ComputerWorld*, October 6, 2014.

23. Carl Benedikt Frey and Michael A. Osborne, "The Future of Employment: How Susceptible Are Jobs to Computerisation?," Oxford Martin Program on the Impacts of Future Technology, September 17, 2013, oxfordmartin.ox.ac.uk.

24. Carl Benedikt Frey et al., "Technology At Work v2.0: The Future Isn't What It Used to Be," Citi Global Perspective and Solutions, January 2016, oxfordmartin.ox.ac.uk.

25. World Economic Forum, "The Future of Jobs Employment, Skills and Workforce Strategy for the Fourth Industrial Revolution," January 18, 2016, www3.weforum.org/docs/Media/WEF_Future_of_Jobs_embargoed.pdf; Larry Elliott, "Robots threaten 15m UK jobs, Says Bank of England's Chief Economist," *Guardian*, November 12, 2015.

26. Jana Kasperkevic, "McDonald's CEO: Robots Won't Replace Workers Despite Tech Opportunities," *Guardian*, May 26, 2016.

27. Sam Machkovech, "McDonald's ex-CEO: $15/hr Minimum Wage Will Unleash the Robot Rebellion," *Ars Technica*, May 25, 2016.

28. Spencer Soper, "Inside Amazon's Warehouse," Lehigh Valley *Morning Call*, September 18, 2011. For a comparable and equally disturbing look at the conditions Amazon's white-collar workers contend with, see Kantor, Jodi and David Streitfeld, "Inside Amazon: Wrestling Big Ideas in a Bruising Workplace," *New York Times*, August 25, 2015.

29. Anthony Wing Kosner, "Google Cabs and Uber Bots Will Challenge Jobs 'Below The API,' " *Forbes*, February 4, 2015.

30. Stuart Silverman, "Target's Cashier Game—Is It Really a Game?," *LevelsPro*, November 29, 2011.

31 Adam Frucci, "Target Makes Cashiering More Tolerable by Turning It into a Game," *Gizmodo*, December 8, 2009.

32. Theatro. "The Container Store Enhances Customer Experience and Operational Productivity with Nationwide Rollout of Theatro's Voice-Controlled Wearable," June 14, 2016, theatro.com.

33. Kazuo Yano et al., "Measurement of Human Behavior: Creating a Society for Discovering Opportunities," *Hitachi Review*, Volume 58, Number 4, 2009, p. 139.

34. Hitachi Ltd. "Business Microscope Identifies Key Factors Affecting Call Center Performance," July 17, 2012, hitachi.com/New/cnews/120717a.pdf.

35. Steve Lohr, "Unblinking Eyes Track Employees," *New York Times*, June 21, 2014.

36. Gilles Deleuze, "Postscript on the Societies of Control," *October*,

Volume 59. (Winter, 1992), pp. 3–7; Steven Poole, "Why the Cult of Hard Work Is Counter-Productive," *New Statesman*, December 11, 2013; David Streitfeld, "Data-Crunching Is Coming to Help Your Boss Manage Your Time," *The New York Times*, August 17, 2015.

37. Tana Ganeva, "Biometrics at Pizza Hut and KFC? How Face Recognition and Digital Fingerprinting Are Creeping into the U.S. Workplace," AlterNet, September 26, 2011.

38. Arlie Russell Hochschild, *The Managed Heart: Commercialization of Human Feeling*, Oakland: University of California Press, 1983.

39. James Downie, "Japanese railway company scanning employees' smiles," *Foreign Policy*, July 7, 2009.

40. Brian Payne, Colin Sloman and Himanshu Tambe, "IQ plus EQ: How Technology Will Unlock the Emotional Intelligence of the Workforce of the Future," Accenture Strategy, January 7, 2016, accenture.com.

41. BetterWorks Systems, Inc. Website, 2016, betterworks.com.

42. Ronald S. Burt, "Structural Holes and Good Ideas," *American Journal of Sociology*, Volume 110, Number 2, 2004, pp. 349–99.

43. David Bicknell, "Sloppy Human Error Still Prime Cause of Data Breaches," *Government Computing*, June 2, 2016.

44. Mark Blunden, "Enfield Council Uses Robotic 'Supercomputer' Instead of Humans to Deliver Frontline Services," *Evening Standard*, June 16, 2016.

45. Jun Hongo, "Fully Automated Lettuce Factory to Open in Japan," *Wall Street Journal,* August 21, 2015.

46. Jim Tankersley, "Robots Are Hurting Middle Class Workers, and Education Won't Solve the Problem, Larry Summers Says," *Washington Post*, March 3, 2015.

47. Nick Dyer-Witheford, *Cyber-Marx: Cycles and Circuits of Struggle in High-technology Capitalism*, Urbana: University of Illinois Press, 1999; see also Lawrence H. Summers, "The Inequality Puzzle," *Democracy*, Summer 2014 No. 33.

48. David Graeber, "On the Phenomenon of Bullshit Jobs," *STRIKE!*, August 17, 2013.

49. Walter Van Trier, "Who Framed 'Social Dividend'?," USBIG Discussion Paper No. 26, March 2002. basisinkomen.nl/wp-content/uploads/020223-Walter-VanTrier-8.pdf. See also John Danaher, "Libertarianism and the Basic Income (Part One)," *Philosophical Disquisitions*, December 17, 2013; Noah Gordon, "The Conservative Case for a Guaranteed Basic Income," *Atlantic*, August 2014.

50. Mike Alberti and Kevin C. Brown. "Guaranteed Income's Moment in the Sun," *Remapping Debate*, April 24, 2013, remappingdebate. org; Rutger Bregman, "Nixon's Basic Income Plan," *Jacobin*, May 5, 2016.

51. Will Grice, "Finland Plans to Give Every Citizen 800 Euros a Month and Scrap Benefits," *Independent*, December 6, 2015; Tracy Brown Hamilton, "The Netherlands' Upcoming Money-for-Nothing Experiment," *Atlantic*, June 21, 2016.
52. John Danaher, "Will Life Be Worth Living in a World Without Work? Technological Unemployment and the Meaning of Life," *Science and Engineering Ethics*, forthcoming, philpapers.org/archive/DANWLB.pdf
53. Hannah Arendt, *The Human Condition*, Chicago: University of Chicago Press, 1958.
54. Amos Zeeberg, "Alienation Is Killing Americans and Japanese," *Nautilus*, June 1, 2016.

8 Machine learning

1. Rob Kitchin, *The Data Revolution: Big Data, Open Data, Data Infrastructures and their Consequences*, London: Sage Publications, 2014.
2. Daniel Rosenberg, "Data Before the Fact," in Lisa Gitelman, ed., *"Raw Data" Is an Oxymoron*, Cambridge, MA: MIT Press, 2013.
3. These questions are explored in greater depth in the excellent Critical Algorithm Studies reading list maintained by Tarleton Gillespie and Nick Seaver of Microsoft Research's Social Media Collective: socialmediacollective.org/reading-lists/critical-algorithm-studies.
4. Nick Bostrom, *Superintelligence: Paths, Dangers, Strategies*, Oxford, UK: Oxford University Press, 2014.
5. For those inclined to dig deeper into such subjects, Andrey Kurenkov's history of neural networks is fantastic: andreykurenkov.com/writing/a-brief-history-of-neural-nets-and-deep-learning.
6. Alistair Barr, "Google Mistakenly Tags Black People as 'Gorillas,' Showing Limits of Algorithms," *Wall Street Journal*, July 1, 2015.
7. Aditya Khosla et al., "Novel dataset for Fine-Grained Image Categorization," First Workshop on Fine-Grained Visual Categorization, IEEE Conference on Computer Vision and Pattern Recognition, 2011, vision.stanford.edu/aditya86/ImageNetDogs; ImageNet, "Large Scale Visual Recognition Challenge 2012," image-net.org/challenges/LSVRC/2012.
8. David M. Stavens, "Learning to Drive: Perception for Autonomous Cars," Ph.D dissertation, Stanford University Department of Computer Science, May 2011, cs.stanford.edu/people/dstavens/thesis/David_Stavens_PhD_Dissertation.pdf.
9. Tesla Motors, Inc. "Your Autopilot Has Arrived." October 14, 2015, teslamotors.com/en_GB/blog/your-autopilot-has-arrived.

10. Alex Davies, "The Model D is Tesla's Most Powerful Car Ever, Plus Autopilot," *Wired*, October 10, 2014; Damon Lavrinc, "Tesla Auto-Steer Will Let Drivers Go From SF To Seattle Hands-Free," *Jalopnik*, March 19, 2015.

11. Roger Fingas, " 'Apple Car' Rollout Reportedly Delayed Until 2021, Owing to Obstacles in 'Project Titan,'" *AppleInsider*, July 21, 2016.

12. Danny Yadron and Dan Tynan. "Tesla Driver Dies in First Fatal Crash While Using Autopilot Mode," *Guardian*, July 1, 2016.

13 Elon Musk, Tweet, April 17, 2016. twitter.com/elonmusk/status/721829237741621248.

14. Tesla Motors, Inc. "A Tragic Loss," June 30, 2016, teslamotors.com/blog/tragic-loss.

15. Tesla Motors, Inc. "Misfortune," July 6, 2016, teslamotors.com/blog/misfortune.

16. Fred Lambert, "Google Deep Learning Founder Says Tesla's Autopilot System Is 'Irresponsible,' " *Electrek*, May 30, 2016.

17. United Nations General Assembly. "Report of the Special Rapporteur on Extrajudicial, Summary or Arbitrary Executions: Lethal Autonomous Robotics and the Protection of Life," April 9, 2013, ohchr.org/Documents/HRBodies/HRCouncil/RegularSession/Session23/A-HRC-23-47_en.pdf.

18. I have often remarked on this propensity in the past, in just about so many words, not least in the 2013 pamphlet cited above. I point it out again here because it keeps happening. Some reflexes are apparently immune to mockery.

19. An image of the brochure can be found at i1.wp.com/bobsullivan.net/wp-content/uploads/2014/09/incident-prevention-close-up-tight.png

20. Richard Kelley et al., "Context-Based Bayesian Intent Recognition," *IEEE Transactions on Autonomous Mental Development*, Volume 4, Number 3, September 2012.

21. Richard Socher et al., "Recursive Deep Models for Semantic Compositionality Over a Sentiment Treebank," *Proceedings of the 2013 Conference on Empirical Methods in Natural Language Processing*, Stroudsburg, PA, October 2013, pp. 1631–42.

22. Bob Sullivan, "Police Sold on Snaptrends, Software That Claims to Stop Crime Before It Starts," bobsullivan.net, September 4, 2014.

23. Ibid.

24. Leo Mirani, "Millions of Facebook Users Have No Idea They're Using the Internet," *Quartz*, February 9, 2015.

25. Ellen Huet, "Server and Protect: Predictive Policing Firm PredPol Promises to Map Crime Before It Happens," *Forbes*, February 11, 2015.

26. Ibid.

27. Robert L. Mitchell, "Predictive policing gets personal," *ComputerWorld*, October 24, 2013.

28. Jay Stanley, "Chicago Police 'Heat List' Renews Old Fears About Government Flagging and Tagging," American Civil Liberties Union, February 25, 2014, aclu.org.

29. Garry F. McCarthy, Superintendent of Police, City of Chicago, "Custom Notifications In Chicago—Pilot Program," Chicago Police Department Directive D13-09, July 7, 2013, directives. chicagopolice.org/directives-mobile/data/a7a57bf0-13fa59ed-26113-fa63-2e1d9a10bb60b9ae.html.

30. Yesha Callahan, "Chicago's Controversial New Police Program Prompts Fears of Racial Profiling," *Clutch*, February 2014.

31. On January 6, 2014, the Chicago Police Department Office of Legal Affairs denied Freedom of Information Act request 14-0023, which had sought information pertaining to the Heat List program, on grounds that its disclosure would "endanger the life or physical safety of law enforcement personnel or any other person." See cdn2.sbnation.com/assets/4020793/Stroud-CPD-FOIA.jpg

32. The problem of police misconduct is so pervasive and of such long standing in the city that the Chicago *Tribune* website maintains a standing category dedicated to it. (Not all of the articles linked concern the Chicago police, but the great majority do.) See, articles. chicagotribune.com/keyword/rogue-cops. A representative article among these is Annie Sweeney, "Chicago Doesn't Discipline Rogue Cops, Scholar Testifies in Bar Beating Trial," *Chicago Tribune*, October 24, 2012.

33. Spencer Ackerman, "The Disappeared: Chicago Police Detain Americans at Abuse-Laden 'Black Site,'" *Guardian*, February 24, 2015; "Homan Square revealed: How Chicago Police 'Disappeared' 7,000 People," *Guardian*, October 19, 2015.

34. Matthew Clark and Gregory Malandrucco. "City of Silence," *Vice*, December 1, 2014. vice.com/read/city-of-silence-117

35. Accenture, "London Metropolitan Police Service and Accenture Police Solutions Complete Analytics Pilot Program to Fight Gang Crime," 2015, accenture.com.

36. Ellen Huet, "Server and Protect: Predictive Policing Firm PredPol Promises to Map Crime Before It Happens," *Forbes*.

37. Nate Berg, "Predicting crime, LAPD-style," *Guardian*, June 25, 2014.

38. Paul J. Brantingham and Patricia L. Brantingham, "Notes on the Geometry of Crime," In P. J. Brantingham and P. L. Brantingham, eds., *Environmental Criminology*, Beverly Hills, CA: Sage Publications, 1981; see also John E. Eck and David Weisburd, "Crime Places In Crime Theory," In J. Eck, J. and D. Weisburd, eds., *Crime And Place. Crime Prevention Studies No. 4.*, Monsey,

NY: Criminal Justice Press, 1995, and Sarah Hodgkinson and Nick Tilley, "Travel-to-Crime: Homing In on the Victim," *International Review of Victimology*, Volume 14, 2007, pp. 281–98.

39. Matt Stroud, "The Minority Report: Chicago's New Police Computer Predicts Crimes, but Is It Racist?," *The Verge*, February 19, 2014.

40. Monica Davey, "Chicago Police Try to Predict Who May Shoot or Be Shot," *New York Times*, May 23, 2016; David Robinson, "Chicago Police Have Tripled Their Use of a Secret, Computerized 'Heat List,' " *EqualFuture*, May 26, 2016.

41. Davey, "Chicago Police Try to Predict Who May Shoot or Be Shot," *New York Times*.

42. Andrew Guthrie Ferguson, "Policing Predictive Policing," *Washington University Law Review*, Volume 94, 2017.

43. Ben Anderson, "Preemption, Precaution, Preparedness: Anticipatory Action And Future Geographies," *Progress in Human Geography*, Volume 34, Number 6 (2010): pp. 777–98.

44. John J. Donohue III and Steven D. Levitt. "The Impact of Legalized Abortion on Crime," *Quarterly Journal of Economics*, Volume 116, Issue 2, May 2001.

45. Daniel Rosenberg, "Data Before the Fact," in Lisa Gitelman, ed., *"Raw Data" Is An Oxymoron*, MIT Press; see also Mary Poovey, *A History of The Modern Fact: Problems of Knowledge in the Sciences of Wealth and Society*, Chicago: University of Chicago Press, 1998.

46. Brian Eno and Peter Schmidt, *Oblique Strategies: Over One Hundred Worthwhile Dilemmas*, London: Opal Ltd., January 1975.

47. Karl Ricanek Jr. and Chris Boehnen, "Facial Analytics: From Big Data to Law Enforcement," *Computer*, Volume 45, Number 9, September 2012.

48. Charles Arthur, "Quividi Defends Tesco Face Scanners after Claims over Customers' Privacy," *Guardian*, November 4, 2013.

49. Amrutha Sethuram et al., "Facial Landmarking: Comparing Automatic Landmarking Methods with Applications in Soft Biometrics," *Computer Vision—ECCV 2012*, October 7, 2012.

50. Judith Butler, *Gender Trouble: Feminism and the Subversion of Identity*, New York and London: Routledge, 1990.

51. Vladimir Khryashchev et al., "Gender Recognition via Face Area Analysis," *Proceedings of the World Congress on Engineering and Computer Science 2012*, Volume 1, October 24, 2012.

52. Shaun Walker, "Face Recognition App Taking Russia by Storm May Bring End to Public Anonymity," *Guardian*, May 17, 2016.

53. Kevin Rothrock, "The Russian Art of Meta-Stalking," *Global Voices Advox*, April 7, 2016.

54. Mary-Ann Russon, "Russian Trolls Outing Porn Stars and

Prostitutes with Neural Network Facial Recognition App," *International Business Times*, April 27, 2016.

55. Weiyao Lin et al., "Group Event Detection for Video Surveillance," 2009 IEEE International Symposium on Circuits and Systems, May 24, 2009, ee.washington.edu/research/nsl/papers/ISCAS-09. pdf.

56. Paul Torrens, personal conversation, 2007; see also geosimulation. org/riots.html. Nan Hu, James Decraene and Wentong Cai, "Effective Crowd Control Through Adaptive Evolution of Agent-Based Simulation Models," *Proceedings of the 2012 Winter Simulation Conference*, December 9, 2012, 10.1109/ WSC.2012.6465040; Andrew J. Park, et al., "A Decision Support System for Crowd Control Using Agent-Based Modeling and Simulation," *2015 IEEE International Conference on Data Mining Workshop*, November 14, 2015, dx.doi.org/10.1109/ ICDMW.2015.249.

57. Greenfield, *Against the Smart City*.

58. Djellel Eddine Difallah, Philippe Cudré-Mauroux and Sean A. McKenna, "Scalable Anomaly Detection for Smart City Infrastructure Networks," *IEEE Internet Computing*, Volume 17, Number 6, November–December 2013.

59. Will Knight, "Baidu Uses Map Searches to Predict When Crowds Will Get Out of Control," *MIT Technology Review*, March 24, 2016.

60. Bruce Schneier, "Technologies of Surveillance," March 5, 2013, schneier.com/blog/archives/2013/03/technologies_of.html.

61. Elias Canetti, *Crowds and Power*, New York: Farrar, Straus and Giroux, 1984.

62. Frank Pasquale, *The Black Box Society: The Secret Algorithms Behind Money and Information*, Cambridge, MA: Harvard University Press, 2015.

63. Elizabeth Dwoskin, "Lending Startups Look at Borrowers' Phone Usage to Assess Creditworthiness," *Wall Street Journal*, November 30, 2015.

64. Amy Traub, "Discredited: How Employment Credit Checks Keep Qualified Workers Out of a Job," *Demos*, March 4, 2013.

65. Elizabeth Dwoskin, "Lending Startups Look at Borrowers' Phone Usage to Assess Creditworthiness," 2015; see also Lori Andrews, *I Know Who You Are and I Saw What You Did*, New York: Free Press, 2011.

66. This is Marilyn Strathern's rather more accessible gloss of Goodhart's original statement, "Any observed statistical regularity will tend to collapse once pressure is placed upon it for control purposes." Marilyn Strathern, "'Improving Ratings': Audit in the British University System," *European Review*, Volume 5, Issue 3, July 1997, pp. 305–21.

67. United States Federal Trade Commission, "Your Equal Credit Opportunity Rights," January 2013, consumer.ftc.gov/articles/0347-your-equal-credit-opportunity-rights.

68. Cathy O'Neil, "Summers' Lending Club Makes Money by Bypassing the Equal Credit Opportunity Act," *Mathbabe*, August 29, 2013; Katie Lobosco, "Facebook Friends Could Change Your Credit Score," *CNN Money*, August 27, 2013.

69. Ibid.

70. Bryce Goodman and Seth Flaxman, "EU Regulations on Algorithmic Decision-Making and a "Right to Explanation," *2016 ICML Workshop on Human Interpretability in Machine Learning*, New York, arxiv.org/pdf/1606.08813v1.pdf.

71. Alice Kroll and Ernest A. Testa, "Predictive Modeling for Life Underwriting," Predictive Modeling for Life Insurance Seminar, May 19, 2010, soa.org/files/pd/2010-tampa-pred-mod-4.pdf.

72. Recall Karl Rove: "We're an empire now, and when we act, we create our own reality. And while you're studying that reality—judiciously, as you will—we'll act again, creating other new realities, which you can study too, and that's how things will sort out. We're history's actors ... and you, all of you, will be left to just study what we do"; Ron Suskind, "Faith, Certainty and the Presidency of George W. Bush," *New York Times*, October 17, 2004.

73. Alex Tabarrok, "The Rise of Opaque Intelligence," *Marginal Revolution*, February 20, 2015.

74. Travis Mannon, "Facebook Outreach Tool Ignores Black Lives Matter," *Intercept*, June 9, 2016.

75. This is easier to do than it is to explain. See rednuht.org/genetic_cars_2/.

76. August C. Bourré, Comment, Speedbird blog, May 28, 2014, speedbird.wordpress.com/2014/05/28/weighing-the-pros-and-cons-of-driverless-cars/#comment-23389.

77. David Z. Morris, "Trains and Self-Driving Cars, Headed for a (Political) Collision," *Fortune*, November 2, 2014.

9 Artificial intelligence

1. Jeff Hawkins, keynote speech, "Why Can't a Computer Be More Like a Brain? How a New Theory of Neocortex Will Lead to Truly Intelligent Machines," O'Reilly Emerging Technology Conference 2007, San Diego, CA, March 27, 2007.

2. The Next Rembrandt project, nextrembrandt.com.

3. David Silver et al., "Mastering the Game of Go with Deep Neural Networks and Tree Search," *Nature*, Volume 529, Issue 7587, pp. 484–9, January 28, 2016.

4. Younggil An and David Ormerod, *Relentless: Lee Sedol vs Gu Li*, Go Game Guru, 2016.
5. Nature Video, "The Computer That Mastered Go," January 27, 2016, YouTube.com.
6. Ormerod, David. "Alphago Shows Its True Strength in 3rd Victory Against Lee Sedol," Go Game Guru, March 12, 2016, gogameguru.com.
7. Yaskawa Electric Corporation, "YASKAWA BUSHIDO PROJECT: Industrial Robot vs Sword Master," June 4, 2015, YouTube .com.
8. See Machii's official website at http://nihontou.jp/syuushinryuu/ intro.htm.
9. Cade Metz, "The Sadness and Beauty of Watching Google's AI Play Go," *Wired*, March 11, 2016.
10. Jo Liss, tweet, December 8, 2015, twitter.com/jo_liss/status/ 674332649226436613
11. Hector J. Levesque, Ernest Davis and Leora Morgenstern, "The Winograd Schema Challenge," *Proceedings of the Thirteenth International Conference on Principles of Knowledge Representation and Reasoning*, 2012, aaai.org/ocs/index.php/KR/ KR12/paper/download/4492/4924.
12. Cara McGoogan, "Uber's Self-Driving Cars Labelled 'Not Ready for Streets' After They Are Found to Cut Across Cycle Lanes," *Telegraph*, December 20, 2016.
13. Timothy A. Salthouse, "When Does Age-Related Cognitive Decline Begin?," *Neurobiology of Aging*, April 2009, Volume 30, Issue 4, pp. 507–14.

10 Radical technologies

1. Bruce Sterling and Jon Lebkowsky, "Topic 487: State of the World 2016," *The WELL*, January 3, 2016, well.com.
2. Mark Bergen, "Nest CEO Tony Fadell Went to Google's All-Hands Meeting to Defend Nest. Here's What He Said," *Recode*, April 13, 2016. f
3. Brad Stone and Jack Clark, "Google Puts Boston Dynamics Up for Sale in Robotics Retreat," *Bloomberg Technology*, March 17, 2016.
4. John Markoff, "Latest to Quit Google's Self-Driving Car Unit: Top Roboticist," *New York Times*, August 5, 2016.
5. Mark Harris, "Secretive Alphabet Division Funded by Google Aims to Fix Public Transit in US," *Guardian*, June 27, 2016.
6. Siimon Reynolds, "Why Google Glass Failed: A Marketing Lesson," *Forbes*, February 5, 2015.

7. Rajat Agrawal, "Why India Rejected Facebook's 'Free' Version of the Internet," *Mashable*, February 9, 2016.

8. Mark Zuckerberg, "The technology behind Aquila," Facebook, July 21, 2016, facebook.com/notes/mark-zuckerberg/the-technology-behind-aquila/10153916136506634/.

9. Mari Saito, "Exclusive: Amazon Expanding Deliveries by Its 'On-Demand' Drivers," Reuters, February 8, 2016.

10. Alan Boyle, "First Amazon Prime Airplane Debuts in Seattle After Secret Night Flight," *GeekWire*, August 4, 2016.

11. Farhad Manjoo, "Think Amazon's Drone Delivery Idea Is a Gimmick? Think Again," *New York Times*, August 10, 2016.

12. CBS News, "Amazon Unveils Futuristic Plan: Delivery by Drone," *60 Minutes*, December 1, 2013.

13. Ben Popper, "Amazon's drone program acquires a team of Europe's top computer vision experts," *The Verge*, May 10, 2016.

14. Danielle Kucera, "Amazon Acquires Kiva Systems in Second-Biggest Takeover," *Bloomberg*, March 19, 2012.

15. Mike Rogoway, "Amazon Reports Price of Elemental Acquisition: $296 Million," *Oregonian*, October 23, 2015.

16. Caleb Pershan, "Startup Doze Monetizes Nap Time for Tired Techies," *SFist*, September 28, 2015; Kate Taylor, "Food-Tech Startup Soylent Snags $20 Million in Funding," *Entrepreneur*, January 15, 2015; Michelle Starr, "Brain-to-Brain Verbal Communication in Humans Achieved for the First Time," *CNet*, September 3, 2014; Frank Tobe, "When Will Sex Robots Hit the Marketplace?," *The Robot Report*, June 8, 2016.

17. Mathew Honan, "Apple Drops 'Computer' from Name," *MacWorld*, January 9, 2007.

18. Richard Barbrook and Andy Cameron, "The Californian Ideology," *Mute*, September 1, 1995.

19. Tim Büthe and Walter Mattli, *The New Global Rulers: The Privatization of Regulation in the World Economy*, Princeton, NJ: Princeton University Press, 2011.

20. Ashlee Vance and Brad Stone, "A Little Chip Designed by Apple Itself," *The New York Times*, February 1, 2010. nytimes.com/2010/02/02/technology/business-computing/02chip.html

21. "Someone who plays video games for ten hours a day, for example, would be considered an idle person, and someone who frequently buys diapers would be considered as probably a parent, who on balance is more likely to have a sense of responsibility." This is the level of sophistication at which decisions that stand to affect the life chances of hundreds of millions of Chinese citizens are being made. Celia Hatton, "China 'Social Credit': Beijing Sets Up Huge System," BBC News, October 26, 2015, bbc.co.uk; see also State Council of the People's Republic of China, "Planning Outline for the Construction of a Social Credit System (2014–2020)," June

14, 2014, chinacopyrightandmedia.wordpress.com/2014/06/14/planning-outline-for-the-construction-of-a-social-credit-system-2014-2020/.

22. Andrew Youderian, "Alibaba vs. Amazon: An In-Depth Comparison of Two eCommerce Giants," *eCommerceFuel*, October 24, 2014.

23. "World's Most Admired Companies 2016," *Fortune*, February 29, 2016.

24. Angela Wilkinson and Roland Kupers, "Living in the Futures," *Harvard Business Review*, May 2013; see also Herman Kahn and Anthony J. Wiener, "The Use of Scenarios," in *The Year 2000: A Framework for Speculation on the Next Thirty-Three Years*, New York: Macmillan, 1967.

25. K. Eric Drexler, "Machines of Inner Space," *Encyclopædia Britannica 1990 Yearbook of Science and the Future*, Chicago: Encyclopædia Britannica, 1989, pp. 160–77.

26. Nick Hall, "Building with Robots and Recycled Plastic," 3D Printing Industry, August 16, 2016, 3dprintingindustry.com/news/building-robots-recycled-plastic-93901/.

27. Navi Radjou, Jaideep Prabhu and Simone Ahuja, "Use Jugaad to Innovate Faster, Cheaper, Better," *Harvard Business Review*, November 8, 2011.

28. Shira Springer, "Embracing Gambiarra in Brazil," *Boston Globe*, August 12, 2016.

29. Brian W. Aldiss, *Billion Year Spree: The True History of Science Fiction*, Garden City: Doubleday & Co., 1973.

Conclusion

1. Alex Kerr, *Dogs and Demons: Tales from the Dark Side of Japan*, New York: Hill and Wang, 2001.

2. Stafford Beer, "What Is Cybernetics?," *Kybernetes*, Volume 31, Issue 2, 2002, pp. 209–19.

3. A representative example is the notion that impoverished traders in the global South would be able to realize a genuine improvement in their fortunes by using mobile phones to access real-time information concerning optimal prices for their goods. In the mobile's early years, this hopeful tale was so often repeated as a justification for public investment in the technology—by manufacturers themselves, as well as their willing enablers in the "futurist" media—that it acquired the status of fact. Later empirical studies conducted in the international development community, however, suggest that this scenario rarely if ever actually transpired in the way either manufacturers or futurists insisted it would. See Wayan Vota, "Surprise! Fishermen Using Mobile Phones for Market

Notes for Pages 305 to 315

Prices Is the Largest Lie in ICT4D," ICTworks, June 3, 2016, ictworks.org.

4. Karl Marx, *The German Ideology*, Amherst, NY: Prometheus Books, 1998.

5. Alan C. Kay, "Predicting The Future," *Stanford Engineering*, Volume 1, Number 1, Autumn 1989, pp. 1–6.

6. Bruno Latour, *Aramis, Or, The Love of Technology*, Cambridge, MA: Harvard University Press, 1993.

7. Jane Bennett, "The Force of Things," *Political Theory*, Volume 32, Number 3, June 2004, pp. 347–72.

8. "They Once Were Giants," *Wall Street Journal*, September 4, 2013.

9. Michel de Certeau, *The Practice of Everyday Life*, Berkeley: University of California Press, 1984; bell hooks, "Marginality as a Site of Resistance," in R. Ferguson et al., eds, *Out There: Marginalization and Contemporary Cultures*. Cambridge, MA: MIT Press, 1990: pp. 241–3; James C. Scott, *Domination and the Arts of Resistance: Hidden Transcripts*, New Haven: Yale University Press, 1990; Gayatri Chakravorty Spivak, "Can the Subaltern Speak?", in Cary Nelson and Lawrence Grossberg, eds., *Marxism and the Interpretation of Culture*, Urbana, IL: University of Illinois Press, 1988, pp. 271–313.

10. Raymond Williams, "Base and Superstructure in Marxist Cultural Theory," *New Left Review*, Volume 1, Issue 82, November–December 1973.

Index